MW01255001

STORIES OF PEOPLE & CIVILIZATION NORTH AMERICA ANCIENT ORIGINS

FLAME TREE PUBLISHING
6 Melbray Mews, Fulham,
London SW6 3NS, United Kingdom
www.flametreepublishing.com

First published and copyright © 2024
Flame Tree Publishing Ltd

24 26 28 27 25
1 3 5 7 9 10 8 6 4 2

ISBN: 978-1-80417-804-1

Cover and pattern art was created by Flame Tree Studio, with elements courtesy of Shutterstock.com/svekloid/Tomacco/ marina_ua. Additional interior decoration courtesy of Shutterstock.com/Vodoleyka.

Judith John (lists of Ancient Kings & Leaders) is a writer and editor specializing in literature and history. A former secondary school English Language and Literature teacher, she has subsequently worked as an editor on major educational projects, including *English A: Literature* for the Pearson International Baccalaureate series. Judith's major research interests include Romantic and Gothic literature, and Renaissance drama.

A copy of the CIP data for this book is available from the British Library.

Designed and created in the UK | Printed and bound in China

STORIES OF PEOPLE & CIVILIZATION NORTH AMERICA ANCIENT ORIGINS

JAMES BALL

Foreword by
DR. NICHOLAS LALUK

Further Reading and
Lists of Ancient Kings & Leaders

CONTENTS

STORIES OF PEOPLE & CIVILIZATION NORTH AMERICA ANCIENT ORIGINS

SERIES FOREWORD

Stretching back to the oral traditions of thousands of years ago, tales of heroes and disaster, creation and conquest have been told by many different civilizations, in ways unique to their landscape and language. Their impact sits deep within our own culture even though the details in the stories themselves are a loose mix of historical record, the latest archaeological evidence, transformed narrative and the unwitting distortions of generations of storytellers.

Today the language of mythology lives around us: our mood is jovial, our countenance is saturnine, we are narcissistic and our modern life is hermetically sealed from others. The nuances of the ancient world form part of our daily routines and help us navigate the information overload of our interconnected lives.

The nature of a myth is that its stories are already known by most of those who hear or read them. Every era brings a new emphasis, but the fundamentals remain the same: a desire to understand and describe the events and relationships of the world. Many of the great stories are archetypes that help us find our own place, equipping us with tools for self-understanding, both individually and as part of a broader culture.

For Western societies it is Greek mythology that speaks to us most clearly. It greatly influenced the mythological heritage of the ancient Roman civilization and is the lens through which we still see the Celts, the Norse and many of the other great peoples and religions. The Greeks themselves inherited much from their neighbours, the Egyptians, an older culture that became weary with the mantle of civilization.

Of course, what we perceive now as mythology had its own origins in perceptions of the divine and the rituals of the sacred. The earliest civilizations, in the crucible of the Middle East, in the Sumer of the third millennium BCE, are the source to which many of the mythical archetypes can be traced. Over five thousand years ago, as humankind collected together in cities for the first time, developed writing and industrial-scale agriculture, started to irrigate the rivers and attempted to control rather than be at the mercy of its environment, humanity began to write down its tentative explanations of natural events, of floods and plagues, of disease.

Early stories tell of gods or god-like animals who are crafty and use their wits to survive, and it is not unreasonable to suggest that these were the first rulers of the gathering peoples of the earth, later elevated to god-like status with the distance of time. Such tales became more political as cities vied with each other for supremacy, creating new gods, new hierarchies for their pantheons. The older gods took on primordial roles and became the preserve of creation and destruction, leaving the new gods to deal with more current, everyday affairs. Empires rose and fell, with Babylon assuming the mantle from Sumeria in the 1800s BCE, in turn to be swept away by the Assyrians of the 1200s BCE; then the Assyrians and the Egyptians were subjugated by the Greeks, the Greeks by the Romans and so on, leading to the spread and assimilation of common themes, ideas and stories throughout the world.

The survival of history is dependent on the telling of good tales, but each one must have the 'feeling' of truth, otherwise it will be ignored. Around firesides, or embedded in a book or a computer, the myths and legends of the past are still the living materials of retold myth, not restricted to an exploration of historical origins. Now we have devices and global communications that give us unparalleled access to a diversity of traditions. We can find out about Indigenous American, Indian, Chinese and tribal African mythology in a way that was denied to our ancestors, we can find connections, plot the archaeology, religion and the mythologies of the world to build a comprehensive image of the human experience that is both humbling and fascinating.

The books in this series introduce the many cultures of ancient humankind to the modern reader. From the earliest migrations across the globe to settlements along rivers, from mountainous landscapes to vast steppes, from woodlands to deserts, humanity has adapted to its environments, nurturing languages and observations and expressing itself through records, mythmaking stories and living traditions. There is still so much to explore, but this is a great place to start.

Jake Jackson
General Editor

FOREWORD

Forming better understandings of the diverse and dynamic origins, histories and cultures of Indigenous peoples in North America is ongoing. Although, as Paulette Steeves (2021:5, see page 29) points out, "Many American archaeologists not only expect but angrily demand that the history of humans in the Western hemisphere, remain unchanged, even though the human history of the rest of the world has recently been radically rewritten through application of new science and archaeological research", many contemporary Indigenous communities are challenging past assumptions, essentialisms and speculations often constructed by non-Indigenous individuals that have come to define the Indigenous past and present in North America. Mackenthun and Mucher (2021:4) also emphasize the importance of critically investigating the making of the American deep past "with perspectives from Indigenous traditional knowledges, multispecies histories, and attention to ongoing systems of intellectual colonialism."

In my own personal and professional experience within the academic, government and Tribal arenas I have witnessed the constant need to truly decolonize and Indigenize research conducted on and with Indigenous communities throughout North America. It is critical that we move on and reassess not only how we portray Indigenous origins, histories and deep-time presence and connections, but also how we foreground embodied interrelated relationships and reciprocal bonds to Mother Earth that truly respect and utilize Indigenous ontologies, epistemologies and realities for a better future. As an Indigenous scholar striving to push decolonial agendas forward, my personal experience in the areas of interpretation and speculation in reference to my own community are worth discussing here in the context of how history is written and understood.

As an Ndee (Apache) Tribal member, one of the primary goals of my research is to demystify and deconstruct how history has been told about my own community – White Mountain Apache – which has been primarily from non-Indigenous researchers. This is a critical point to make in reference to this volume, because in the book various Indigenous Nations are categorized into ten major locations throughout North America. However, moving forward with exploring Indigenous pasts how do we rethink such categorizations through Indigenous interpretations? How do we go beyond such academic boundaries to see Indigenous presence and movement across time and space that is not curtailed by non-Indigenous interpretation? The point is, for various disciplines to more forward effectively with forming better understandings of the Indigenous past, present and future, Indigenous voices need to be foregrounded as empirical, and researchers need to modify ongoing overreliance on outdated non-Indigenous models and perceptions of Indigenous origins and histories.

It is of the utmost importance that readers of this volume understand that many Indigenous communities in North America state that they have been here since time immemorial. Moreover, by acknowledging such long-standing Indigenous connections, we need to work to create tangible benefits and better the lives of the members of the Indigenous communities we are researching and working with, while respecting their own cultures, identities and deep-time associations to the environment and landscape. As Mackethun and Mucher (2021:3–4) state "The past's ongoing appeal reveals the relevance of these narratives to current-day concerns about individual and collective identities, pursuits of sovereignty and self-determination, and questions of the origin – and destiny – of humanity."

Dr. Nicholas Laluk

STORIES OF PEOPLE & CIVILIZATION NORTH AMERICA ANCIENT ORIGINS

INTRODUCTION
& FURTHER READING

INTRODUCTION

Most people have a mental image that appears when they hear or read the words 'Native American'. I imagine even Native Americans do. For many people, this might include feathered headdresses, peace pipes and circled wagon trains.

And while this is a wholly inaccurate view of the vast majority of Native American cultures and lived experiences, it is perhaps an inevitable consequence of the prism through which many of us have viewed indigenous Americans. So many of the books and films that have been made over the years only address Native American history after 1492. And then only in terms of their interactions with European settlers. The fact that so many of these books and films have also been created by the descendants of European settlers means that, even when the intentions are good, the portrayal of Native Americans has not been entirely accurate and certainly not as nuanced as it should be. All too often, Native Americans have been rendered down into simple, crude caricatures, and these are the images that many of us carry around in our heads.

The truth is that the cultures, histories and lived experiences of the Native people of North America are far too broad and varied to whittle down into a single, simple image for us to conjure up whenever we hear them referenced. One of the intentions of this book is to convey just how varied the Native peoples of North America are.

These different cultures did not live in blissful harmony. Like humans anywhere, different groups engaged in trade, entered into fierce rivalries and waged brutal wars against each other. When Europeans entered the mix, they were often initially viewed in terms of how they would impact the conflicts with rival tribes. These relationships and rivalries, and the way in which they were forever altered by the European colonizers, are also explored in this book

WHAT'S IN A NAME?

Columbus was famously unable to distinguish the Americas from the Indies and so, for many years, the inhabitants of the Americas were referred to as 'American Indians' or simply 'Indians'. Despite the glaring inaccuracy, the misnomer continued to be used and was generally considered acceptable – even by some Native Americans – for centuries. However, perspectives on Native Americans, both in terms of their treatment and the terminology used to describe them, have changed over the years.

All 'umbrella terms' are problematic to a greater or lesser extent, and attitudes and terminology will no doubt continue to change. As will become apparent, no people are indigenous or native to the Americas and all are descended from people who moved there from one place or another. It is for this reason that Canadians use the term 'First Nation People' to describe their country's oldest inhabitants, and it is a term that is increasingly used in the United States. Wherever possible, this book will use the term used by the tribe, band or nation to identify themselves. Where a broader brush is required, despite their imperfections, the terms 'Native Americans' and 'indigenous people' will be used. When the occasion demands it, such as referencing the Indian Removal Act of 1830 or the Permanent Indian Frontier, the word 'Indian' will be used, but only ever as part of a historical term.

Similarly, you may be familiar with the vast herds of buffalo that once inhabited the Great Plains of North America. However, in much the same way as the Europeans misidentified the people of the Americas as Indians, they misidentified the bison as buffalo. The term 'buffalo' was used so much and for so long that, even after zoologists pointed out its inaccuracy, people seemed reluctant to change. In the interests of factual accuracy, these animals will be referred to as bison in this book.

Terminology is so important and potentially so problematic exactly because of the preconceptions that we all have when it comes to Native Americans. But what will become clear as you read this book is that there is no such thing as a typical 'Native North American'. Before the arrival of Europeans, the continent was populated by people living rich and varied ways of life, speaking different languages, following different religions and practicing different social systems. Trying to render them down to a 'typical Native American' is as futile and pointless as trying to describe a 'typical European'.

It is also important not to think of Native Americans in the past tense. At the time of writing, there are over five hundred federally recognized indigenous communities and nations that are made up of nearly three million United States citizens. But it needs to be understood that these are the descendants of perhaps as many as fifteen million people who inhabited North America when the European settlers first arrived. This book is the story of the origins of the indigenous communities who live in America today. Those origins go back a long way, but all of their histories have been dramatically shaped by events since 1492. This book endeavours to tell the story of the Native Americans before, during and after the arrival of the Europeans.

REGION BY REGION

As so much of a people's culture, customs and diet are shaped by their environment and immediate surroundings, this book will divide the Native American peoples up by their geographical locations. The different cultural regions are:

The Arctic

This encompasses the people who live in modern-day Canada, Alaska and Greenland. The people here, known as the Inuit and Aleut, are located the furthest north of all the Native American peoples but are also probably among the most recent arrivals from Asia.

The Subarctic

Heading south into the still mostly frozen Subarctic, we will examine the customs and beliefs of the Athabaskan and Algonquian-speaking peoples of the tundra. With a different genetic ancestry to the Inuit and Aleut, as well as enjoying slightly more forgiving climactic conditions, the people of the Subarctic provide a fascinating case study in similarities and differences with their northern neighbours.

The Northeast

Whereas the harsh climate of the Arctic and Subarctic may have delayed contact with European settlers, the Northeast region was in many ways the battleground where various European nations fought for supremacy in North America. As a result, the people of the temperate Northeast were among the first to feel the full impact of colonization. It is home to Algonquian, Iroquoian and Siouan-speaking peoples, the site of the *Mayflower*'s landing and the famous Native American government known as the Iroquois League.

The Southeast

The area that stretches from modern-day Virginia down to Florida and across to Texas is even more fertile than the land to the north of it. This led to the development of probably the most advanced agrarian civilization in North America. The ample rainfall and long growing seasons meant that beans, maize, squash and sunflowers were all extensively cultivated by people who spoke variants of the Muskogean language. These include the nations of the Cherokee, Chickasaw, Choctaw, Creek and Seminole.

The Great Plains

This vast area, which stretches from the Mississippi River in the east to the Rocky Mountains in the west and from Canada in the north to the Gulf of Mexico in the south, was home to many tribes. It is the braves of the Plains who people have come to most associate with the term 'Native Americans'. Yet, the nomadic lifestyle comprising horses, tepees and bison hunting was only adopted after the arrival of horses that were brought by Europeans. And many tribes only moved on to the Plains after being forced off their ancestral territories.

The Southwest

Although not as large an area as the Great Plains, the Southwest region stretches from Texas to Arizona and from Utah to Mexico. It is home to Native Americans who fall into two broad groups. The first have become known as the Pueblo people, or Puebloans, and are descended from some of the first humans to live in the Americas. The Pueblo are farmers who built spectacular homes out of rock and adobe. Other more recent arrivals in the Southwest include the Apache and Navajo. Traditionally, these were nomadic hunters who also raided villages for resources.

The Great Basin

Early European colonizers considered the Great Basin, which has no rivers running in or out of it, boiling summers and frozen winters, to be inhospitable. The fact that it had been home to people for thousands of years proved otherwise, but surviving in the Great Basin took enormous skill and expert knowledge. The traditional lifestyle of the Washoe, Ute, Paiute and Shoshone was nomadic and took advantage of every seasonal cycle. Life in a land where food and fresh water is so rare is extremely challenging.

California

The area of California is one of specular variety in terms of landscapes. It has redwood forests, snowcapped mountains, rich farmlands, arid deserts and an ocean coastline. This meant that its original inhabitants lived equally varied traditional lifestyles. The ample resources available also meant it was the most densely populated area of North America before the arrival of Europeans. Coastal people lived off the abundant fish, oysters and clams, while forest dwellers hunted deer, elk and antelope and collected acorns. Farming also took place along the Colorado River. Well-known Californian tribes include the Hula, Yurok, Pomo, Yuki, Winton, Baidu, Miwok, Yokuts, Yana and Chumash.

The Northwest

This narrow strip that stretches from the Alaskan border to northern California is just 241 kilometres (150 miles) wide. Yet the plentiful food available in this temperate and rain-soaked region means it is home to a comparatively large number of nations. Bountiful food meant that, despite being hunter-gatherers, the people of the region had the time to develop sophisticated societal cultures and art – particularly woodcarving. This is reflected most in the Northwest's development of one of the most iconic aspects of Native North American culture: the totem pole.

The Plateau

This region spans the current border that divides Canada and the United States and is surrounded by mountains. It is home to some of the most spectacular archaeological finds in North America, providing evidence of human presence in the region up to 10,000 years ago. It is an area of low rainfall and, as a result, the Native nations developed along the banks of the rivers. Fish, particularly salmon, are central to the history, culture and survival of the people of this region.

FURTHER READING

Barnes, Ian, *The Historical Atlas of Native Americans* (Chartwell Books, 2011)

Curtis, Edward S., The North American Indian: The Complete Portfolios (multi-volume, originally published c. 1907; reprint edition: Taschen, 2022)

Debo, Angie, A *History of the Indians of the United States* (Folio Society, 2003)

Dunbar-Ortiz, Roxanne, *An Indigenous Peoples' History of the United States* (Beacon Press, 2014)

Duval, Kathleen, *Native Nations: A Millennium in North America* (Random House Inc, 2024)

Hämäläinen, Pekka, *Indigenous Continent: The Epic Contest for North America* (W.W. Norton & Co. Inc., 2023)

Mackenthun, Gesa, and Christen Mucher eds., *Decolonizing 'Prehistory': Deep Time and Indigenous Knowledges in North America* (University of Arizona Press, 2021)

Nies, Judith, *Native American History* (Ballantine Books, 1996)

Ortiz, Alfonso, *American Indian Myths and Legends* (Pantheon, 1985)

Steeves, Paulette F.C., *The Indigenous Paleolithic of the Western Hemisphere* (University of Nebraska Press, 2021)

Townsend, Kenneth W., *First Americans: A History of Native Peoples* (Routledge, 2018)

Trigger, Bruce G., *The Cambridge History of the Native Peoples of the Americas. Volume 1: North America* (Cambridge University Press, 1997)

Wertz, Jay, *The First Americans* (Welbeck Publishing, 2018)

Wilson, James, *The Earth Shall Weep: A History of Native America* (Picador, 1999)

James Ball (author) is a writer specializing in history and education. A former secondary school history teacher, he has been authoring highly successful books for publishers including Oxford University Press and York Press for over 15 years. James has written titles on topics as diverse as the American West, the history of medicine, medieval China and Henry VIII.

Dr. Nicholas Laluk (Foreword) is a member of the White Mountain Apache Tribe (the Ndee) located in east-central Arizona and is an Indigenous archaeologist interested in the continued decolonization and Indigenization of the archaeological discipline. He received his PhD from the Department of Anthropology at the University of Arizona, took a postdoctoral position at the Center for Race and Ethnicity in America at Brown University, and followed this with a position with his own Tribe as Deputy Historic Preservation Officer. He has worked for the U.S. Forest Service as a Tribal liaison-archaeologist, as well as a wildland firefighter and wildland fire cultural heritage resource advisor. He continues to advocate for epistemic and social justice, inclusion and the critical need for the Indigenous voice to be included in all stages of research-related and real-world activities.

ORIGIN THEORIES OF NATIVE AMERICANS

Indigenous North Americans' sacred oral histories affirm that they have lived on the continent since time immemorial. As the anthropological geneticist Jennifer Raff says, "Native Americans truly did originate in the Americas, as a genetically and culturally distinctive group. They are absolutely indigenous to this continent." This must be borne in mind and does not have to be incompatible with the generally accepted view that we are all descended from the *Homo sapiens* that first developed in Africa. But exactly how, where and when humans populated the Americas is still contested. And this is despite the advent of DNA technology that many people expected to close the debate. So what are the different theories? Why are they contested? And how come DNA has not given us all the answers?

EARLY THEORIES

You may not be surprised to learn that this debate is not new. As far back as 1590, Spanish Jesuit missionary Fray Jose de Acosta proposed that people had crossed into North America from Asia over a land bridge that he believed was still there.

This was advanced thinking, particularly for a theologian whose contemporaries assumed that people had been in the Americas since the creation of the world. In essence, Acosta proposed that Columbus was not the first to 'discover' the New World. It was an idea that captured the imagination, and his book, *Historia Natural Y Moral De Las Indias*, was quickly translated into Dutch, French, German, Latin and English.

The Land Bridge Theory

The Russian Tsar, Peter the Great, was obsessed with all things maritime. In the eighteenth century, he founded the Russian Navy from scratch and, in a country with no seagoing traditions, recruited large numbers of foreign naval experts, shipyard superintendents, academics and navigators. One of these foreign recruits was a Danish explorer named Vitus Bering.

In 1724, Peter put him in charge of an expedition to discover whether Acosta was right and Asia and North America were indeed connected by land. By navigating the waters that separated modern-day Alaska from the Siberian peninsula of Chukotka, he travelled from the Pacific to the Arctic Ocean. In doing so, Bering confirmed that there was no existing land bridge from Russia to North America. He also inadvertently ensured that the straits that divided the two peninsulas were named after him. In addition to this, Bering's travels confirmed what the people living on Siberia's Chukotka Peninsula had known for thousands of years: that there were people living on the great landmass across the water.

Captain James Cook may be best known for his voyages to Australia and the South Pacific, but he also played an important role in exploring the Bering Strait. The detailed maps of the Alaskan Coast produced by Cook's 1778 expedition fired people's imaginations. The Bering Strait was very narrow. If a land bridge does not exist today, what were the chances of one existing thousands of years ago?

As our scientific understanding of the Pleistocene Epoch, or Ice Age, increased, so did the number of people who began to believe that North America and Asia were once connected by land. The last Ice Age began around 100,000 years ago and only ended around 11,500 years ago. For much of that time, enormous areas of the planet were covered by glaciers. These glaciers locked in trillions of gallons of seawater, which resulted in much lower sea levels. This, it is widely believed, led to the emergence of 600,000 square miles of flat, grassy, treeless plain between Alaska and Siberia. It was no mere narrow strip of land that is implied by the word 'bridge', but a large landmass in its own right. It has come to be known as Beringia. And Beringia became home to people migrating from Asia.

Another reason it is perhaps inaccurate to call Beringia a land bridge is because, for much of its existence, the route east into North America was blocked by glaciers. But, in around 16000 BCE, a gradual warming of temperatures led the enormous Cordilleran and Laurentide ice sheets to slowly retreat. This opened up the route east but also led to rising sea levels and the subsequent shrinking of Beringia. The people living on Beringia had a choice; move west into Siberia or east into Alaska and Canada.

By 11000 BCE the waters had risen to such an extent that Beringia had been cut in two. The stretch of water that was eventually to be called the Bering Strait had come into existence. For those who had made the decision to travel east into North America, there was now no way back to Asia. And there was no easy or straightforward way for subsequent waves of Asian migrants to follow them.

According to the land bridge theory, within less than 1,000 years, the heirs of these Siberian nomads had populated the entire Americas. What began with a handful of families following some animals on to Beringia had ended, just a few centuries later, with their descendants arriving at the southernmost tip of Chile. Initially, these first human settlers of this vast land hugged the western coast as they journeyed south. But gradually, they moved eastwards and inland. From as few as perhaps seventy individuals who made that first journey east from Beringia, a vast patchwork of different social, cultural and ethnic groupings became established right across the Americas. Over the course of thousands of years, an enormous variety of ways of life became adopted as people adapted to the climate and landscape they found themselves in.

Who Were the Clovis People?

The so-called 'Clovis People' have long been held up as evidence to support the land bridge theory. They are named after the village of Clovis, New Mexico, where stone spearheads were found at the start of the twentieth century. These distinct spearheads, known as 'Clovis points', are unlike any found in Europe or Asia. They have, however, been found in the thousands over a vast area in both North and southern America.

It is not possible to carbon date stone spearheads, but the ones at Clovis were found within the remains of a mammoth. This puts the hunters as being active around 13,000 years ago, which fits in perfectly with the land bridge theory. The apparent lack of any earlier physical evidence of human presence in the Americas, combined with the fact that Clovis points have been found in so many different locations, led to claims that the Clovis people were the first to arrive on the continent.

For decades, there was something approaching a consensus around both the land bridge and 'Clovis First' theories. But in recent years, all that has started to fall apart. Some scientists believe that, although the retreating glaciers may have produced a corridor from Beringia into present-day Canada between 13,500 and 15,000 years ago, this corridor would have remained impassable to humans for thousands of years. The land the glaciers exposed would have been free of vegetation and animals. There would have been no food to eat and no wood to burn. This means that humans would have been unable to sustain themselves on a journey that would have taken months or even years. Core samples have revealed that vegetation first began to appear around 12,600 years ago and trees, fish, moose and elk did not arrive until 11,500 years ago. This is a considerable time after archaeological evidence suggests the Clovis people were living in the Americas. So if humans didn't arrive via a land bridge, how did they reach the continent?

The Kelp Highway Hypothesis

One theory for how humans arrived is the Kelp Highway. This is similar to the explanations given for how humans settled in Australia and Japan. It does not dispute that people migrated from Asia in to Beringia; or that people travelled from Beringia to the Americas. It just refutes the assertion that they travelled there on foot through the corridor left by the retreating glaciers.

Instead, it states they used the vast forests of seaweed, known as kelp, to sustain them on their journey south by boat. These undersea forests once existed all along the Pacific Rim of northeastern Asia and Beringia and as far south as modern-day Chile. The dense kelp forests would be filled with edible sea life and would also help to lessen the impact of waves. The prehistoric travellers would stay close to the shore, where they could collect fresh water. They could travel faster as well as have greater access to food than if they travelled by foot.

Compelling as the Kelp Highway hypothesis might be, there is little archaeological evidence to support it. This may not be due to any weakness in its argument, but rather to the extent that sea levels have risen since the Ice Age. The places where the Beringian migrants may have come ashore and built settlements could now be many miles out to sea and under several metres of silt on the seabed.

The Solutrean Hypothesis

Another explanation for how humans settled in the Americas is that they travelled from Europe and crossed the Atlantic on pack ice. The Solutreans were people who originated in modern-day France, Spain and Portugal between 17,000 and 21,000 years ago. They were notable for their unique tool-making techniques that were far in advance of their contemporaries. It is the similarities in the techniques used by the Clovis people to make their spearheads and the Solutreans in the manufacture of their tools that forms the basis of this argument. The existence of glaciers and ice shelves in the Atlantic would have supposedly enabled the Solutreans to collect fresh water and hunt sea mammals to sustain them on their epic journey west.

Many experts are skeptical of the existence of the ice shelves that would have been necessary to enable the crossing of the vast Atlantic Ocean. Other critics point to the large gaps in time between the Solutrean era and the Clovis people. There is also a total lack of evidence that the Solutreans did any kind of seafaring, let alone crossed the Atlantic.

ARCHAEOLOGICAL EVIDENCE

Many people have come to discount the land bridge theory in general, and the 'Clovis First' argument in particular, due to recent archaeological discoveries. The layers of flaked stone in a cave in Chiquihuite, Mexico point to possible human activity 30,000 years ago. Layers of bones with cut marks in Uruguay indicate butchery may have taken place 34,000 years ago. The remains of a mastodon (an ancestor of the mammoth) in California in close proximity to what some claim to be hammer stones and anvils put the date of human activity in the Americas back as far as 130,000 years ago.

It has to be stressed that each of these claims is heavily contested and disputed. To their critics, the evidence of 'butchery marks' just isn't strong enough to prove human presence. The oldest undisputed evidence of human activity has been found in modern-day Alaska (or Ancient Beringia) and dates back 13,485 years. Charcoal pieces from a well-used hearth, cooked animal bones and stone tools with resharpened blades all combine to provide incontrovertible physical proof that humans were present. Carbon dating of the charcoal gives us an almost precise date. This kind of evidence just does not exist to prove an earlier human presence. Or does it?

The Footprints in the White Sands

It is hard to imagine a more evocative form of evidence of human presence than footprints. In 2021, on what was once the muddy edge of a lake in New Mexico, archaeologists began examining what were assumed to be prehistoric footprints. While physical evidence such as footprints cannot normally be dated, with every step these people took, they pushed tiny seeds into the mud. These seeds can be used for carbon dating. The result is physical evidence of human presence in the Americas a staggering 25,000 years ago.

This is a paradigm-shifting discovery. So much so that the conclusions are heavily disputed. Whether these disputes are down to errors in the science or because they undermine long held and fiercely argued beliefs remains to be seen.

Indecisive Evidence of DNA

Samples of Native American DNA, both ancient and modern, have been collected and sequenced. Unfortunately, these sequences have perhaps created as many questions as they have provided answers.

Based on the known and constant rates at which DNA bases mutate, the genetic evidence indicates that the last common ancestor of all Native Americans lived somewhere between 15,000 and 30,000 years ago. This is at least 2,000 years before the physical evidence left by the Clovis people so, if nothing else, it seems to disprove the 'Clovis First' theory.

After this, things get a lot more complicated and a lot less clear-cut. The genetic evidence points to a small group of people in East Asia breaking away from the larger ancestral populations around 36,000 years ago. This group then split in two, although both started independently interacting with ancient northern Siberians around 24,000 years ago. One of these groups stayed in East Asia and the other moved to Beringia.

DNA evidence supports the idea that Beringia served as a home and a refuge from the ice rather than a bridge that was quickly crossed. The mitochondrial DNA from both ancient and contemporary Native Americans shows that their ancestors underwent a period of isolation around 21,000 to 20,000 years ago. This fits in with the dates when enormous glaciers were believed to have blocked the routes both east and west from Beringia.

When the glaciers retreated and the routes east and south from Beringia opened up around 17,000 years ago, the lineages began to diversify as different groups spread out and stopped encountering each other. Geneticists have identified two major genetic groups, and one minor group, that resulted from this migration into the Americas.

The minor branch did not stray much below the Arctic Circle and remained in modern-day Canada and Alaska. The first major branch is referred to by geneticists as Southern Native Americans (SNA). These are the ancestors of all the Native peoples who live south of the present-day United States. Many indigenous people who live in the United States can also trace their forefathers back to this genetic group.

The second major branch is referred to as Northern Native Americans (NNA). These are the ancestors of the peoples who speak the Algonquian, Salesian, Tsimshian and Na-Diné languages that are found in North America.

Rapid Expansion and Dispersal

The DNA evidence also supports the idea that, once free from the confines of Beringia, the SNA group dispersed very fast and very far. The genetic remains of a man who lived in Nevada 10,700 years ago indicate that he was closely related to five people whose remains were discovered in Lagoa Santa, Brazil. They lived 10,400 to 9,800 years ago, making them near contemporaries. But they were 9,600 kilometres (6,000 miles) away from their genetic Nevadan relative at the time of their deaths. Travelling such large distances in such a short time certainly supports the idea that people journeyed south by boat rather than by foot.

Genetic evidence also indicates a rapid population growth. This is perhaps an unsurprising and inevitable result of moving into lands of ample resources, with little or no competition from other humans, that were filled with animals who had not yet learned to fear people.

The Australasian Connection

The weight of physical evidence points to a migration from Beringia. DNA evidence seems to support this and indicates that at least part of the journey south was by boat. So far, so clear. But what could possibly explain why two per cent of the DNA of some Native South Americans is closely related to that found in ancient Australians? Or how this ancient Australian DNA was present in people living in modern-day Brazil 10,000 years ago?

If the idea of Solutreans crossing the Atlantic is unfeasible for many experts, the idea of people crossing the Pacific is surely laughable. Not only this, these ancient Australasian travellers would have had to cross both the Andes Mountains and the Amazon River without leaving any trace of their genes on the western side of them. As things stand, the presence of the 2% of Australian DNA has scientists stumped.

So the advent of DNA has strengthened some arguments, destroyed others and raised some frankly baffling questions. What is clear is that the presence of humans in the Americas cannot be quickly or simply explained. The search for answers goes on.

INDIGENOUS CRITICISMS

The holes that DNA evidence punched through the former land bridge consensus came as no surprise to many indigenous people. Attempts to explain the origins of the peoples of the Americas were all too often things that happened *to* them rather than *with* them. The fact that the Natives of North America did not develop a written language meant that their evidence and histories were all too often discounted as anecdotal. This, they believe, completely ignores the sacred nature of their stories. It also dismisses the great care and attention that is given to maintaining their traditions and the sharing of their histories in this way.

Members of the Mohawk Nation were explaining that their people had counted over 33,000 winters in North America long before DNA evidence disproved the 'Clovis First' argument. If nothing else, perhaps this will herald an era of closer ties between research scientists and the descendants of the people whose lives and stories they are exploring.

For too long, the deep ties and insights that Native communities have to their lands have been excluded from academic research. When the historic treatment of Native North Americans by Europeans and Euro-Americans is taken into account, a reluctance to engage with scientific research can come as no surprise. From a Native American perspective, the extraction of the genome from one of their long-dead ancestors does not appear any different from the countless desecrations they have suffered since 1492. Making indigenous people part of the process may not only lead to more respectful research but, in all likelihood, will result in more accurate conclusions.

It may also help redress the cultural bias of the 'conquering people' that many people believe is present in multiple theories of how the Americas were populated. If the starting point of the research is that the indigenous people are a homogenous mass who are culturally and technologically inferior to their contemporaries elsewhere on the planet, it is bound to have an impact on the judgements reached.

FUTURE POSSIBILITIES

There are so many gaps in our knowledge of the pre-1492 lives and histories of Native North Americans. The lack of written documents makes this inevitable to a certain degree. After all, writing is not simply a way of communicating, it is a way of storing knowledge and information. But that's not to say it is impossible to fill in many of the gaps that exist in Native North American history. It must be remembered that writing is a fairly recent human development and the first writing system to be developed anywhere on earth was created in Mesopotamia in around 3200 BCE. The first Chinese writing system appeared between the eighteenth and twelfth century BCE and the Latin alphabet, which is what this book is written in, originated in the seventh century BCE. Yet there is a great deal of understanding about the people who pre-date these systems. This book helps outline much of what is known of the history of the descendants of North America's original inhabitants, cultures and ways of life that they developed. In years to come, as archaeologists, anthropologists and linguists continue to do their work, there will undoubtedly be more to learn.

THE ARCTIC

The Arctic is not just one of the harshest environments in North America, it is one of the harshest environments on Earth. The North American section of the Arctic encompasses parts of northern Alaska from the US, the Yukon Territory, Northwest Territories, Nunavut, Quebec and Labrador from Canada and Greenland, which is part of Denmark's commonwealth. These are lands where the sun does not rise from November to January. From May to August, it becomes the land of the midnight sun, but the constant daylight does not stop the snow from frequently falling in June. This most inhospitable of regions, which experiences average temperatures of minus forty degrees Celsius for parts of the year, has been home to a number of cultures for many thousands of years.

THE SAQQAQ AND DORSET PEOPLES

The first people that have been identified as inhabiting the Arctic region of the New World have come to be known as the Saqqaq culture. They inhabited lands in southern Greenland and are named after the Saqqaq settlement, which has been the site of many archaeological finds. The latest evidence indicates that the Saqqaq culture first developed around 2400 BCE and lasted until around 800 BCE. Archaeology points to a life lived in tents and spent hunting caribou and birds.

Succeeding the Saqqaqs were a people who anthropologists have named the Dorsets. These people survived through hunting walrus and other sea mammals, and the first evidence of their culture was discovered in 1925 in what was then called Cape Dorset (now Kinngait) in Nunavut, Canada. They are believed to have been active from around 500 BCE to around 1500 CE when the Dorset, for reasons that are not entirely clear, appear to have gone extinct.

Recent DNA research, which utilized the DNA from over 150 ancient human remains, shows that the Saqqaq and the Dorset peoples shared the same genetic lineage. They all stemmed from the same migration across the Bering Strait from Siberia around 6,000 years ago and are now collectively referred to as Paleo-Eskimos. This came as a great surprise to many archaeologists who had concluded that the Saqqaq and Dorset must have had distinct and separate origins. The fact that the Saqqaq used the technology of bows and arrows, and yet the later Dorset did not, certainly pointed to this. People have since surmised that, due to a subsistence built entirely on hunting sea mammals through holes in the ice, the Dorset may have simply failed to continue to make bows and arrows as they were no longer of any use to them. Within a few generations, there were no tribespeople who had any memories of bows and arrows, and the technology was lost.

Also, DNA evidence cannot explain why the Paleo-Eskimos suddenly disappeared. However, it provides hints that a second, separate migration of people across the Bering Strait around 1,000 years ago may have been key.

THE THULE

Archaeological evidence indicates that there may have been an overlap between the Dorset and the Thule peoples in both Greenland and northern Canada for several centuries. That overlap, however, is not evidenced by either the technology they employed or their DNA. This indicates that there was absolutely no mixing between the two people. This lack of genetic mixing and the complete disappearance of one of the peoples has raised questions in many experts' minds about the possibility of a prehistoric genocide. Much of this is speculation. But the fact remains that a whole Dorset population, with its cultural tradition that had survived for thousands of years, disappeared within the space of around a century.

Whether they were responsible for the demise of the Dorset people or not, the Thule migration across the Bering Strait took place around 1000 CE. Thanks to their use of dogsleds and skin-covered boats called *umiaks*, they were able to travel large distances and in large numbers. They expanded eastwards from the Alaskan Coast and occupied Canada and eventually Greenland. It is from the Thule that today's Inuit are directly descended.

MODERN-DAY INHABITANTS OF THE ARCTIC

The people who inhabit the Arctic regions of North America can be roughly divided into two groups: the Inuit and the Aleut.

Anthropologists are not exactly sure of the origins of the Aleut, but it is widely believed that the first people arrived on the Aleutian archipelago from Siberia around 9,000 years ago.

The stone tools that these earliest settlers left behind are quite distinct from the tools and technology of later people. This has led some archaeologists to conclude that the original culture may have been replaced around 5,000 years ago. Whether this was a violent displacement or a gradual transition is unknown. What is clear is that the Aleutian traditions that were present at the time of European contact were established around 3000 BCE.

The Aleut people remain centred in and around the Aleutian Islands that are scattered between Siberia and Alaska. The Inuit's ancestors, the Thule, split from the Aleut and expanded eastwards across the Arctic. Eventually, they inhabited, albeit sparsely, an area of over 9,600 km (6,000 miles) that stretches from Siberia to Greenland.

Physiological Characteristics and Adaptions

Even before the current advances in genetics, scientists had identified physical characteristics in the Aleut and Inuit peoples that set them apart from other Native Americans. One of these is the epicanthic eye fold. This is when the skin of the upper eyelid folds over to give the eye an almond-shaped appearance. It is a physical characteristic that is shared by both the Aleut and Inuit, as well as many Asian people, but is not apparent in Native Americans in other parts of the New World. In the main, Aleut and Inuit are also shorter and more heavily set than other indigenous American groups.

Although their arrival in the Americas is relatively recent, scientists believe some of the physical characteristics of these Arctic dwellers may be the result of adapting to the uniquely demanding environment in which they live. Studies have shown an Inuit person's ability to produce body heat, known as the basal metabolic rate, is thirteen to thirty-three per cent higher than that of a non-Inuit person.

Perspiration is one of the body's main ways to reduce its temperature, and Inuit have been shown to have fewer sweat glands. The blood vessels on the extremities such as hands and feet have also been shown to dilate quicker among Inuit. This leads to increased blood flow, which helps stave off the worst effects of the subzero temperatures.

Arctic Similarities and Differences

They may have been scattered over an enormous area but, aside from the Aleut-Inuit divergence, the inhabitants of the North American Arctic remained much more unified in terms of culture compared to indigenous people of other areas. From 1000 CE onwards, many of the most commonly known aspects of Arctic culture were universally adopted. This included the hooded fur parka, the use of dogs for transport and travelling in small boats such as kayaks.

Although the languages of the Inuit and Aleut belong to the same Eskimo-Aleut family, they have diverged over the centuries. Even among the Inuit, separate subgroups have developed, and dialects can vary quite widely. Put simply, the further apart two groups are, the less likely they are to be able to understand each other.

Social Structures

For many Native North Americans, the tribe or the nation is the most important aspect of their society. Their precarious existence of life in the Arctic means close co-operation is essential merely to survive. As a result, life has been lived on a more intimate scale with the family unit becoming key for the Aleut people. Based on the male line, several nuclear families would live together in one large house. For example, a married couple would often live in one building along with their adult sons and their wives and children. The men of the family would then all work together to hunt and the women would work together to butcher and process the animals that were brought home.

Conversely, in some of the larger Inuit settlements, it was not uncommon for all of the men of the village to live together in a separate house known as a *kashim*. A man's seniority in the group was reflected by the position of his space within the kashim, with the most senior man occupying the spaces furthest from the cold and draughts of the entrance.

Gender Imbalances

Traditionally, both the Aleut and Inuit had very gender-specific roles. This involved men bringing home the animals they had killed and the women butchering and preserving the carcasses. In Inuit society, women would also bring food to the kashim for their husbands and sons, who would join their fathers from the age of five. It was the custom for men to keep their weapons and tools at their wives' homes where they usually spent time with their spouses during the day.

The isolated nature of both Aleut and Inuit communities meant there was often an imbalance in the genders in the group. With girls usually marrying shortly after reaching puberty and males expected to marry a few years later, they often found there was a lack of suitable marital matches. This shortage of suitable suitors sometimes led to a man taking a second wife or a woman taking a second husband.

Boys would accompany their fathers on hunts to observe and learn from an early age. Girls would be taught how to cook, sew, butcher animals and tan hides by their mothers, grandmothers and aunts. Elders were cared for by the community and were both respected and valued for their accumulated wisdom.

Deadly Disputes

Disputes within communities could often prove deadly. This was not because of any violence involved in the dispute, but because the breakdown in vital co-operation would often lead to food shortages. When people's existence is on a knife edge, as it so often is in the Arctic, even a temporary interruption in the supply of sustenance can have catastrophic effects on a community. Perhaps as a result of this, both the Aleut and Inuit adopted a system of verbal duelling for when conflicts arise. Participants take turns insulting each other, sometimes in the form of song, and the person who loses control is deemed to have lost the duel. The intention is to clear the air and to get all grievances out in the open, but some feuds still fester for many years.

Culling Caribou

In a land of very little vegetation, hunting animals dominated both the thoughts and actions of the Arctic people. Successful hunting was not just essential as a source of food, every facet of their lives depended on regular access to the carcasses of animals. Exactly which animals were hunted depended on geographical location. Traditionally, the lives of the Inuit, who mainly lived away from the coast, greatly depended on their ability to successfully hunt caribou. These large, hoofed deer are very closely related to the reindeer and migrate in enormous herds to reach their summer grazing grounds. This migration could involve travelling distances of over 1,200 km (800 miles), and the Inuit knew the caribou's routes intimately.

For centuries, large piles of rocks, called 'cairns', were built in anticipation of the caribou's arrival. To increase their effectiveness, the cairns would be decorated with furs and feathers that moved in the wind and alarmed the caribou. This would funnel them towards the waiting hunters who would dispatch them with bows and arrows and spears. Smaller groups of Inuit, who did not have the numbers or resources to build cairns, would attack caribou as the animals slowed to cross a river or lake. These attacks were often launched from kayaks.

Once they had killed as many animals as they needed, the meat had to be removed, sinews and tendons made into ropes, and hides stretched, tanned and dried. The meat was preserved either by smoking or by simply burying it in storage pits where the year-round subzero temperatures ensured that the meat would not spoil. Hides were extremely valuable, not only for clothing, bedding and housing, but as items they could trade with coastal groups. In exchange, inland Inuit would receive whale and seal oil. In a treeless land, access to these oils gave them light, heat and the ability to cook. This could often mean the difference between life and death.

Hunting on the Ice

Unlike the caribou, which are hunted in the early summer, seals are primarily hunted during the winter. In the past, the Inuit would leave the coastal areas and move out on to the freshly formed ice. The most common seal hunted was the ringed seal and, at around five feet in length and weighing around sixty-eight kilograms (150 pounds), killing one using the traditional method took great strength as well as skill and patience.

Ringed seals can stay submerged for up to 15 minutes at a time and often access a variety of breathing holes between dives. Hunters sometimes used dogs to identify which breathing hole to watch. When the numbers were available, they worked in teams to cover several holes at once. The method of killing was brutal but effective. Once a seal came up for air, the hunter would stab it in the head with a spear that was attached to a rope made of sinew or leather. The hunter then held on to the rope until the seal drowned or succumbed to its injuries. The corpse was then dragged up on to the ice, which often involved enormous exertion.

If they were hungry enough, and they often were, hunters might start eating the seal on the ice right next to the breathing hole. People in the Arctic usually ate meat raw anyway, so this would not represent any kind of hardship. If it had been caught as part of a team effort, the seal would be dragged back to the village for the women to butcher and divide up among the hunters. The man who did the killing would traditionally receive the best cuts. The precious oil was then rendered from the blubber and stored in sealskin containers to be used later or to be traded.

Whaling

Another source of invaluable oil was the numerous types of whales that inhabit the Arctic waters. Traditionally, whales were hunted towards the end of winter when the ice would start to break apart and whales could be more easily trapped and isolated between the ice sheets. The Aleut would use kayaks to drive whales towards their fellow hunters who lay in wait on the shores of shallow bays. When the whales came close enough, they would be harpooned and dragged ashore.

The Inuit's larger boats, called umiaks, could hold as many as ten people. Traditionally, umiaks were used to attack whales in open water in a process that was dangerous and physically demanding, sometimes it was deadly. The hunters would chase a whale and attempt to position their boat alongside it when it came up for air. They would then stab it with harpoons that were attached to inflated seal skins. This both made it more difficult for the whale to dive to safety and easier for the hunters to keep track of the whale's movements. It would take several harpoons to kill the whale and it often only succumbed once its vital organs were pierced. The whale was then dragged ashore and given to the wife of the leader of the hunt. She would then oversee the butchering and ensure that the crew all received a share.

Fish

Migrations to spawning grounds mean that, in the early summer, the Arctic rivers are often full of fish. As a result, many groups head to temporary camps on riverbanks to take advantage of this nutritious, and comparatively easily caught food source.

Traditionally, the fish were caught in a variety of ways: nets made from caribou sinews, hook and line (with the hook made from bone) or by simply standing in the water and stabbing the fish as they swam past. Larger groups would even construct weirs to corral the fish towards the waiting spears and nets. The haul was often plentiful and certainly more than could be consumed at once. Like most other animal flesh, it was often preserved by burying it in the frozen ground. But salmon was also dried on racks in the sun or in the smoke of fires. Unlike the hunting of other animals, the catching of fish was often the preserve of women.

During the near-constant sunlight of the short summer, women and children were also responsible for gathering the berries that grow in the Arctic. Blueberries and cranberries were gathered, and either dried or squashed into a flat sheet to preserve them and added to stews in the winter.

A WORLD WITHOUT WOOD OR METAL

All of this hunting, butchering and processing of animals was undertaken by people who had limited access to wood and almost no access to metal of any kind. Although rare, driftwood was collected and highly prized, and wood could also be occasionally traded with other groups. Metal, however, was almost non-existent to the people of the Arctic. The only exception was the deposits of copper that were found along what is today the Copper River on Victoria Island in Canada. The Inuit there, who subsequently became known as the Copper Inuit, crafted tools and weapons by beating the soft, malleable metal they had found and moulding it into the desired shapes. Even rarer were the iron knives that are believed to have been made from the iron found in meteors.

But the Copper Inuit are very much the exception. Almost all of the traditional tools and weapons used by the Inuit and Aleut were made from stone, bone, ivory, antlers or wood. From these materials, a wide variety of spears, harpoons, bows and arrows were made. Each one was designed with a specific animal or situation in mind.

Women had an equally great variety of traditional tools in their kits. Needles to create clothes, bedding and even boats were made from ivory and bone. Stone oil lamps and stone bowls were used for cooking, although meat was mostly eaten raw. They had a number of stone-bladed tools that were used to butcher animals and prepare hides. Perhaps the most important among these was the *ulu*, a triangular-shaped knife with a curved blade on its broadest side. An ivory or wooden handle would be attached to the point of the triangle that is directly opposite the blade. Made of ground slate, the ulu was invaluable as both a cutting implement and a tool to scrape flesh and fat from the inside of hides. Women became extremely adept with ulus and, such was its versatility, it was used for tasks as varied as cutting ice blocks and cutting hair.

Arctic Shelter

The precise cutting of ice blocks was a key part of constructing temporary winter housing. The domed structures of igloos have become synonymous with the lives of Native Americans in the Arctic. However, these were only built by the Inuit when they went out on to the ice in winter to hunt seals and to give them respite from the extreme winter weather.

Igloos were extremely effective because they could be built in around an hour and, although the temperature would still be around freezing inside, it gave protection against the wind. Igloos were usually around five feet high and seven feet across and were only ever intended to be used for short periods. When whole villages were out on the ice, much larger snow houses were built. These could be rectangular as well as domed and were intended for use over a more prolonged period. As a result, extra snow was often piled over the top to provide an extra layer of insulation, while clear blocks of ice made from freshwater were installed in walls to serve as windows. They were insulated with skins that were anchored in the floor and ceiling in a way that kept them suspended and prevented direct contact with walls. Some communities dug tunnels between snow houses to remove the need to go outside when visiting neighbours.

It was, however, rare for entire communities to move out on to the ice. Usually, the elders and the women would stay in permanent houses on the land. The Inuit built houses that were sunk into the ground and made of whatever materials they could muster. This included stone, earth, bone and wood. Depending on the season, the Inuit used one of two doors to their houses. In the mild summer months, they would use a door that was built at ground level. During the winter, the use of this door caused too much heat to be lost and entry and exit were gained through a tunnel that could be twenty feet long and six feet deep.

The Aleut lived in permanent villages and built substantial structures that housed as many as twenty people. With no trees on their islands, they made the frames from whale bones and, where possible, driftwood. The frames were then covered in skins and a layer of grass. This was then topped with cut blocks of earth and another layer of grass. Entry to Aleut houses was gained through holes in the roof with notched logs acting as ladders. Inside, cubicles were created by hanging woven grass mats that were also used to cover the floor. A lack of fuel meant there were no open fires and all light and heat was provided by lamps that burnt whale and seal oil.

During the short summer, when many Inuit groups travelled to temporary sites to hunt caribou or to catch spawning salmon, they would live in a conical tent made from animal skins. These were more dome-shaped than the tepees seen on the Great Plains and elsewhere and were not made of bison hides. Instead, Inuit used the skins of caribou, seals, walruses and even salmon to make their tents.

Arctic Transport

Materials derived from animal carcasses were also essential in helping both Aleut and Inuit people travel around using traditional methods. Kayaks were made from a wood and bone frame over which seal skins were stretched and stitched tightly together. Traditional kayaks were around 18 feet long and were extremely light and manoeuvrable. They were single-person vessels and almost fully enclosed apart from a small hole in the centre in which the paddler sat. They enabled hunters to cover large distances in a short period and often animals were hunted directly from them. The larger Inuit umiak, which was also made from a light framework and sealskins, was key to enabling them to successfully pursue and kill many species of whales.

The fastest way to travel over land and ice in winter was by dogsled. Dogs had been domesticated by the people of the Arctic thousands of years ago and, harnessing them into teams to pull sleds was key in enabling the Inuit to spread across the region. Much like the frameworks of kayaks, the sleds were made from a combination of bone, wood, animal skins and sinews. The runners were made of bone and often had fresh water poured on them before the journey commenced. As the water froze, it helped create an almost frictionless surface that glided across the frozen seascape. Sleds were also essential in helping the hunters return the cumbersome animal carcasses to their villages.

Arctic Clothing

Every element of the traditional clothing worn by the Aleut and Inuit people was made from the animals that they hunted. In winter, this consisted of two complete layers of clothing. The inner layer of a long-sleeved shirt and a pair of trousers was worn with the fur against the skin, as it trapped escaping body heat. The outer layer of trousers and a parka was worn with the fur facing outside to prevent the wind and cold from penetrating through to the body. Parkas often extended down to the knees and were even longer for women, to allow an infant to be carried inside. Inuit parkas had hoods for both men and women but Aleut preferred fur hats. The outer layer was normally removed in the summer and the inner layer reversed so the fur faced outwards.

Of all the items of clothing worn, perhaps the most important to be developed were waterproof boots. These were made from seal or walrus skin and were lined with thick fur socks. Depending on the conditions, snowshoes and studs were also attached to the boots to help give the wearer a sure foot in deep snow or on slippery ice.

Two pairs of mittens enabled the wearer to stave off frostbite while also allowing them to be dexterous enough to fire a bow and arrow or throw a spear. Men who hunted whales frequently wore a one-piece waterproof suit made of seal gut. A drawstring at the neck would be pulled tight to prevent as much water as possible from gaining entry and, when kayaking, the large flap around the waist would be stretched over the hole in the boat to prevent water coming aboard.

In addition to keeping their wearer alive, clothes were also a status symbol: They were a physical display of a man's prowess as a hunter and reflected the skill of the women in his family to prepare hides and make suits.

An Inuit and Aleut person's individuality was also expressed through tattoos and piercings as well as clothing. As most of the body was covered for most of the time, facial tattoos were particularly common. Similarly, piercings were mainly undertaken on the head and face with noses, ears, lips and cheeks being adorned with specially carved pieces of bone and ivory.

Arctic Spirituality

Such was the importance of hunting to their traditional existence that it is perhaps not surprising that the religious beliefs of the Aleut and Inuit were greatly shaped by their relationship with the animals they relied upon. In common with nearly all Native Americans, the people of the Arctic still widely believe that all living things have spirits. These spirits can affect their mental and physical wellbeing, so they try to live their lives in ways that don't offend them.

This belief led to a strict separation of sea and land animals. Parkas never contained the hides of both a seal and caribou, for example, nor was the meat of the caribou ever cooked or served alongside the meat of a seal. One of the great fears of the people of the Arctic is that upsetting the spirits will make successful hunting impossible. Most communities have shamans whose task is to prevent the community from offending the spirits and to placate the spirits when offended. In addition to this, traditionally, they acted as medics when wounds needed cleaning and bones required setting.

Religious ceremonies are often linked to major hunts and to the animals on which the people subsisted. For example, for the Inuit who live away from the coast, the Caribou Festival in early summer is the most important religious festival of the year and coincides with the major caribou hunt. Despite the variety of animals that are the focus of their multiple religious festivals, every celebration shares themes of renewal, marking new starts and requesting future bounty.

The Bladder Festival of the Inuit involved inflating and decorating the bladders of all the seals that had been caught over the past year. The Inuit believed, and widely still do, that the soul or spirit of the seal resided in the bladder and, on the day of the festival, the decorated bladders were taken down, deflated and transported to a hole that had been cut in the ice nearby. The bladders were then submerged in the water in the hope and belief that they would become new animals that would return to be hunted and help sustain the community.

Summer fairs are still extremely important for many people in the Arctic. Although their primary purpose is to facilitate trade and social intercourse, traditionally, they were also an opportunity to trade any surpluses a group might have for resources they required. They enable meetings with relatives who might not have been seen from one summer fair to the next and are events where many weddings are arranged. Games are played, stories are told and dances are held. Arctic people continue to travel far and wide to attend summer fairs, as they have for centuries, and the events continue to be some of the highlights of the Arctic year.

Arctic Origin Stories

The origin stories of the Native people of the Arctic vary from group to group, but a feature that is common to many is the key role played by the raven. It is the raven that is credited with creating the earth. Plants started to grow from this earth and so did the first man. The raven showed the man the world he had created and taught him the skills he would need to survive. He then created a woman out of clay to act as a companion and, when more men grew out of the earth, he made them companions too. The raven went on to create pairs of birds, fish and animals from clay and he taught the men how to hunt them. As a result, the raven is considered a sacred bird by both the Aleut and the Inuit although his role is also that of a trickster in some communities.

Another common Arctic origin story is that of Sedna. She was a beautiful woman who refused to marry until a strange handsome hunter arrived in the village. She left with him and travelled to his home where he revealed he wasn't a man at all, but a bird. When Sedna's father visited, he saw how unhappy she was and decided to return her to her home village. Whilst they were on the journey back, Sedna's husband pursued them and conjured a huge storm to overturn their boat. Scared for his life, Sedna's father attempted to throw her overboard but she managed to hold on to the side of the vessel with her fingers. Growing desperate, Sedna's father slashed at her fingers which fell into the water as they were chopped off. These fingers became transformed into the whales, walruses, seals and fish. Sedna sank to the seabed where she became the goddess of the sea. Success at hunting sea mammals is often attributed to a group's ability to please Sedna.

CONTACT WITH EUROPEANS

Some communities in the North American Arctic were among the first to have contact with Europeans when Vikings travelled from Iceland in 985 CE and settled on Greenland's south west coast. Conversely, communities in the North American Arctic, specifically the Copper Inuit in the Central Arctic region of Canada, were among the very last to be contacted by Europeans and continued to live an almost entirely traditional lifestyle into the twentieth century. Once contact was made between Euro-Americans and the Copper Inuit in 1908, as with all Arctic communities, their lives and lifestyles were changed quickly and irrevocably.

Viking Settlements

Although much of what is proclaimed about the Viking expeditions to North America in the tenth century is speculation, it is widely believed that Eric the Red set off from Iceland with twenty-five longships. So perilous was the crossing that eleven were lost in the attempt but two Viking settlements were still successfully established. Livestock of sheep, cattle and goats were brought from Scandinavia, and they thrived on the lush pasture of Greenland. Over the next couple of centuries, the Vikings travelled back and forth to Iceland to trade and also established some sort of contact with the Inuit to the north – whom they called *Skraellings*. They undoubtedly launched expeditions to the west during this time and it is likely that they made contact with Subarctic communities in modern-day Canada.

For reasons that are not entirely clear, the Viking settlements in Greenland disappeared at some point in the 1300s. A combination of the danger and distance of the journey back to Iceland, attacks by Inuit and the onset of a mini Ice Age probably all combined to end their presence in North America. Despite having stayed for centuries, they left little mark and their influence on the Inuit was minimal. As the years passed, Inuit stories of the Norsemen gradually became myths and legends.

The Northwest Passage

It was the desire to find the fabled Northwest Passage to Asia that brought Europeans back to the American Arctic and into contact with its people. In 1576, English explorer Martin Frobisher led an expedition to find the passage and sailed into what is now the Labrador Sea between Greenland and the Labrador Coast. There he made contact with the Inuit, which quickly turned into conflict. During the fighting, three Inuit were captured by Frobisher's crew and taken back to England. Five members of the English expedition were captured and carried off on to the ice by the Inuit.

Subsequent expeditions failed to find a shortcut to Asia, but they did bring back furs of startling quality that were enough to motivate others to head to the frozen north. One such expedition leader was English explorer Henry Hudson, and he ended up perishing in 1611 after being abandoned by his crew in the frozen bay that now bears his name. His expedition may have failed but it directly led to the foundation of the Hudson Bay Company in 1670. This company set up trading posts in the Arctic with the intention of buying furs from the Natives. The consequences for the Natives were devastating on several levels.

Insidious Trading

Firstly, the goods that were offered by the company in exchange for furs were highly desired by the Inuit. They included firearms, steel knives and axes and loom-woven cloth and blankets. This led the Inuit to swiftly abandon their usual hunting patterns and prioritize the animals with the most valuable fur, such as beaver and mink. The adoption of European weapons and hunting methods meant animals could be killed much more efficiently and this soon began to impact their numbers. The natural cycles had been broken and the delicate balance with nature had been suddenly and permanently upset.

On top of this, along with their technology and metal goods, the traders brought death and disease. It was a tragic tale that was to be repeated again and again as Europeans came into contact with the indigenous peoples of the Americas. Diseases such as smallpox, influenza, measles and mumps were deadly even in the overcrowded cities of Europe, when the populations had acquired a degree of immunity. There was no such protection for the Inuit and epidemics tore through their communities. In 1781, ninety per cent of those who traded with the Hudson Bay post on the northern shore died of smallpox.

A similar fate befell the Aleut, although it was at the hands of Europeans of a different nationality. Tsar Peter the Great first sent Vitus Bering to explore the region in 1724. On the back of his reports describing the richness of Arctic furs, unscrupulous Russian merchants sent brutal hunters to the region. The result was conflict with the Aleut who tried to prevent their islands and hunting territories from being overrun by the newcomers. The Aleut were unable to resist either the guns or the diseases that the Russians brought with them and the fur hunters quickly worked their way across the Aleutian Island chain. By the time they reached Kodiak Island in 1762, the Aleut population had been reduced from 20,000 to just 4,000. The animal population of the islands suffered a similar precipitous decline, and the Russians turned their attention to the Alaskan mainland and the Subarctic in search of more furs.

The Return of the Vikings

In nineteenth-century Denmark, it was widely believed that descendants of Eric the Red's medieval settlers still lived in Greenland. Inspired by the whaling expeditions around Greenland and motivated to spread their Protestant faith to the descendants of those early Norse settlers, an expedition was sent in 1721 to re-establish contact.

When no such descendants were found, they attempted to convert the Inuit to Christianity instead. Merchants soon followed in the wake of the missionaries, and firearms, tobacco and alcohol inevitably began to infiltrate Inuit lives. Settlements started to grow around both trading posts and religious missions and the Europeans started to exert an ever-greater influence over the lives of the Inuit. Conscious of this, the Danes introduced regulations in 1782 which prevented the sale of alcohol to the Inuit. They also established a relief fund to act as a safety net for the Greenland Inuit when times were hard.

Denmark scaled back its missionary work in the nineteenth century but always considered Greenland part of its territory. But, by the late twentieth century, there were concerted calls for increased autonomy from the Danish mainland. In response, the Greenland Home Rule Act was passed in 1978. This gave Greenlanders control of their political affairs while keeping them as part of the Danish commonwealth, and therefore entitled them to receive financial support.

Western Canada

Captain George Vancouver had claimed the entire West Coast of Canada for England on an expedition in 1708. However, most of the Inuit of that region did not have any contact with Europeans until the whaling ships arrived in the nineteenth century. As usual, the new arrivals brought new technology and diseases with them, but also devastated the whale populations. At the beginning of the nineteenth century, much of Europe was lit by whale oil and it was also highly prized as a lubricant. In a world without plastic, the flexible plates used by whales to filter krill, known as baleen, were also eagerly sought. Baleen was used to make a wide variety of products such as buttons, combs and corsets. The desire for oil and baleen meant European whalers quickly hunted most species to extinction. Many Inuit groups relied on these whales for their very existence, and they were forced to radically change their way of life or perish.

American Alaska

Russia had laid claim to Alaska in the 1740s and through a combination of trade and terror via the Russian-American Company, it had grown its influence right across the peninsula in the first half of the nineteenth century.

The United States approached Russia about purchasing Alaska as far back as the 1840s but had been firmly rebuffed. However, defeat at the hands of Britain and France in the Crimean War changed both Russia's finances and its attitude towards a sale. On 30 March 1867, the Treaty of Cession was signed, which transferred ownership of Alaska from Russia to the United States for the princely sum of $7.2 million. At the stroke of a pen, all of the surviving Aleut and Inuit people of this territory found themselves living on American land.

Finite Amount of Fur

In much the same way as European technology and techniques devastated the whale populations, the introduction of quick-loading cartridge rifles meant seals could be easily killed from long distances and in great numbers. Metal traps meant even more could be killed with minimal effort. Whereas every part of a seal had previously been used, Inuit were soon killing them just for their skins, with the carcasses being left to rot on the ice. Similarly, the millions of caribou that once roamed the Arctic were rapidly reduced to numbers in the thousands thanks to the arrival of modern rifles.

The respect and reverence for the animals that sustained the Inuit was gone, and with it went a way of life that had guaranteed a never-ending supply of meat and skins. They had abandoned a lifestyle that had fed and clothed them for thousands of years in pursuit of the money and goods that were being offered by

Europeans. It was a decision that was as short-sighted as it was tragic. By the start of the twentieth century, a combination of animal extinction and changing European fashions meant Inuit could no longer support themselves by hunting and selling fur.

Canning Salmon and the Clamour to Klondike

The whales, caribou, mink, arctic foxes and seals may have been hunted to unsustainable numbers, but the large population of salmon in and around Alaska offered the prospect of employment and drew many Inuit to the fishing industry. This was seasonal work, and the Inuit would relocate in order to catch fish during the summer months and then return to their ancestral home when the canneries shut down in the winter.

The discovery of gold in the Yukon Territory of Canada in 1896 attracted prospectors from all over the world. Further discoveries in Alaska brought yet more gold hunters and many Inuit realized they could gain employment as guides. The boom town of Nome, Alaska was home to 20,000 prospectors in 1900 and many Inuit moved there in search of work. A great number decided to stay and take up an urban way of life that was totally alien to their forefathers.

CHANGES IN THE TWENTIETH CENTURY

The discovery of oil in 1957 led to Alaska becoming a state in 1959. Attempts to extract the oil and introduce new ways of life, such as herding reindeer that had been imported from Norway, were met with increased activism from Native communities. Although they were unable to prevent oil from being drilled, the Alaska Natives Settlement Act secured hundreds of millions of dollars in compensation in return for drilling rights in a designated forty-four million acres of land. Similarly, when the Canadian province of Quebec decided to build a series of hydroelectric plants in James Bay in 1971, the Native people were compensated for the 363,000 square kilometres (140,000 square miles) that were affected.

The Emergence of Nunavut

From the late 1970s, members of the Inuit communities in Canada's Northwest territories started to lobby for more social and political autonomy. In 1982, a referendum was held to decide whether a new province called Nunavut ('Our Land') should be created; fifty-six per cent of those who voted were in favour.

The 33,000 people of Nunavut now have a legislature and a premier. Through self-determination, they have taken steps to preserve their identity, culture and customs, and serve as an example and inspiration to indigenous communities across North America. Other regions of Canada soon followed suit and in 2005 the Labrador Inuit Land Claims Agreement was passed. This recognized Inuit rights to the land and surrounding waters and enabled the Labrador Inuit to govern themselves. The Inuit Territory in Labrador became known as *Nunatsiavut*, which translates to 'Our Beautiful Land'.

The Challenge of Climate Change

Traditional Inuit lifestyles have long since been threatened by the technology, disease and alcohol brought by Europeans. In recent years, the threat of a changing climate has been added to that list. When Barack Obama became the first US president to visit the Arctic in 2015, he saw that the spring seal hunt that usually lasted three weeks only lasted for three days due to the thin ice. Winters are already six weeks shorter than their historical length and the amount of sea ice has shrunk by a third in the last fifteen years. As a result, animals that are traditionally hunted are changing their patterns of behaviour and many are heading even further north in search of colder waters. In their place, new species are increasingly entering Arctic waters.

There are also concerns about the impact of a disappearing Arctic on the Inuit and Aleut psyche. It is a habitat that has both shaped their lifestyles and defined them as people. The experience of losing it has led to reports of increased incidents of drug and alcohol abuse.

Arctic Tradition in the Twenty-First Century

The modern world has penetrated every aspect of the lives of people in the Arctic. They stream music, play video games and go on social media. But they are also trying to maintain and revive ancient traditions such as dances, dialects, throat singing and winter games. The Arctic Winter Games feature internationally played sports such as ice hockey and curling alongside traditional Inuit tests of strength and endurance. Such events aim to ensure that their cultural traditions survive for generations to come. The population numbers that suffered so greatly from the arrival of Europeans have also revived. According to the latest census data, there are just under 20,000 members of the Aleut Nation living today. The Inuit are spread across three modern-day countries and there are around 60,000 in Canada, 50,000 in Greenland and 30,000 in Alaska.

THE ARCTIC

THE SUBARCTIC

The Subarctic is a vast area that encompasses most of modern-day Canada and Alaska. Its northern border is around 2,500 kilometres (1,600 miles) south of the North Pole and the region extends a further 2,200 kilometres (1,400 miles) south. It is a flat land that has a covering of evergreen forests in the south, which gradually thin out into a bleak and desolate tundra as you move north. The winters are long, hard and cold with average temperatures ranging from -1 degrees Celsius to -53 degrees Celsius. The summers are short and are accompanied by clouds of bloodsucking insects.

The people who have inhabited this unforgiving region can be broadly divided into two groups based on their language and geographical location. Generally speaking, the people who live in the east of the Subarctic speak a form of Athabaskan while those in the west speak a type of Algonquian. There is a smaller third group, known as the Central Alaskan Yup'ik, who speak a dialect from the Eskimo-Aleut language family. These people are related to the Inuit and their culture blends Arctic and Subarctic practices more than any other.

The groups that make up the Athabaskan speakers in the west include the Slave (also known as Awokanak or Etchareottine), the Deg Hit'an, the Dogrib, the Kaska, the Carrier (also known as the Takulli) and the Tanaina. The Algonquian-speaking groups of the east include the Cree, the Innu and the Ojibwa or Chippewa.

The vast majority of Subarctic Natives, now known as First Nation People in Canada, do not share the same genetic ancestry as the Inuit and Aleut to the north. They are descended from people who have been present in the Americas for much longer. However, many Subarctic people do share similar environments and have had regular contact with the people in the Arctic for centuries. As a result, they share multiple traits and customs with the Inuit and Aleut. Within the Subarctic region, however, time, distance, climate and the arrival of Europeans led to distinct differences emerging within the groups who live there.

SURVIVING IN THE SUBARCTIC

The climate of the Subarctic is not suitable for supporting any kind of horticulture. Therefore, the Natives of the region survive by hunting and gathering. Exactly what is hunted varies depending on the group's location, but caribou, moose, black bear, beaver, hare, marmot and groundhog are all killed to provide both food and clothing. Fish such as pike, lake trout, grayling and salmon help to sustain those who can access lakes, rivers and coastlines. Waterfowl are hunted as they migrate through the Subarctic, and bison are hunted by those in the south of the region.

The indigenous people of the Subarctic are highly skilled hunters with a variety of techniques and tools to catch wild animals. Traditionally, these included bows and arrows and spears and lances. The stone or bone tips used on these weapons varied depending on the prey being hunted. They also used pit traps, snares and dead falls that caused heavy logs to fall on animals once triggered. Fish were caught in basket traps and nets as well as on lines.

Successfully hunting moose and caribou was especially important due to their thick hides, as well as their meat. Traditionally, it was the role of the women of the group to process the skins, tan the hides and turn them into clothing. This was a highly involved procedure that involved scrubbing the wet rawhides with the brains of the dead animals to help break down the membranes that needed to be removed. Once the skins were tanned and pliable enough, they were then cut and sewn into clothes using needles made from animal bones and sinews. A Subarctic Native typically wore trousers, shirts and thick robes made from warm and waterproof furs. Moccasins were usually attached to the trousers and hoods and mittens stopped the other extremities from freezing. Although they were a matter of life and death, clothes were often decorated with porcupine quills and beads made from seeds. At night, people would sleep under blankets made from strips of rabbit skin that were woven together.

Despite the skill and variety of approaches used to catch animals, the threat of starvation was never far away. Whenever they could, food would be preserved so it would be available to eat all year round and especially during the depths of winter. Berries were dried and stored and then pounded together with dried meat or fish and mixed with melted fat to make a substance called pemmican. Once cooled, it was sewn into animal-hide bags and became a highly transportable, high-protein and high-energy foodstuff that sustained travellers throughout the winter.

Subarctic Spiritual Beliefs

Most of the Algonquian-speaking groups believe in the *manitou* or 'creator' concept. This is the belief in a personal relationship with a spirit being who accompanies them at all times. The manitou has the power to affect a person's strength, skill and wisdom and the way a person lives their life impacts the relationship with the creator. If they conduct themselves in a way that pleases the manitou, they believe they will be treated more favourably.

Algonquian speakers also believe that the supply of the animals which they hunt is controlled by spirits. As a result, the remains of their prey are treated with reverence and never given to dogs to chew. Bears are afforded particular respect with feasts, dances and offerings of tobacco held in their honour after a successful hunt. Both men and women commonly undertake vision quests in their youth to gain insights into how they should behave to achieve success.

The belief in spirits was and is widespread across the Subarctic. It is believed that they inhabit and govern everything from storms, to rocks, to animals and humans. They have the power to harm and to help. They can bring sickness or cause starvation by sending animals far away from a camp. Some tribes believe in a spirit or phantom of starvation known as the Wendigo. During the deep midwinter, when the threat of starvation is at its highest and people rarely leave their shelters, the Wendigo is believed to stalk the woods looking to prey on the hungry and the sick.

Historically, shamans played an important role in interacting with and influencing spirits for groups all across the Subarctic. Shamans were both male and female and they were central figures in healing the sick and prophesying the future. One common ritual that was performed to aid the sick was known as the Shaking Tent. An afflicted person was placed inside a small cylindrical tent made from animal skins and branches. Outside, the shaman's prayers, chants and dances were believed to cause the spirits to enter the tent. The spirits' arrival would be marked by the violent shaking of the tent and, reportedly, the appearance of sparks and noises in the surrounding air. When the ceremony ended at dawn the following morning, the afflicted person was believed to have returned to health. In some groups, such as the Innu, a caribou shoulder blade was placed in a fire to gain guidance from the spirit world. Predictions and decisions were made based on the interpretation of the cracks that appeared on the bone as it was enveloped by the flames.

Subarctic Art

The spiritual beliefs of the Subarctic region are also reflected in the rock art that can be seen in over 500 sites located between Quebec and Saskatchewan. They are estimated to be thousands of years old, and some have been painted using fingers while others were daubed with brushes made from the fibres of plants or animal fur. A wide range of subjects are depicted, but the mythical thunderbird is repeatedly featured.

The thunderbird is an important mythological creature in many regions other than the Subarctic, particularly in the Northwest and Northeast culture areas. It is usually depicted as having enormous wings and a curling beak like a bird of prey and is believed to have magical powers. These powers include creating thunder by flapping its wings and shooting lightning from its eyes. To the Cree, thunderstorms are the result of a struggle between the thunderbird and a horned serpent. Any person lucky enough to survive being struck by lightning is believed to have been imbued with the thunderbird's powers and traditionally became a shaman.

Masks perform an important role in the spiritual and cultural life of people in the Subarctic. They are worn in ceremonial dances and are often made to represent the spirits of salmon, caribou, foxes, etc. They are worn exclusively by men in dances and ceremonies designed to connect with the spirit world. A great deal of time and effort goes into creating the masks to ensure that a world that is usually invisible is rendered visible to the assembled village.

Subarctic Shelter

The people who lived in the Subarctic before the arrival of the Europeans were semi-nomadic and moved with the availability of animals. In the summer months, they lived in temporary structures made from pine wood frames and covered in animal skins. A fire was built in the centre of these tepees or tents and a hole at the top allowed smoke to escape. Animal skins were also used as carpets and blankets to provide extra warmth. In the winter months, more substantial and semi-permanent dwellings were constructed. These were partially dug into the ground to create the lower part of the walls, which were then built up with horizontally laid logs. The gaps between the logs were filled with mud and moss to prevent any draughts. With temperatures reaching such dangerous lows, the entire outer walls were covered with a layer of earth that acted as both an insulator and draught excluder. Inside, the walls were usually lined with animal skins.

THE ARRIVAL OF THE EUROPEANS

When the French explorer Jacques Cartier sailed along what is now the Labrador Coast of northeastern Canada in 1534, he was not impressed by what he saw. He was unwilling to believe that anybody could live in such an environment and claimed he had not seen even 'one cartload of earth and yet I landed in many places'. But people were there, and the Algonquian speakers who he met were eager to trade. In exchange for the knives and glass beads he had on his ship, Cartier took beaver furs home with him.

Beaver pelts were greatly valued by French milliners, who transformed them into fashionable hats. The popularity of this headwear led to scores of French ships sailing for what is now Canada and, by the start of the seventeenth century, thousands of French people had moved to northern North America to seek their fortune in the fur trade. In 1608, Samuel de Champlain founded the city of Quebec on the banks of the Saint Lawrence River. This soon became the central hub in a network of French fur trading posts that eventually stretched the entire breadth of the Subarctic from the Atlantic to the Pacific Coasts.

Russian Competition

The Russians arrived in the Subarctic region somewhat later than the French, but for similar reasons. In 1818, a man named Petr Korsakovski built the first Russian trading post in what is now Bristol Bay in Southwest Alaska. Shortly after, the Russian-American Company was founded to further exploit the natural resource of North American furs. As was the case with the French, the Russians were aided in their collection of pelts by the Native populations who all too gladly traded them for European goods. The sheer scale of this trade is difficult to comprehend. According to Russian-American Company accounts, in 1821 alone, they purchased 1.3 million fox pelts, 73,000 sea otter pelts and 31,000 sable pelts from indigenous peoples. In addition to this, they purchased the furs of thousands of bears, wolves, walruses and lynx. This vast trade in furs was to have a profound and permanent impact on both the people and wildlife of the Subarctic.

Social Structures

There was no overriding government or infrastructure to organize or co-ordinate the people of the Subarctic. Traditionally, people lived fairly isolated and autonomous lives in groups of twenty-five to thirty people. Although there may have been individuals who members of the groups looked to for leadership and decision-making, there were no formal chiefs in the majority of Subarctic bands. It was only with the arrival of the European fur traders, and their desire to have a specific individual whom they could control and intimidate, that chiefs became prevalent in the region.

The commonality of dialect, as well as familial ties, usually acted as bonds between groups. Regular contact between local bands, intermarriage and common territories used for hunting and gathering often led to kinships and the use of familial terms when communicating with each other. Over time, this led to bands, tribes and even loosely organized nations emerging that were present when the first Europeans arrived in the Subarctic. Some, such as the Métis, continued to emerge post-contact with Europeans.

THE CREE

Today, the Cree are the most populous and widely distributed of all the indigenous peoples in Canada. For more than 6,000 years, these Algonquian-speaking people were limited to living near the Arctic Circle among eastern Canada's rivers, lakes and forests. However, their success as hunters enabled them to spread out over an enormous area. From Quebec in the east to Alberta in the west and stretching from the Arctic Circle all the way down to the Great Plains, of all the Native North American groups, the Cree are the most widespread.

This huge geographical spread resulted in the development of different Cree Nations: Plains Cree, Woodland Cree, Swampy Cree and Eastern Cree. The sheer scale of the area inhabited by the Cree meant that considerable variations in the customs and beliefs have developed within the various groups themselves.

Travelling such long distances meant the Cree, and other nations, developed techniques and technologies to aid them. In winter, toboggans were dragged to enable heavy loads to be easily moved. To help them walk through deep drifts, snowshoes were constructed by stretching animal tendons across light wooden frames. These spread the weight of the wearer, prevented them from sinking into the snow and allowed them to move fast enough and far enough to track down the animals they were hunting. During the summer months, canoes allowed people to travel much more quickly and easily than by travelling by foot.

Cree Creation Stories

A trickster figure named Wisakedjak is central to the Cree's worldview. He is believed to be very clever but also devious and liable to get himself into trouble. The Cree believe that life lessons, both good and bad, can be learned from observing the examples set by the trickster. Creation stories vary from Cree Nation to Cree Nation but they often feature a creator or manitou figure and the Wisakedjak trickster figure. In the accounts of many groups, the creator told the trickster to teach the people how to live in peace and to take care of them. When Wisakedjak repeatedly failed to do this and fighting subsequently broke out among the people, the creator was bitterly disappointed and decided to flood the lands. This left only Wisakedjak, Otter, Beaver and Muskrat alive and floating in the water. Wisakedjak told the animals to dive down and collect some of the mud, which he could then turn into new land. Otter and Beaver died in their attempts but Muskrat eventually emerged from the deep with a paw full of wet earth. The Cree believe this is where the Earth of today came from.

Cree Contact with Europeans

An aspect of Cree history that perhaps sets them apart from most other Native North Americans is the nature and impact of their interaction with Europeans. Unlike most other indigenous peoples, the Cree saw the arrival of the Europeans as an opportunity that could be exploited to their advantage. Contact with Europeans certainly acted as a catalyst in the Cree expansion and inhabitation of much of Canada.

The first Europeans to make contact with the Cree were probably the Jesuit missionaries who arrived in the James Bay area in 1640. Their impact on the Cree was very limited but the arrival of the fur traders, and the Hudson Bay Company in particular, profoundly altered the way the Cree lived their lives.

The first change was the wholesale transformation of the Cree's hunting habits. Their skills and knowledge were switched from being used to kill animals that provided food to killing animals with thick fur which the Europeans badly wanted. They were so successful in their endeavours that they were soon able to purchase large numbers of rifles, steel animal traps, knives, axes and iron pots from the Europeans. Before long, they had given up the traditional tools, clothes and ways that had served them so well for thousands of years. They had identified an opportunity to play middleman between the fur traders and the other indigenous peoples that they believed would bring them wealth, power and prestige.

Middlemen in the Fur Trade

Between the 1660s and the 1680s, the Cree established themselves as the middlemen with the fur traders. They combined their intimate knowledge of the land and wildlife with the use of modern firearms to devastating effect. Their search for ever more animals took them far and wide and brought them into contact with tribes that the Cree had not previously encountered. These tribes often feared and respected the Cree, especially as the Cree were armed with rifles. Furs were purchased from these tribes, often in exchange for goods that the Cree had purchased from fur traders. This meant the Cree were responsible for introducing European technology, and therefore disrupting traditional practices, deep into the Subarctic.

The Cree traded with the British posts in the north and French posts in the south and, through a combination of enterprise and intimidation, prevented other tribes from accessing the posts directly. As a result, the Cree turned a profit on nearly every pelt purchased by the traders and became the wealthiest and most powerful indigenous nation in the Subarctic.

The name Cree itself is directly derived from involvement in the fur trade. It is believed to be derived from *Kristineaux*, the name the French used for the tribe, which was then shortened to Kri or Cree. It is believed that *Kristineaux* is most likely a corruption of

Kenistenoag, which is a term that some of the tribespeople used to describe themselves and means 'the people' in Algonquian.

The Cost of Commerce

Early exposure to European technology may have brought dividends to the Cree but it inevitably meant exposure to European disease and alcohol. It is thought that around two-thirds of the Cree became infected and died of diseases that they had no previous exposure to and zero immunity from. But unlike many other Native groups, they were able to regrow their populations.

By the 1730s, many of the Woodland Cree had decided to escape epidemics and the heavily depleted hunting grounds of their traditional lands in eastern Canada and relocate to the Great Plains of the west. For well over a century, the move appeared to be a dramatic success. The woodland trappers and beaver stalkers had become highly successful horse-mounted bison hunters and fearsome warriors. Within a couple of generations, horses and firearms had become central to the existence of many Cree and they frequently waged war against other Plains tribes. But the tragic story of the Woodland Cree was destined to be repeated on the Plains.

The destruction of the bison herds in the 1870s and 1880s combined with the attritional effects of repeated epidemics to devastating effect. The result was that the Plains Cree surrendered to the wishes of the Canadian government and relocated to reserves. There, they attempted to eke out an existence through farming and ranching while keeping their culture alive. This was considerably undermined by the onslaught of the Canadian residential school system. By removing the young from their families, their language and their environment, it was a brutally effective way to cut the ties to their traditions and assimilate them into wider Canadian society.

THE ALASKAN ATHABASKAN

Alaskan Athabaskan is the term that is used to refer to the eleven groups of North American Natives who live to the south of the Arctic and speak the Athabaskan language. The Athabaskan speakers are thought to descend from some of the earliest arrivals in the Americas and, in around 500 CE, split into three major divisions. One branch headed for the Plains, another to the Southwestern region and the third, after successfully battling the Inuit, settled in the Subarctic interior of Alaska. The Alaskan Athabaskans often refer to themselves as the Dene, meaning 'the people'.

Unlike the Cree and other Subarctic groups to the east, the Alaskan Athabaskans did not rush to exploit the opportunities presented by the arrival of Europeans. Perhaps forewarned by stories of enslavement by Russian fur traders and motivated by fears that the Europeans would kill them and steal their hunting grounds, the Alaskan Athabaskans did their best to keep the new arrivals at bay.

In 1796, 1818 and 1847, successive Russian expeditions had all of their members massacred as they attempted to explore the interior of Alaska. The Alaskan Athabaskans developed a reputation for being fiercely protective of their territory and unwelcoming to trespassers. This helped keep European encroachment to a minimum for most of the nineteenth century. However, once gold was discovered in the Yukon Territory of Canada in 1896, it triggered a stampede through Alaskan Athabaskan Territory that even the fiercest reputations could not repel.

Alaskan Athabaskan Groups

The Deg Hit'an built villages along the banks of the Lower Yukon and Upper Kuskokwim Rivers. Their lifestyles shared many commonalities with the Inuit just to the north, such as wearing parkas, hunting with harpoons and building their villages around the *kashim* men's houses. It was in these buildings that disputes were heard and ruled upon and seasonal ceremonies were performed.

Unlike most Subarctic people, the Deg Hit'an society was divided into three social classes. Around eighty per cent of the village made up the 'normal' working class with around fifteen per cent belonging to families that were particularly effective hunters or gatherers. They could sell their excess produce, accrue wealth and establish social distinctions with elaborate clothing. It was these families that would lead the group's ceremonial life. The remaining five per cent were something of an underclass that did not contribute to hunting or gathering and lived off the work of others. Although they were not left to starve, members of this group were not respected and often died unmarried.

Deg Hit'an Beliefs

The Deg Hit'an revere the raven, in much the same way as the Inuit and Aleut, and believe him to be the creator, God. However, they also believe the raven to be a trickster figure whose behaviour frequently gets him into trouble. Stories of these misadventures enable the Deg Hit'an to both teach and learn life lessons and gain insights into how they should behave.

The Slave

The Slave, or Awokanak or Etchareottine, were given their name by the Cree who, armed with rifles, plundered traditional Slave territories in search of animal pelts. As the name implies, the Cree enslaved large numbers of these Athabaskan speakers and the term was then picked up by the British and French.

The Slave developed a reputation for pacifism and treated the women and the elders of their tribes with a level of respect that was not typical of all Alaskan Athabaskans. Their society was loosely organized into small independent bands. They sheltered in tepee-like structures in the summer and more substantial rectangular timber-framed huts in the winter. Like many others, they believed in guardian spirits but, less commonly, believed that a deathbed confession of sins could help forestall death.

The Carrier

One explanation for how the Carrier, or Takulli, were given their name is that English settlers named them after the custom of widows carrying the ashes of their deceased husbands in rucksacks for three years. This is disputed and others believe it is a corruption of English translations of the name other tribes used for them. Takulli means 'People Who Go upon the Water' which is perhaps a misleading name for a semi-sedentary people who divided their time between fishing camps and living in semi-subterranean houses.

Although they hunted various animals and foraged for wild plants, their economy was centred around the plentiful salmon of the upper branches of the Fraser River in what is now British Columbia. The Carrier were divided up into subgroups with each having exclusive rights to certain territories for hunting. The

Carrier's spiritual belief centred around a great sky god and they contacted spirits through rituals, dreams and visions. Much like tribes of the Pacific Northwest to the south, the Carrier often depicted these spirits in carved pillars that have come to be known as totem poles. The Carriers believe in both the afterlife and reincarnation.

The Gwich'in

The Gwich'in are Athabaskan speakers who traditionally lived in the basins of the Yukon and Peel Rivers in the east of Alaska. Their geographical location meant they shared cultural traits with the Inuit in the west, with whom they traded and fought, and the tribes to the east and south. This has led to their customs and cultures becoming something of a melting pot with parkas and hoods being worn while also using face paint and decorating their clothes and hair with feathers, beads and fringes. Like so many nations and tribes, the name Gwich'in is believed to mean 'people'. But there is no precise agreement over exactly which groups constituted the Gwich'in and it has been used as a catch-all term for Athabaskan-speaking people of this region.

The Chipewyan

Traditionally, the Chipewyan inhabited the land that was bordered by the Churchill River to the south and stretched some 1,130 kilometres (700 miles) to the north. The caribou were the main source of their subsistence but, much like the Cree, the arrival of Europeans triggered a change in their hunting priorities.

When the Hudson Bay Company opened a trading post at the mouth of the Churchill River in 1717, the Chipewyan switched to hunting animals whose fur was prized. And, in much the same way as the Cree, they took advantage of their location, knowledge of the land and contacts with the British to establish themselves as middlemen in the fur trade. When the Yellowknife and Dogrib tribes to the west sold their furs, it was to the Chipewyan. This led to enormous profits for the Chipewyan but also spelt disaster. Exposure to European disease in general, and the smallpox epidemic of 1781 in particular, completely decimated the Chipewyan. And, unlike the Cree, the Chipewyan were unable to rebuild their numbers or move to new lands.

The Yup'ik

The Yup'ik traditionally inhabit the wetlands of Central Alaska. In the Eskimo-Aleut dialect that they speak, the word for April translates to 'bird place'. This reflects the fact that it is during this month that their lands becaome the destination for millions of migrating birds. Geese, ducks and cranes were traditionally hunted with bows and arrows and eggs were gathered from the nests.

In June, it was the turn of the salmon to migrate up the Yukon River. The Yup'ik word for the Yukon roughly translates as 'provider for all' and reflects how ample the fish were and how important a role the river played in their lives. As well as providing enough food to feed the Yup'ik all year round, salmon skin was also used to make waterproof boots, mittens and even parkas.

Like most other nations and tribes, the hunting habits of the Yup'ik were transformed by the arrival of the Europeans. Pelts became the most prized items because they could be traded for European goods. In the process, they also collected European pathogens and it is estimated that sixty per cent of the Yup'ik population succumbed to smallpox in the 1838 epidemic alone.

Métis

The Métis are an entirely post-contact indigenous nation that grew directly from the seventeenth and eighteenth century fur trade. It is believed the term Métis comes from the French term *métisser*, which means 'to mix races', and reflects the nation's origins. Its people are descended from unions between European fur traders and indigenous women from tribes such as the Cree. The offspring of these unions often found they were accepted by neither the indigenous tribes nor the European traders, and they developed their own culture and collective consciousness.

The Métis grew with the fur trade and many gained employment as interpreters, negotiators, guides and fur packers for the Hudson Bay Company. Communities settled along the fur trade routes with their homeland stretching across modern-day Manitoba, Saskatchewan, Alberta, Ontario and British Columbia. They developed a language, called Michif, which is a portmanteau dialect made up of Cree verbs and French nouns.

In 1885, the Saskatchewan Métis took up arms against the Canadian government in protest against perceived discrimination and lands being taken from them and given to railroad companies. The uprising was crushed and its leader, Louis Riel, was executed for treason. The Métis communities continued to be dispersed from their land, have their communities broken up and derided as "half-breeds" but it was a key moment in their development as a people.

The twentieth century bore witness to a long political struggle for official recognition and protection of Métis rights. This finally culminated in the Constitution Act of 1982. This legally identified the three culturally distinct indigenous peoples of Canada: the Inuit and Aleut, the First Nation People and the

Métis. It is estimated that there are around 450,000 members of the Métis Nation who are Canadian citizens and many others all over the world. The Métis may be the youngest of all of the Native North American nations, but they still existed long before both Canada and the United States.

THE SUBARCTIC TODAY

The Subarctic undoubtedly remains less developed than other regions of North America and therefore retains more of the wilderness that supports traditional native ways of life. However, there has been development and disruption, and the struggle to preserve the delicate ecosystems continues in the twenty-first century.

The discovery of gold in the Klondike region of the Yukon, Canada, in 1898 triggered a Subarctic gold rush. This was compounded by the discovery of gold near Nome, Alaska just two years later. The result was the arrival of over 100,000 prospectors in the Subarctic and, just as with every other gold rush, led to violence, drunkenness, disease and the establishment of boomtowns. When the rush came to an end in 1910, many Euro-Americans decided to stay in Alaska and began to demand the development and infrastructure building that had occurred in other states.

They got their wish when the 470-mile railroad from Fairbanks to Seward was built in 1914. Unfortunately for the Native peoples, it both cut straight through their lands and had the effect of bringing more people to the state. Faced with the prospect of ever more migrants moving to Alaska, leaders of the Native nations met with state and federal officials in 1915 to discuss their future and the future of the Alaskan wilderness. The notion of reservations for each nation was rejected and instead, the Natives accepted the idea of being recipients of individual plots of land. They were also given promises that the land on which indigenous villages stood would not be sold to commercial developers.

In Canada, territories that First Nations people had hunted and fished on for thousands of years were sold by the government and put behind fences. As Canada continued to develop, highways, airports, oil pipelines and railroads were all built during the twentieth century. All of these developments interfered with traditional ways of life, even after laws passed in 1930 granted people the right to trap, fish and hunt on all unoccupied land.

As we entered the twenty-first century, Native people in the Subarctic have become more strident and self-confident in their efforts to protect their ways of life and the habitats that have shaped their cultures. In 2002, plans were announced to build North America's biggest open-cast mine in Alaska. The Yup'ik argued that the damage caused by extracting the estimated $120 billion of gold would severely interfere with their hunting and fishing grounds. Finally, in 2014 the American Environmental Protection Agency ruled in favour of the Yup'ik and the plans for the enormous mine were abandoned.

In Canada, when the government planned to weaken environmental protection laws, it led to the formation of a grass-roots, female-led indigenous movement called Idle No More. The movement snowballed and spread across Canada and into the United States. It continues to campaign to protect native sovereignty as well as the land, water and sky of the Subarctic.

There are currently around 1.4 million First Nations people living in Canada and a further 110,000 Native people living in Alaska. Their lives may be unrecognizable from those of their ancestors who lived two centuries ago, but they continue to fight to preserve their culture, their history and their ways of life.

THE SUBARCTIC

THE NORTHEAST

The Northeast region begins on the Atlantic Coast and stretches 900 miles west to the banks of the Mississippi River. Its northern border lies in southern Canada and extends down as far as the Ohio River. The climate is temperate and mild and there is no shortage of rainfall to provide fresh water. It is also a land that is rich in food sources.

Its extensive coastline, lakes, rivers and streams provide fish and shellfish. The woodland that covered most of the region before the arrival of Europeans was home to animals that were widely hunted. However, many Native Americans in the Northeast also developed a sophisticated system of horticulture to help support and sustain them.

The people of the Northeast can be roughly categorized based on three language families: Algonquian, Iroquoian and Siouan. These three main language families also help provide the strongest evidence as to the origins of the respective groups that populated the Northeast.

ALGONQUIAN SPEAKERS

Forms of Algonquian are spoken by groups right across the region. It is believed that the Algonquian language can be traced back as far as 1000 BCE with geographical origins in the Great Lakes region on the current US-Canada border.

It is through a commonality of language that linguists identify a common ancestry. In the case of Algonquian, this not only includes tribes and groups of the Northeast region, but also those of the Subarctic such as the Cree and Innu. The shared dialect supports the theory that it was these Algonquian-speaking Subarctic groups that moved south into warmer and less demanding climates. Once there, they thrived and splintered into various new tribes and groups.

The many Algonquian-speaking groups of the Northeast include the Algonquin, Wampanoag, Mohican, Mi'kmaq, Abenaki, Mohegan, Penobscot, Pequot, Massachusetts, Delaware, Kickapoo, Illinois, Ojibwa, Fox (Meskwaki) and Sauk. People often mistakenly believe that the term 'Algonquin' refers to all Algonquian-speaking peoples. The Algonquins are, in fact, a specific people who traditionally occupied the densely wooded areas of the Ottawa River valley near present-day Quebec.

THE MOHICANS

Of all the groups, tribes and nations of North America, the Mohicans have possibly entered the popular consciousness more than any other. This could be due to the 1826 novel *The Last of the Mohicans*, by James Fenimore Cooper, and its subsequent movie adaptations in the twentieth century. In Britain, it could be due to the adoption of the name Mohican to describe a type of haircut popular with punks in the 1970s. Whatever the reason, it is probably the same reason for the Mohicans being subject to more misconceptions and mythologizing than any other Native North American group.

According to the Mohicans' own oral histories of their origins: 'A great people travelled from the Northwest: crossed over the salt waters, and after long and weary pilgrimages – planting many colonies on their track – took possession and built their fires upon the Atlantic Coast, extending from the Delaware on the south to the Penobscot on the north. They became, in the process of time, divided into different tribes and interests; all, however, speaking one common dialect.'

The Mohicans settled near a river which they called the Mahicannituck, now called the Hudson, and called themselves the Muh-he-con-neok: the People of the Waters That Are Never Still. As the years passed, the name evolved and they became known as the Mohican.

Daily Life Among the Mohicans

The Mohican lands are centred around modern-day Albany in New York State and extend from the Hudson River Valley in the north down to Vermont, Massachusetts and Connecticut. Like many Native groups, the roles and everyday life of individuals were dependent on their sex and the season of the year.

Women were responsible for planting, weeding and caring for the crops of corn, beans and squash as well as being in charge of the home and raising children. Men served as warriors and hunters and brought back wild turkeys, pheasants, deer and moose that thrived in the woodland that surrounded them. Meat, vegetables and berries that were foraged were preserved by being dried and buried in pits that were lined with bark to help keep out moisture.

The woods also provided trees containing sap that the Mohicans tapped and boiled to make maple syrup. The running of the sap coincided with early spring, so tapping the trees was accompanied by ceremonies to mark the end of winter and a return to warmer temperatures.

Winter was a time to repair hunting and trapping equipment, make baskets and utensils and teach the young. Storytellers not only gave youngsters practical advice on their duties, roles and responsibilities, but they also taught them about Mohican religious beliefs.

Mohicans believe that when the creator had finished making the world, he divided it into four quarters and gave each section to a powerful being called a mani'towuk. Each was responsible for taking care of its own region and it is because of the different mani'towuks that winds blow in different directions. Winter is explained as being the result of a game of dice between the mani'towuks of the north and south – an especially cold winter is the result of the north mani'towuk winning the game. Every year, herbs and tobacco are gathered and offered with prayers to the four mani'towuks.

As with many tribes who relied on agriculture for food, over time the Mohican settlements became larger and more fortified. They were often positioned on hills between fields and woodland and usually surrounded by stockades or palisades of logs driven into the ground. Some Mohicans lived in longhouses that sheltered several families from the same clan. These could be as long as 30 metres (100 feet) and represented more permanent structures than the we-ko-wohm they also lived in when on hunting expeditions. Sometimes referred to as wigwams, these circular buildings were framed with bent saplings and covered with bark.

Mohican Contact with Europeans

The Dutch were the first Europeans to sail up the Mahicannituck and into the lands of the Mohicans. Led by Henry Hudson, after whom the river was destined to be renamed, the expedition of 1609 found an area rich in beavers and otters. By 1614, the Dutch had established a trading post and a war was raging between the Mohicans and the neighbouring Iroquoian-speaking Mohawks over who controlled the land and therefore access to the lucrative furs.

It was the Mohawks who eventually prevailed and the Mohicans who were driven from their territory along the Mahicannituck/ Hudson River. They moved east and settled near the Housatonic River in what is now Massachusetts, but the arrival of Europeans in ever greater numbers had caused irretrievable disruption to the Mohican way of life. The English replaced the Dutch as the dominant European power in the region and, along with their technology and disease, they brought a zeal to convert the Natives of what they called 'New England' to Christianity.

By 1734, the European newcomers were prospering to such an extent that some Natives began to attribute their success to their God. A missionary named John Sergeant was permitted to live in the Mohican village of Wnahktukuk, where he preached and baptized those he converted. A church and school were built and, before long, the European settlers began to refer to the Mohican village as Stockbridge. The Mohicans who lived there were simply called the 'Stockbridge Indians' and, when the Revolutionary War erupted in 1775, they fought on the side of the colonists.

Despite their war service, it was soon clear that they were not welcome in the newly independent nation and pressure grew to remove all Native Americans from New York State. The Mohicans moved several times until eventually settling in

Wisconsin. There, they were joined by another Native group called the Munsee. Now known as the Stockbridge-Munsee Band of Mohican Indians, they still live there today.

So, in spite of the impression given by the title of Fenimore Cooper's novel, there has yet to be a 'last Mohican'. It is also very likely that parts of the novel were inspired by events of the Pequot War. In this conflict, members of the Mohegan Tribe sided with the British in their fight against the Pequot. The Mohegan, who are also Algonquian-speaking, were led by a man named Uncas – which also happens to be the name of the main character in the novel. The Mohegan is today a federally recognized Indian Nation with its own reservation. Uncas, in the real world, was neither the last of the Mohegans nor the last of the Mohicans.

As for the haircut, shaved at the sides to leave a central stripe, it was never adopted by the Mohicans. In the United States, the same haircut is usually referred to as a 'Mohawk' despite the Mohawks never adopting that style either. The only Native people of North America who did wear their hair like this were the Pawnee, and they lived over a thousand miles away on the plains of modern-day Kansas.

THE WAMPANOAG

The Wampanoag are another Algonquian-speaking group that has entered Western popular culture more than most indigenous North American tribes. The ancestors of the Wampanoag have lived in what is now known as Martha's Vineyard for as long as 10,000 years and, like the Mohicans, they hunted and fished but also farmed extensively.

It is believed that, at the start of the seventeenth century, there were as many as 40,000 people living in the sixty-seven villages that comprised the Wampanoag Nation. These villages were spread along the East Coast, and the Wampanoag Territory covered Cape Cod, Nantucket and Rhode Island.

The Wampanoag are most commonly associated with their interactions with the English pilgrims on the ship *Mayflower*. But the insidious impact of Europeans had started to devastate Wampanoag communities long before the 'Pilgrim Fathers' had ever set sail in 1620.

Ships from England had been arriving in North American waters from the start of the 1600s. It was not uncommon for these vessels to capture Native Americans and take them back to Europe as either slaves or exotic curiosities to be displayed. One Native who suffered this fate was called Tisquantum, although the Europeans called him Squanto. It is believed he was first captured on the coast of what is now Maine by an expedition led by Captain George Weymouth in 1605.

Some say he was taken to England but, by 1614, he was back in his homeland where he was unfortunate enough to be captured a second time. This time, it was another English explorer called Thomas Hunt, who sailed for Spain. Once there, Tisquantum and twenty-three other Native Americans were sold into the European slave trade. Exactly how he won his freedom is unknown, but he recrossed the Atlantic in 1619 acting as an interpreter for Captain Thomas Dermer. Although back in his homeland, he was never able to return to his people. By the time he got there, his home village of Patuxet no longer existed. It been completely wiped out in the 'Great Dying' – the period between 1616 and 1619 when mysterious European diseases ravaged the Native coastal communities of the Northeast. Tisquantum was then captured by the Wampanoag.

The Arrival of the *Mayflower*

At the time that the *Mayflower*'s passengers made land in 1620, the Wampanoag were already experiencing a time of great change and turmoil. Different Wampanoag groups usually co-operated and worked together under the leadership of chosen leaders called sachems. The impact of the Great Dying led to the loss of a great many sachems and meant that traditional bonds and structures had broken down. Land had been lost to rival tribes and new sachems were working to build new unions between the surviving Wampanoag groups.

It is in the context of this restructuring and existential threat from both epidemics and other tribes that the Wampanoag watched the men, women and children of the *Mayflower* come ashore. They must have seen the arrival of the new Europeans as a threat but, in their present circumstances, they also saw it as an opportunity to forge a powerful new alliance.

Tisquantum, with his knowledge of English, was used by the Wampanoag to help develop relations. He instructed the new settlers on how to plant corn and where to fish and hunt. Once trust had been established, he was able to introduce the English to the Wampanoag chief Ousamequin, also known as Massasoit.

This led to a peace treaty between the two groups, and the Wampanoag undoubtedly saved the *Mayflower* pilgrims from starvation. Like the majority of indigenous peoples, the Wampanoag gave thanks by holding feasts and ceremonies during times of harvest. The autumn of 1621 was no different and, at some point between 21 September and 9 November, the people destined to be known as the Pilgrim Fathers held a three-day celebration of their successful harvest. It is not known if any members of the Wampanoag were present. However, during the nineteenth century, this event entered popular American culture and imagination as the First Thanksgiving.

The foothold that was established by the *Mayflower* was consolidated by arrivals of other ships in 1621 and 1623. More settlements were established and the door was held open for more European Puritans wishing to escape religious persecution. As early as the 1630s, the Wampanoag were a minority in their own lands. With Plymouth Colony established as a base, the English Puritans went on to found the towns of Windsor in 1632, Wethersfield in 1633, Hartford in 1635 and Springfield in 1636.

Tisquatum, like so many others, died of a fever brought by the Europeans and his remains lie in an unknown grave. Others were killed in a more direct and deliberate way by the Europeans. The Pequot people were brutally wiped out by the colonizers of Massachusetts Bay in 1637. For the Wampanoag, the Pequot War was a harbinger of things to come.

King Philip's War

When the Wampanoag chief Ousamequin died in 1662, he was succeeded by his son Metacomet. Metacomet had grave misgivings about the alliance that his father had forged with the colonists and began to see that a cuckoo had been allowed into the nest. The colonists continued to arrive in ever greater numbers from Europe and continued to expand into Wampanoag land. At the same time, they were making ever greater demands and claimed that the peace treaty required the Wampanoag to hand over any guns that they owned.

Metacomet, perhaps seeing that this was the last opportunity to remove the new arrivals from his lands, launched an uprising that comprised not only the Wampanoag but also the Nipmuck, Pocumtuck and Narragansett tribes. In 1675, Metacomet, who was known as King Philip by the English, co-ordinated a series of ruthless raids on colonist settlements. Initially, the war went well for the Natives and many of the frontier towns were devastated. But the targeting of Wampanoag crops by the colonial militia raised the spectre of starvation and the tide slowly turned against the indigenous people.

After fourteen months of fighting that saw entire villages burnt to the ground and thousands killed or sold into slavery, the rebellion was finally put down. The Wampanoag, Narragansett and other tribes had been all but wiped out. Those who could fled west, and their land was soon occupied by new arrivals from England.

Metacomet was captured and was hung, drawn and quartered. His head was displayed on a spike at Plymouth Colony for the next twenty years. The Wampanoag had helped the English to survive, and their reward was to lose their land, liberty and lives.

Many centuries later, in 1970, the Wampanoag leader Frank James gave a speech to mark the 350th anniversary of the *Mayflower*'s sailing and the First Thanksgiving. He said: 'Ousamequin, the great Sachem of the Wampanoag, and his People welcomed and befriended the settlers of the Plymouth Plantation. Perhaps he did this because his Tribe had been depleted by an epidemic. Or his knowledge of the harsh oncoming winter was the reason for his peaceful acceptance of these acts. This action by Massasoit was perhaps our biggest mistake. We, the Wampanoag, welcomed you, the white man, with open arms, little knowing that it was the beginning of the end; that before fifty years were to pass, the Wampanoag would no longer be a free people. What happened in those short fifty years? What has happened in the last three hundred years?'

The Wampanoag Today

Of the nearly seventy Wampanoag tribal communities that were present in New England in 1600, only six remain today. The 5,000 residents of New England who are the descendants of those who watched the *Mayflower* arrive on their shores work tirelessly to honour their ancestors and keep their culture alive. Descendants of the Wampanoag have also recently been identified in the islands of the Caribbean. Their forefathers had been sold into slavery in the aftermath of King Philip's War.

THE EXTINCTION OF THE PEQUOT

Unlike many other tribes of the Northeast who, although severely depleted and robbed of their lands, managed to survive the arrival of the Europeans, the Pequot did not. They were an Algonquian-speaking people who shared the same origins as the Mohegans but had split from them at some point before contact with the English. The Pequots had aggressively expanded to take land in the Connecticut River valley from numerous tribes including the Mohegan and the Wampanoag. This was an attempt to corner the lucrative fur trade that had been established by the Dutch, and it was with the settlers from Holland that the Pequot forged an alliance.

Tensions grew as different nations, both Native and European, manoeuvred to control access to furs. The murders of several fur traders at the hands of the Pequot led to a collapse of their alliance with the Dutch, as well as the launching of reprisal raids by the English. Angered by these raids, the Pequot laid siege to the English Fort Saybrook in 1636 and attacked Wethersfield in 1637.

The Mystic Massacre

The leaders of the Puritan towns raised a militia of ninety men who were accompanied by seventy Mohegan warriors to pursue the Pequot. On 26 May 1637, they surrounded the fortified Pequot village at Mystic and attacked at dawn. The combination of a ferocious fire inside the village and the soldiers waiting outside the fort meant that, of the 500 who were originally sheltering within, only seven were taken prisoner and another seven escaped into the woods.

The slaughter of so many of their warriors and the brutality of the assault led many Pequot to abandon their lands and their villages and to seek refuge with the Mohawk. Led by a chief named Sassacus, they were relentlessly pursued and many were captured or killed before they reached safety. When Sassacus did finally arrive at Mohawk Territory in present-day New York, he was murdered and his head and hands were sent to the English.

The Treaty of Hartford was signed in 1638. It declared that the Pequots were now extinct and that any surviving members must submit to the authority of the Mohegans or Narragansett.

IROQUOIAN SPEAKERS

The Iroquoian-speaking peoples of the Northeast are perhaps most notable for the intertribal links that they established between themselves. The Iroquois League (or Iroquois Confederacy) has been described as the most famous Native government in North America and was established before the arrival of the Europeans. The exact date of its creation remains a matter of academic debate. Many archaeologists put its formation at around 1450, although others argue that it was established much earlier. Some believe it was formed after the adoption of corn as a staple crop, whereas others think the evidence of the Iroquois oral history points to the solar eclipse of 1142. According to their founding tradition, it was created after centuries of inter-Iroquois warfare when the different tribes were persuaded to live in peace and harmony by a mourning chief named Hiawatha.

The Iroquois League/Confederacy is considered significant because many believe it to be one of the oldest democratic institutions in the world. Some claim that the Great Law of Peace, as the confederacy's constitution is known, greatly interested Benjamin Franklin and could even have been a source of inspiration for the Constitution of the United States of America.

The Iroquoian language family is thought to date back to around 2000 BCE and have its origins in the area around the southern shores of Lake Ontario and Lake Erie. By around 1000 CE, five tribes or distinct groups emerged in this area: the Mohawk, the Seneca, the Cayuga, the Onondaga and the Oneida.

NATIONS OF THE LEAGUE

The Mohawk, or 'People of the Flint', had their territories farthest east of all the Nations of the Confederacy – which is why they were sometimes referred to as the 'Keepers of the Eastern

Door'. Some historians believe that the Mohawk hairstyle, which involved shaving or plucking all but a square of hair on the top of their heads, was intended to make their heads more attractive targets to scalp hunters over any women and children present.

The Seneca, or 'People of the Great Hill', were the largest of the nations that made up the initial confederacy. At their height, the Seneca could assemble 1,000 braves on the battlefield, which was as many as the other nations of the league combined. As the member of the confederacy that was positioned furthest west, they were sometimes called the 'Keepers of the Western Door'.

The Cayuga, or 'People of the Great Swamp', had a traditional homeland that stretched from the northern shore of the St. Lawrence River to the Finger Lakes region. Despite the reference to swamps, the Cayuga were highly successful farmers.

The Onondaga, or 'People of the Hills', occupied the territory in the centre of Iroquois land. As a result, they became the centre of the league's political life, as the sachems or leaders travelled to Onondaga lands for councils.

The Oneida were probably the smallest of the nations that made up the Iroquois Confederacy. Meaning 'People of the Standing Stone', they were made up of three clans and occupied a single village in what is now north-central New York State. Their name is derived from the legend that a large stone would appear to mark the location of their next village.

Iroquoian Life

The region these nations occupied is sometimes called Iroquoia, and the woodland that covered it provided seemingly inexhaustible resources. Timber and bark were utilized for construction and the woods were filled with food such as walnuts and berries to forage. Archaeological evidence also points to whitetail deer, who lived in the forests, as being an important food source.

Larger villages could be home to over 1,000 inhabitants. These were surrounded by palisade walls that could be anywhere between four and six metres high and encircled an area of up to three acres. Shelter was provided by timber longhouses with roofs made of elm bark shingles or tiles. Fields of corn, maize, beans and squash surrounded the fortified village.

Every twenty years or so, the entire village would be abandoned and rebuilt at a new location. This was done for a variety of reasons. As the years passed, the distances that needed to be travelled to gather firewood grew longer and longer. After so many years, timber longhouses would be in need of repair. This was an opportunity to rebuild near soil that had not been exhausted of nutrients by two decades of cultivation.

Moving villages would not only require new houses and palisades to be built, but fields also had to be cleared. This was achieved through a combination of burning and felling trees with axes. Horticulture was very much the responsibility of women and, working in teams, they planted the maize, beans and squash seeds in hillocks. They then weeded them throughout the summer and harvested and processed the crops in the autumn. Crops were rotated annually from field to field in an attempt to maintain yields, but this delayed rather than prevented the loss of fertility in the soil.

Family Life

Extended families, and therefore occupants of longhouses, were organized along maternal lines. So grandparents would live with their daughters and their daughters' husbands as well as their children. Most longhouses were organized under the informal authority of a senior matriarch. On a wider level, membership of clans was also based on the matrilineal line.

It was the custom of these clans to reuse ancestral names, of both men and women. This was done both to keep the memory of cherished figures alive and to impose high expectations on the new recipient of the name. The clan unit was important to the way the members of the Iroquois League operated and organized themselves. Each clan would hold regular councils in which leaders were appointed and decisions made. This enabled the opinions of individuals to be shared in councils held by villages, tribes or even nations and ensured their voices were accurately represented.

Five Nations

As part of the Iroquois League, the five nations would meet in a longhouse and consider themselves to be one people. Whatever the exact date and circumstances of its foundation, it was apparent to seventeenth-century Europeans that the confederacy had been in existence long before the white man's arrival. When meeting with Iroquois leaders in 1635, the Dutchman Harmen Meyndertsz van den Bogaert had it explained to him: 'Here it is Mohawk, Oneida, Onondaga, Cayuga and Seneca all over – the Iroquois League.'

Decades later, in 1654, the Frenchman Simon Le Moyne recorded being told: 'We the five Iroquois Nations compose but one cabin; we maintain but one fire; and we have, from time immemorial, dwelt under one and the same roof.' As in any family, there were rivalries, disputes and even outright conflict between the various nations of the league. However, the arrival of the Europeans in the seventeenth century had an undeniable galvanizing effect on the Iroquois League.

In fact, the arrival of the Dutch and the English heralded a prolonged period of warfare, death and destruction. Perhaps counterintuitively, these wars were not waged against the new arrivals from Europe but against rival indigenous groups. The Iroquois quickly understood that access to furs meant access to European technology. Above all else, this meant access to firearms. Unfortunately for the Iroquois, the beaver – which was especially prized by the Europeans – had never been particularly common in their territories and was very soon extremely scarce. To increase their access to furs, and therefore firearms, they sought to take over neighbouring land and eliminate competition.

At the same time that they fought for beaver pelts, they were being assaulted by the highly infectious pathogens that had been brought by the Europeans. Some estimates claim that over sixty per cent of the entire Mohawk population died in the first smallpox epidemic of 1634. Once established on American shores, these diseases continued to exact a deadly toll and, by 1646, it is thought that the Mohawk population stood at less than a quarter of what it had in 1600.

Intertribal Warfare

Rival indigenous tribes joined forces and formed confederacies in the face of the onslaught from Europeans – and the epidemics they brought with them. The Iroquois League saw itself in an existential struggle and the violence against other Native peoples intensified. The Beaver Wars saw the Iroquois attack the Neutral Confederacy to the east between 1647 and 1651 and the Huron Confederacy to the north in 1648 and 1649. They assaulted the Tobacco Tribal Alliance in Ontario between 1649 and 1651 and the Erie Nation in northern Ohio between 1654 and 1656. The Susquehannocks in Pennsylvania, Quapas in Ohio, Shawnees to the south and Abenakis in the northeast were all attacked in 1662. During the 1670s and 1680s, the Iroquois League extended their attacks into the Midwest where they assaulted the Illinois, Ottawas, Foxes and Ojibwas.

The desire for a continuing supply of guns, cloth, kettles, metal axes, etc., meant that war was not waged against the English. Commercial ties led to the creation of what became known as the Covenant Chain. This was a series of contracts between the Iroquois and the English and the Iroquois and other smaller, Native groups. The Iroquois positioned themselves to be useful to the point of being indispensable to the English. Their ability to successfully mediate and negotiate with diverse groups undoubtedly helped reduce conflict between the English and indigenous people. This secured the Iroquois status as well as wealth.

Relations with the French were less convivial and there were French attacks on major settlements of the Mohawks, Senecas, Oneidas and Onondagas in the 1680s and 1690s. Hostilities were finally brought to an end in 1701 when the Iroquois League signed the Grand Settlement. This secured peace with France by formally declaring the league's neutrality in the Anglo-French struggle for control in North America.

Expanding South

The Grand Settlement meant an end to fighting between the league and the French-aligned Native groups. As a result, the Iroquois Confederacy looked south for new rivals to fight and new lands to control. For the next fifty years, they were engaged in almost constant conflict with the Choctaws, the Creeks, the

Catawbas and the Cherokees. This expansion into the south also led to the Tuscarora tribe joining the league and, from 1723 onwards, the Iroquois Confederacy was comprised of six nations. The Tuscarora were Iroquoian-speaking descendants of a group that had left the Lake Ontario and Lake Erie region around 500 BCE and had settled in modern-day North Carolina and Virginia.

The first half of the eighteenth century saw the Iroquois reposition themselves as being essential to the interests of both the English and the French. While this succeeded in the short term and gave the league both power and prestige, by the middle of the 1700s, the rules of the game had changed. The Europeans no longer wanted furs, they wanted land.

The Iroquois sold land they had captured to the English colonists but, by the late 1740s, they had nothing left to sell. At the same time, more and more colonists were arriving and encroaching on Iroquois Territory.

Victory for England against France in the Seven Years' War that raged between 1754 to 1763 meant that the Iroquois League lost its position as a power broker. When war broke out between the American colonists and the British government, the league left tribes and even individuals free to choose which side they would back. The Oneida chose to fight alongside the colonists and, as a result, are sometimes known as 'America's first allies'. The vast majority of Iroquois however, believing that the British represented a more secure source of manufactured goods, ended up fighting for Britain.

Moving North

After the war, the British government set aside land alongside the Grand River in Ontario for members of the league to settle on. About 1,000 members, from all six tribes, moved there and their leaders established a council to govern what became the Six Nations Reserve.

South of the border in the United States, around 2,000 league members re-established its existence at Buffalo Creek in what was Seneca Territory. They moved to Onondaga land near Syracuse in 1847 and remain a reservation government to this day.

SIOUAN SPEAKERS

The other major language family present in the Northeast region is Siouan. Even though Siouan is most commonly associated with the people of the Plains, its origins can probably be traced back to the Northeast. Linguists believe that, over 1,000 years ago, a large number of Siouan-speaking people migrated west and occupied an enormous area of the centre of the continent. The reasons for the migration are unknown, but a sizeable number of Siouan speakers remained present in the Northeast. They were still there when the Europeans arrived in the seventeenth century.

The most notable of the Siouan-speaking people of the Northeast are the Ho-Chunk. For many years, the Ho-Chunk were commonly referred to as the Winnebago. This English term was derived from the Algonquian word for 'people of the dirty water' and is thought to refer to the Fox River and Lake Winnebago which become clogged with dead fish in the summer. As a result, the term Winnebago is now considered derogatory. The name Ho-Chunk comes from the word Ho-Chungra which means 'people of the parent speech' and reflects the subsequent spread and popularity of the Siouan language.

The exact origins of the Ho-Chunk are unclear and the subject of contesting theories. One suggests that they migrated from the East Coast along the Ohio River and then branched north to the Wisconsin area somewhere between 800 and 1200 CE. Others argue they arrived in Wisconsin as recently as the 1500s after migrating from the lower Mississippi Valley.

Like their Algonquian and Iroquois neighbours in the Northeast, the Ho-Chunk partially sustained themselves by growing and storing crops. Using canoes made by digging out the centres of tree trunks, they travelled far and wide along the Fox and Wisconsin Rivers in search of game to hunt. The Ho-Chunk also crossed the Mississippi and hunted bison on the Plains.

Traditionally, the Ho-Chunk lived in rectangular longhouses in a few villages situated in the Winnebago area. They were organized along paternal lines and, at the time of first contact with Europeans in the 1630s, were divided into 12 clans. These clans belonged either to those in the Air or Earth division. The clans in the Air division were Thunder, Eagle, Hawk and Pigeon and those of the Earth were Bear, Wolf, Water Spirit, Buffalo, Deer, Elk, Fish and Snake. A member of an Earth Clan always found a marriage partner from an Air Clan and vice versa. Some clans had specific roles or responsibilities. For example, the Hawk Clan played an important role in warfare and the Buffalo Clan was responsible for spreading news and sharing information throughout all the Ho-Chunk people.

Ho-Chunk Contact with Europeans

A French explorer named Jean Nicolet was the first to make contact with the Ho-Chunk when he arrived in the Green Bay region in 1634. The Ho-Chunk soon engaged in the fur trade and were described as powerful and skilled warriors by the French traders. It was the expansion, aggression and determination of the Iroquois Confederacy to dominate the fur trade that spelt disaster for the Ho-Chunk. Although they were not attacked directly, Algonquian-speaking refugees who were fleeing the Iroquois onslaught moved into Ho-Chunk territories. The diseases the refugees brought with them led to new epidemics. Competition for resources led to warfare and starvation. Some estimate the reduction in Ho-Chunk numbers during this period was as high as ninety per cent.

Intermarriage with Algonquin tribes helped numbers recover but, alongside the switch to prioritizing hunting animals for their fur, led to a diluting of Ho-Chunk identity and loss of long-held traditions. The disruption caused by the arrival of so many people fleeing the Iroquois Confederacy caused them to move from the Green Bay region and settle in Wisconsin between Lake Winnebago and the Mississippi River. When they moved, they switched to living in smaller, more scattered villages and abandoned the rectangular longhouses in favour of domed wigwams. Trade with the British and French for guns, traps, tools and cloth meant that horticulture, while still practised, was not given the priority it once was. It also meant that, in search of ever more beaver pelts, they expanded west and south throughout the 1700s.

Ho-Chunk War with the United States

Decades of trade led to the Ho-Chunk developing a strong attachment and sense of loyalty towards the British – even after Wisconsin became part of the United States in 1783. When war broke out between Britain and the United States in 1812, the Ho-Chunk fought on the side of the British.

By the 1830s, large numbers of Euro-American settlers had moved to Wisconsin and were eager to take over Ho-Chunk lands. A treaty was signed in 1837 that ceded all Ho-Chunk Territory to the federal government and gave them just eight months to vacate their lands. When this deadline was widely ignored, the army moved in to remove them in 1841. They were initially moved to Minnesota and then on to South Dakota before finally being given a reservation in Nebraska in 1865. But the government had failed to remove all of the Ho-Chunk from Wisconsin and many who had been removed simply moved back in the intervening years.

Their continued presence greatly angered the Euro-American settlers and the government tried to remove the Ho-Chunk again in 1873 and 1874. This again failed and, during the 1880s, they were allowed to take up land claims and remain in Wisconsin. Many supported themselves by working as travelling fruit pickers and agricultural labourers and hunting and trapping animals through the winter.

At the start of the twentieth century, Ho-Chunk performance programmes and craft sales were established in the city of Wisconsin Dells that were designed to appeal to tourists. The success of this programme brought economic benefits and caused more Ho-Chunk to settle in the area. This helped establish a Wisconsin Ho-Chunk identity despite not being identified by the federal government at this time. In 1963, the Wisconsin Ho-Chunk were finally given recognition and sovereignty.

THE NORTHEAST

THE SOUTHEAST

The area of the Southeast stretches up from the Gulf of Mexico to the Ohio River Valley. It also extends from the Atlantic Ocean in the east to the Mississippi River in the west. The climate in the north of the region is warm and becomes subtropical in the south. Much like the Northeast before the land was settled by Europeans, it was mostly covered in deciduous forests. However, the Southeast also contains areas of wetland and coastal scrub. At the time of the arrival of the Europeans, the Southeast was more densely populated than the Northeast and was among the most densely populated areas of all of North America.

THE PEOPLE OF THE SOUTHEAST

Dialects

The people of the Southeast speak languages derived from several language families, the most common being Muskogean. This is spoken by the Seminole, Creek, Choctaw and Chickasaw, among others. Siouan is also present and spoken by the Catawba, Cheraw and Waccamaw, as well as many smaller tribes. Some languages are spoken by only one tribe, most notably the Iroquoian-speaking Cherokee. The Natchez, believed to be direct descendants of prehistoric Mississippian peoples, spoke a language that was entirely unique to them and is now believed extinct.

Diet

The diet of the people of the Southeast was underpinned by agriculture. Several varieties of corn were farmed and were commonly baked or roasted on the cob. Beans and squash were also cultivated and often combined and stewed in a pot to make dishes such as succotash. Sunflowers were grown and harvested for their oil, and the diet of most groups was supplemented by foraging nuts, berries and greens.

The length of the growing season in the Southwest meant that it was possible for many tribes to plant and harvest twice a year. The first planting took place during spring. By midsummer, produce was available and a second planting was undertaken. The crop yields were increased by burning off the remaining stalks of the previous harvest. In early autumn, the primary harvest took place and was marked by major communal celebrations.

Hunting

Meat was added to the diet through the hunting of the ample wildlife that was present in the Southeast. Turkeys, deer, rabbits, bears, raccoons, otters and squirrels were killed and eaten while their populations and habitats were carefully managed. Controlled use of fire cleared large areas of land which enabled the bushes and trees that supported deer, rabbits, turkeys and squirrels to take root and thrive. Trees were protected from the fires by placing a ring of wet clay around the trunk – a process known as girdling. In what is now Florida, alligators and turtles were hunted, and oysters, mussels and crabs were consumed in coastal areas.

Hunting would mostly take place during the winter months and many villages would empty of men as they took to the woods on extended hunting expeditions. Meat, supplemented by dried corn, squash and beans, was an essential component of the diet in the winter months.

Settlement and Shelter

The greatest determining factor in the location of many settlements was the quality of the soil. Most people lived in small villages or hamlets that were satellites of more substantial towns. The towns were protected by the timber ring of a palisade and often contained a square, communal house or temple. In many cases, the communal houses or temples were built on top of large mounds that can still be seen today. The population of the surrounding hamlets would gather in the towns for ceremonies and celebrations.

Most people in the Southeast built circular winter houses that were tightly sealed and had cone-shaped roofs made of thatch. Summer dwellings were often built in a rectangular shape and had walls made from wattle and daub. This involved plastering clay over a framework of woven branches and gave shade and protection from strong winds without becoming stifling in the summer heat. The precise style of houses varied across the region and often reflected the climate. The Seminole, who lived in the sweltering heat and swampy terrain of the modern-day Florida Everglades, developed a form of housing called the chickee. These were built on stilts, raising the floor off the wet ground and with open sides to enable air to circulate. Protection from downpours of rain was afforded by a dense thatch roof.

The climate also meant that, unlike in some regions, clothing wasn't a matter of life and death. Tanned deerskin was fashioned into breechcloths, shirts and cloaks for men in summer and women usually wore a skirt with a tunic. In winter, in the more northerly areas of the region, bear fur and bison hides were used to make leggings and robes.

Feathers were highly prized for their value in ornamentation, with the feathers of cranes, eagles, hawks and swans being particularly valued.

Social Structures

Most cultures of the Southeast were ruled by chiefs. However, the degree of power and reverence that chiefs enjoyed varied greatly between nations. The chief of the Natchez was a godlike figure who was called the 'Great Sun', while the chief of the Timucua was literally carried by his followers, such was his elevated status. The Choctaw, Creek and Cherokee had chiefs who were much more earthly figures. Rather than inheriting their position, they would earn it through achievements and accomplishments.

Perhaps reflecting the more pragmatic nature of their chiefs, the societies of the Choctaw, Creek and Cherokee were much less stratified. The Natchez, on the other hand, had strict rules regarding potential marriage suitors and the Chitimacha, who resided in modern-day Louisiana, had what is believed to be the only caste system present in all Native North American societies.

Across the Southeastern peoples, families were organized and descent was traced matrilineally. Extended families usually spread across several villages, which created links and fostered a sense of kinship instead of rivalry between settlements.

The influence of women was also felt in many other ways. Farming was almost entirely their responsibility along with preserving and preparing the food. Clothing, pottery and baskets were all made by women and the early education of both girls and boys was undertaken by the children's female relatives.

Men were often absent from villages for extended periods because they were responsible for hunting, trading and waging war. Trade in particular could lead to prolonged absences as it not only took place on a local level, but also with people in the Northeast and on the Plains. Archaeological evidence indicates that there was trade with the Antilles islands in the Caribbean, and there is significant cultural evidence of exchanges with people in both Central and South America.

In comparison to many regions, the Southeast was an easy place to live, with plentiful food and resources available. As a result, trade often involved luxury items. People who lived on the coast provided the shells that were used to make beads and decorate clothing and objects. In exchange, they received resources that were scarce in their territory, such as furs or flint.

While at home, men built houses and helped clear fields and harvest crops. They were also responsible for the education of boys. Unlike girls, who had very short childhoods and were soon working alongside their mothers and aunts, boys were allowed to learn the skills necessary to fulfil their roles by playing with other boys. This involved stalking small animals such as squirrels and hunting them with blowpipes, or wrestling and playing ball games.

Spirituality

The belief that all humans, animals and plants have a spirit was universal across the Southeastern region. A failure to treat the spirits of slain animals with adequate respect could result in disaster, with the spirit taking its revenge. Most illness and disease was attributed to disrespecting animals that had been hunted and killed.

Plant spirits were considered to be friendly to humans and in many cases offered an antidote to disease caused by animal spirits. The Green Corn Ceremony, or Busk, was celebrated in midsummer by nearly all the people and tribes of the Southeast. Reflecting both the importance of corn as a crop and its annual return, all fires were allowed to die throughout the village before being ceremoniously relit. This symbolized renewal and heralded a new beginning.

Certain objects were believed to be imbued with a spiritual energy or power. Wood that came from a tree that had been struck by lightning and crystals such as quartz were believed to have sacred power. The people of the Tukabahchee Creek tribe held embossed copper plates to have sacred power.

Origin Stories

Across the Southeast, the story of a great flood and the earth being created from mud rescued from beneath the waters was commonplace. Myths and legends centred around the struggle between hero figures and tricksters were also widely believed – both in the Southeast and across North America.

First Contact with Europeans

The geographical location of the Southwest meant it was blessed with a wonderful climate. It also meant the inhabitants were among the first Native North Americans to have contact with Europeans and the first to experience the horror of what that entailed.

The very first Europeans to reach the United States were Spanish. In 1512, Juan Ponce de León led an expedition from Puerto Rico to search for land to the north of Cuba. Believing he had discovered a large island, he named it *Pascua Florida* and claimed the land for Spain. The name, which roughly translates as Flowery Easter, reflects that it was both Easter and that the vegetation was in bloom at the time of his arrival.

Spanish expeditions and attempts to colonize Florida continued throughout the sixteenth century – most notably Hernando de Soto's expedition of 1539, which managed to cross the Mississippi River. The failure to discover gold during these incursions tempered the desire to occupy the land, but ownership of Florida and beyond was seen as strategically vital to protect the colonies in the Caribbean. Enough Spaniards arrived to devastate the Native populations with disease and as many as ninety per cent succumbed to sicknesses such as smallpox.

French Florida

In the 1560s, French protestants, known as Huguenots, attempted to establish colonies in what is today Florida and South Carolina. Fleeing religious persecution in the Catholic homeland, they hoped to create a Protestant society where they were free to worship as they wished. Fort Carolina, as the settlement was known, was attacked by the Spanish in 1565 and all the Huguenots were either killed or fled into the wilderness.

The English Influence

The English may have been the last of the European nations to explore the possibilities of colonizing North America, but they were obviously the most successful. By the late seventeenth century, their colonies stretched across the whole eastern seaboard from Maine to the top of the Florida peninsula. The thirteen colonies that were established in the seventeenth and eighteenth centuries attracted Protestants in search of religious freedom, ambitious younger sons of the nobility who were keen to amass their own land and fortune and patriotic pragmatists who looked upon Spain's colonies in the New World with envy. All of these ambitions were enabled and empowered by the establishment of trading companies by the English crown.

The result was that, by the beginning of the eighteenth century, when the English started to exert the greatest influence in the Southeast, the Natives of those lands had been adapting to and recovering from the impact of Europeans for over two centuries.

THE CREEK

The existence of the Creek Nation was a direct result of the arrival of Europeans. When Columbus landed in 1492, there were no Creeks. The threats posed by the arrivals of the Spanish and the appalling impact of the epidemics they brought with them led the Native peoples from an area that stretched from the Ocmulgee River in the east to the Tallapoosa River in Alabama to form a complex political alliance. These peoples spoke a variety of different languages, with Muskogean being the most popular, but were united in their wish to stave off the threat from the Europeans and remain at peace with one another.

By 1715, when the English from the soon-to-be-established colony of Georgia began to build relations with these allied peoples, they referred to them as Creeks. Initially, it was a shorthand term for those who were living on Ochese Creek, but was soon being used to refer to every Native person of the Deep South.

By the time Georgia, the last of the thirteen colonies, was founded in 1732, relations between the English and the Creek were well established. Initially, trade centred around the exchange of European goods like textiles and ironware for enslaved people. Soon, however, it was deer skins that were being supplied and tens of thousands were soon crossing the Atlantic every year. English factories then processed the skins and turned them into breeches and gloves or stretched them over books.

Guns and rum soon became integral parts of Creek culture and the increase in trade led to a degree of integration between the Creek and the newcomers. Some Georgia traders lived among the Creek, married Creek women and had children. Some of these dual heritage children, such as William Macintosh and Alexander McGillivray, grew up to become important tribal leaders. Creek communities were further bolstered by the arrival of Africans who had escaped enslavement. They, too, settled by the hundreds in Creek villages throughout the eighteenth century.

The result of this trade was that the Creek Nation became the most powerful confederation of indigenous people in the Southeast region. They occupied millions of acres of land that stretched across modern-day Alabama and Florida as well as Georgia. All this was to change in the years following the American War of Independence.

THE ROAD TO REMOVAL

When the thirteen colonies went to war to win their independence in 1775, many Native Americans chose to side with the British. It was with the British that they had established secure trading relationships, and the great fear was that independence would lead to yet more immigrants from Europe and more encroachment on their lands.

When the Treaty of Paris was signed in 1793 and the War of Independence was brought to an end, Britain agreed to hand over all land east of the Mississippi, south of the Great Lakes and north of Florida. It made no mention of the fact that much of this land had been promised to several Native American nations in treaties they had signed with the British.

One legacy of the war was that the victorious colonists viewed all Native Americans as treacherous savages who had sided with their great enemy. For their part, the indigenous people viewed the colonists as double-crossers whose treaties were worthless.

Wars between Native Americans and the United States raged throughout the 1780s and 1790s – encouraged and enabled by the British who were hoping to make life for the government of their former colony as difficult as possible. Britain retained a presence in Canada and when war broke out between Britain and the United States in 1812, once again many Native American warriors fought under the British flag.

To many Americans, this merely confirmed what they already believed – that the indigenous peoples were their intractable enemy and were an obstacle in the way of America fulfilling its destiny. They simply had to be removed.

The Indian Removal Act

Many American presidents, such as Thomas Jefferson, had advocated a relatively peaceful approach towards the Native Americans living within the United States. They encouraged conversion to Christianity and a peaceful integration into American society through property ownership and commerce.

When Andrew Jackson was elected president in 1828, however, it became immediately apparent that he had a less conciliatory approach. Jackson had fought in the War of 1812 against the British and their Native American allies and had personally led a brutal subsequent campaign against the Seminole in what is modern-day Florida.

The vicious treatment meted out to the Natives under his presidency earned him the nickname 'Indian Killer'. But it also won him many supporters, and he was elected for a second term in 1832. As far as Jackson was concerned, the Natives were not members of foreign nations – they were Americans. As such, they were subject to the same rules and laws as every other American.

Jackson believed any form of self-rule would only be possible if they abandoned their ancestral homelands and moved to officially designated reservations that were west of the Mississippi River. In his eyes, this was the merciful thing to do. If the Native nations remained where they were, Jackson was convinced that the ever-increasing number of settlers would completely wipe them out in a few short years. But he also believed it was the right thing to do. As he asked Congress: 'What good man would prefer a country covered with forests and ranged by a few thousand savages to our extensive Republic, studied with cities, towns and prosperous farms, embellished with all the improvements which art can devise and industry execute, occupied by more than 12 million happy people, and filled with all the blessings of liberty, civilization and religion?'

To ensure that large numbers of Native American people could be moved as he wished, Jackson wanted to pass new legislation that meant relocation could be legally enforced. It was called the Indian Removal Act. Support for Jackson and his legislation was far from universal, and many spoke out against it – including Davy Crockett who had become a congressman for the state of Tennessee. There was an impassioned debate in both Houses of Congress but, on 26 May 1830, the Indian Removal Act was signed into law by Andrew Jackson.

Less than six months later, the forced relocation of indigenous people in the Southeast began.

The Removal of the Creek

There had been concerted efforts throughout the 1820s to remove the Creek from the land they occupied. A Creek Chief who had a Scottish father and was known as William McIntosh or Tustunnuggee Hutkee (White Warrior) signed the Treaty of Indian Springs in 1825. This signed over all Creek land in Georgia and some in Alabama. In return, he was given land to the west of the Mississippi, known as Indian Country, and $200,000.

McIntosh had acted without the approval of the Creek National Council and, as a result, he was punished by death. A delegation of Creek leaders was dispatched to Washington in 1826 to attempt to get the Treaty of Indian Springs overturned, and was partially successful. The Treaty of Washington was signed, which superseded the Treaty of Indian Springs, and returned all land within Alabama to the Creek. All land in Georgia, however, remained in federal hands.

Over the next few years, several hundred Creek crossed the Mississippi to Indian Territory, but these were mostly former supporters of McIntosh. Increased encroachment on their lands by settlers led to another Creek delegation travelling to Washington in 1832. This resulted in the Treaty of Cusseta – which proved to be a disastrous move. Under the terms of the treaty, the Creek surrendered their sovereign claim to the land in exchange for being given a legal entitlement to it. Each Creek family was given 320 acres of land and each chief received 640 acres. The owners of the land were free to do with it as they wished but, as individual landowners instead of a sovereign nation, the door to being divided and conquered had been pushed wide open.

Settlers began moving on to Creek land, clearing forests and building farms. When the US government refused to do anything to stop this blatant encroachment, the Creek took matters into their own hands. In 1836, a Creek war party attacked and overwhelmed the Georgian town of Roanoke and killed its defenders. In the following weeks, more farms were attacked and settlers killed. It gave President Jackson the pretext for Creek relocation he had been looking for.

Fourteen companies of US Army soldiers were dispatched to Georgia, supported by 400 Marines and five US Navy steamboats that travelled along the Chattahoochee River. They had defeated the Creek war bands by the middle of 1837 but remained in Georgia to round up the tribes. Around 15,000 men, women and children were assembled at Fort Mitchell. From there, they were forced to march the 750 miles to Fort Gibson on the other side of the Mississippi River. No wagons were provided to transport belongings, children or the elderly.

By the time they had reached Fort Gibson, three months had passed and exposure to the elements, disease and starvation had claimed around 3,500 Creek lives. Those who survived were issued with a US Army blanket and left to their own devices. It is believed that there were around 22,000 Creek living in Georgia and Alabama in 1832. By 1837, there were no Creek left living in those states and just 12,000 clinging to existence in Indian Territory.

THE CHOCTAW

The Creek were not the first people displaced by the Indian Removal Act. The Choctaw are a Muskogean-speaking people who had occupied the land that is now southeastern Mississippi for centuries. It is estimated that around 20,000 Choctaw lived in approximately seventy settlements that were built along the Pascagoula, Chickasawhay and Pearl Rivers during the 1750s.

They were highly skilled farmers and routinely produced surplus crops to trade with. Reflecting the agricultural nature of their society, the Green Corn Festival at midsummer was the most important ritual of the Choctaw year. The funerals of the Choctaw were distinctive for their practice of removing the bones of the diseased. This was undertaken by bone-gatherers who were heavily tattooed and had very long fingernails.

Contact with Europeans led to a great desire for, and even reliance on, manufactured goods. Firearms, alcohol and woolen cloth all became central to the lives of many Choctaw and were purchased with deer skins. But extensive hunting resulted in deer becoming increasingly rare in the territories and, under the leadership of a chief from the eastern division of the Choctaw named Mushulatubbee, they began to diversify.

Mushulatubbee was keen to maintain the supply of manufactured goods so the Choctaw began to raise livestock, including horses, grow cotton and even own slaves. But by the start of the nineteenth century, it was the Choctaw lands that the settlers wanted. In 1820, Mushulatubbee signed the Treaty of Doak's Stand, which agreed to give the US government some of the Choctaw lands in present-day Mississippi and Alabama. In return, the Choctaw would receive land west of the Mississippi River in what is now Arkansas.

In practice, the effects of this treaty were negligible. Few, if any, Choctaw moved to the lands across the river and the territory that had been ceded to the government was already swarming with illegal settlers. This meant that, just four years later, the land to the west of the Mississippi River that had been granted to the Choctaw was ceded back to the government in return for money and the formal recognition of Mushulatubbee as the chief of all Choctaw people.

Mushulatubbee signed the Treaty of Dancing Rabbit Creek with the government in 1830. This exchanged eleven million acres of land in modern-day Mississippi for fifteen million acres in Indian Territory. The difference this time was the existence of the Indian Removal Act – and President Jackson was eager to prove its effectiveness.

Trail of Tears

The relocation began in the late autumn of 1831 and the plan was to remove all of the Choctaw people in three waves that took place in successive years. There was little enthusiasm for the move among the Choctaw, but there was an acceptance that resistance against it by this stage was futile. As one Choctaw chief put it: 'Our doom is sealed. There is no other course for us but to turn our faces to our new homes toward the setting sun.'

Around 7,000 people left in the first wave and were taken by steamboat up the Arkansas and Ouchita Rivers. However, the final several hundred miles were to be travelled on foot and the winter of 1831–32 proved to be the worst in living memory. There was insufficient clothing and provisions to cope with the subzero temperatures and delays caused by enormous snow drifts, frozen rivers and subsequent floods. It is estimated that only 5,500 of those who embarked on the journey arrived in Indian Territory alive.

Their new home was named Oklahoma – derived from the Choctaw words for 'red' and 'people'. When asked to describe his journey by a reporter from the *Arkansas Gazette*, the Choctaw chief named Little Rock said it was a 'trail of tears and death'. The Trail of Tears has come to be the term used to describe all of the removals of indigenous peoples from the Southeastern region in the mid-nineteenth century.

Despite the death toll and suffering, the first wave was considered a success by the government, the only concern being the financial cost that was twice what had been estimated. As a result, when the second wave of around 7,000 Choctaw departed in 1832, the amount of provisions and the number of wagons provided were reduced. The requirement for nearly all of the Choctaw to walk, regardless of age or illness, led to great suffering that was compounded by a deadly cholera outbreak.

It is perhaps not surprising that the third wave, which took place in 1833, struggled to attract the same numbers as the previous two once word of the suffering and hardship inevitably spread. Around 900 Choctaw joined this journey, which meant that, by 1834, around 11,500 Choctaw had been relocated and settled in Indian Country.

This left around 6,000 Choctaw still in Mississippi and they became the target of ever greater threats, intimidation and violence. In 1848, one Choctaw chief who had decided to stay in Mississippi said: 'We have had our habitations torn down and burned, our fences destroyed, cattle turned into our fields and we ourselves have been scourged, manacled, fettered and otherwise personally abused, until such treatment that some of our best men have died.'

Attempts to remove the Choctaw from Mississippi continued into the twentieth century. Those in Oklahoma operated a quasi-autonomous government but, in time, the land there also became desired by settlers. When Oklahoma became a state in 1907, some of the land was allocated to individuals from the Choctaw and other Native nations while the rest was opened up to Euro-American homesteaders.

It is believed that there are around 160,000 descendants of the Choctaw alive today.

THE SEMINOLE

At some point around the middle of the eighteenth century, groups broke away from the Creek settlements and occupied the Everglades of northern Florida. By 1775, they were being referred to as the Seminole and had become fierce rivals and enemies of the Creek alliance to which they once belonged. It is believed that the word Seminole is derived either from the Muskogean word for 'runaway' or 'separatists' or from the Spanish word *cimarrón* which means 'wild'.

The Seminole made their homes among the thickets and wetlands that, until 1819, belonged to Spain. Although this landscape limited the amount of horticulture that took place, they did manage to grow corn on the higher, dryer land. Mostly though, they subsisted by foraging, hunting and fishing. What the Everglades lacked in suitable agricultural land, it more than made up for in providing protection, isolation and innumerable hiding places from outsiders. As a result, the Seminoles were joined by those attempting to escape enslavement or being drawn into the battle for dominance between European colonizers.

The First Seminole War

But encroachment and interference from colonizers and settlers could only be put off for so long. The First Seminole War of 1817 was triggered by attempts by the US government to recapture enslaved African-Americans who had escaped and started living among the Seminoles. When American soldiers destroyed a garrison that served as a refuge for those escaping the plantations and killed 270 people, the Seminole responded by raiding American settlements that were situated on the Georgia-Florida border.

The Army general and future president Andrew Jackson was given command of the forces in the area and led a brutal scorched earth campaign against the Seminole villages on Lake Miccosukee and the Suwannee River. Jackson also seized Spanish military posts and the Spanish town of Pensacola – leading to Spain ceding its territories in Florida in the Transcontinental Treaty of 1819.

Four years later, the US government granted the Seminoles a reservation just below what is now Tampa Bay as part of the Treaty of Camp Moultrie. Although the reservation was in Florida, it was both unsuitable for farming and lacked the wildlife to support the Seminole through hunting. Fresh drinking water was also in short supply. The result was starvation, suffering and disease.

As a consequence, the opportunity to move to new lands in Indian Territory was welcomed by many Seminoles when it was offered in the Treaty of Payne's Landing in 1832. As part of the treaty, a small party of Seminole chiefs were allowed to travel to and inspect their newly designated lands before the full removal took place. The inspection party were appalled to discover that their new home was to be shared with their sworn and bitter enemies the Creek – who had already taken up residence.

Despite their severe misgivings, the chiefs were pressured into signing a statement declaring that the Seminole would locate to this land. Once the news about sharing land with the Creek spread, it caused deep divisions within the Seminole. The vast majority refused to move and the leader of one of the groups in favour of removal was murdered in 1835. Around 400 of his followers decided to make the break and move into Indian Territory.

Four hundred and seven tribal members embarked on steamers from New Orleans on 23 April 1836. Just 320 arrived in Fort Gibson on 23 May, the arduous overland portion of the journey being afflicted by disease and torrential rains.

The Second Seminole War

Tensions between the Seminole who refused to leave Florida and the US Army spilt over when, in late 1835, a band of warriors attacked and killed 110 US soldiers in what became known as the Date Massacre. It triggered the Second Seminole War that dragged on until 1842, taking the lives of 1,600 US troops and at least double that of Seminole people. Any prisoners who were captured were shipped off to Indian Territory which led to the numbers of Seminole that had relocated rising to around 4,000 by the war's end.

The Third Seminole War

An equal number remained in Florida and steadfastly refused to budge, preferring instead to retreat into the remotest areas where contact with Euro-Americans was limited. However, minor clashes occurred frequently whenever there was contact between settlers and the Seminoles. As a result of one of these clashes, the US Army was sent into the area in December 1855. When one of their camps was attacked and a number of soldiers killed, open conflict erupted once again in what became known as the Third Seminole War.

The US government established a new Seminole Reservation in Indian Territory that was completely separate and some distance away from where the Creek were situated. By offering passage there and a further incentive of $500 for every man and $100 for every woman, the Seminole agreed to cease hostilities and relocate to the reservation west of the Mississippi.

Not everyone made the move however, and there was a continued, if limited, Seminole presence in Florida. As relations with the US government improved during the twentieth century, the Seminole Tribe of Florida gained federal recognition and regained 80,000 acres of land. They have since developed numerous economic programmes that include tourist attractions such as a tribal museum, a casino and a private airstrip. There are around 27,000 individuals of Seminole descent alive today.

THE CHICKASAW

The Chickasaw speak the language of the Muskogean family and inhabited the lands that make up what is now northern Mississippi and Alabama. It is believed by many that the Chickasaw and the Choctaw may have once been a single tribe, such are the cultural and social similarities.

The Chickasaw were traditionally a semi-nomadic people whose influence spread over an immense territory and involved them raiding, conquering and assimilating many different tribes. Their settlements were usually stretched along the banks of rivers and streams rather than being surrounded by circular palisades.

Contact with Europeans occurred comparatively early in relation to other peoples of the Southeast and probably dates back to Hernando de Soto's expedition of 1540–41. In the eighteenth century, the Chickasaw sided with the British in their struggles against the French and the colonists. By the start of the nineteenth century, the extent of Chickasaw lands had been steadily chipped away by a series of treaties with the United States. This had started in 1786, when their northern territorial boundary was fixed at the Ohio River, and by 1837 they were confined to a small area in what is today northwestern Alabama and northern Mississippi.

They had adapted well to living in smaller territories and had abandoned the hunting and gathering way of life of their ancestors, establishing instead prosperous farms and plantations. This success was not enough to help them resist the pressure from the US government and ever greater numbers of settlers who wanted the Chickasaw removed from the Southeast completely.

This pressure was intensified considerably when the state legislatures of both Alabama and Mississippi made following tribal laws a crime that was punishable by fines. The Chickasaw leaders, perhaps seeing the writing on the wall, adopted a pragmatic approach and began to negotiate their relocation to Indian Territory.

As they were not in armed conflict with the United States, unlike the Seminole and Creek, the Chickasaw were given time to sell their homelands and receive a fair value for their lands' worth. Between 1835 and 1837, they raised more than $3 million from the sale of their land and used some of this money to pay for their relocation to Indian Territory.

It was still a long and difficult journey, especially for the young and the elderly, but when the first relocation began in 1837, it was well provisioned with horses, wagons, clothing and food. The last Chickasaw left their homelands in Mississippi and Alabama in 1850 and, although the journey was not as traumatic as those of other Southeastern nations and certainly had a lower death toll, life in their new territory was difficult.

Their new neighbours in the form of Kickapoo, Shawnee, Comanche, Choctaw and Kiowa were not welcoming and violence was a common occurrence. The land was of poorer quality than that which they had been forced to abandon and the threat of starvation from failed crops was a feature of life in Indian Territory. Outbreaks of disease and droughts were frequent, and the trauma caused by the forced dislocation from all they had ever known was felt keenly.

There are an estimated 40,000 descendants of the Chickasaw in the early twenty-first century, many of whom are living on tribal landholdings or reservations in Oklahoma.

THE CHEROKEE

The roots of the Cherokee Nation can be traced back to the north and the southern shores of Lake Ontario and Lake Erie. Archaeological and linguistic evidence indicates that they moved to the Southeast in around 1400 CE to escape conflict with their fellow Iroquoian-speaking tribes. In subsequent centuries, the Cherokee remained sworn enemies of the Iroquois League.

The name Cherokee is derived from a Muskogean term meaning 'people of a different speech' and is considered by some to be a pejorative term. Many members of the Cherokee prefer to be known as Keetoowah or Tsalagi.

The move to the Southeast had proven to be a great success and they became one of the largest and most powerful nations of the region. Language aside, they adopted much of the culture and many customs of the other tribes, such as the Creek, whom they lived among. By 1650, the Cherokee Nation comprised around 22,500 people and encompassed around 100,000 square kilometres (about 40,000 square miles) of territory that stretched across parts of modern-day Georgia, Alabama, eastern Tennessee and the western Carolinas.

Contact with Europeans

When Spanish explorers first made contact with the Cherokee in the mid-sixteenth century, they described how they lived in towns of thirty to sixty dwellings and slept in windowless log cabins that had holes in their bark roofs to allow smoke to escape. They cultivated corn, squash and beans, and like the other tribes of the Southeast, celebrated the Green Corn or Busk Festival at midsummer.

By the eighteenth century, the Cherokee had sided with the British in terms of both trade and warfare. When war between the American colonists and their former British masters erupted, the Cherokee threw their lot in with the British, convinced that the Crown would protect the integrity of the borders of their land.

They entered the war enthusiastically and, despite British attempts to prevent them, launched attacks on the colonist forts at Fort Watauga and Eaton's Station in what is now North Carolina. Both raids were led by Chief Dragging Canoe and took place in July 1776. Both raids failed and resulted in vicious and violent reprisals by the Southern militias throughout the autumn.

With their crops burned, villages destroyed and warriors scattered across the region, the Cherokee faced starvation. In order to obtain peace, they had to pay a high price and forfeit huge areas of land in what is now North and South Carolina in the treaties of DeWitt's Corner and Long Island of Holston in 1777.

Over the following decades, sporadic episodes of Cherokee rebellion or uprisings inevitably led to the yielding of yet more territory. But from the start of the nineteenth century, there followed a period of remarkable integration and assimilation of settler culture by the Cherokee. They adopted farming, weaving and home-building techniques learned from the Euro-Americans, and adopted a form of government that was directly modelled on that of the United States. The Cherokee Nation had elected officials, a Senate and a House of Representatives. One of its first acts was to make the sale of Cherokee land a capital offence.

Perhaps most remarkably, they developed and adopted a written language. Known as the *syllabary* and developed by a Cherokee named Sequoyah who had served in the US Army, it provided a visual symbol for each syllable in the Cherokee's form of Iroquoian. Before long, nearly every single Cherokee became literate in the syllabary and it led to translations of Christian Scriptures, and the first Native American newspaper in the form of the *Cherokee Phoenix*, which was first published in 1828. It also led to a formal, written constitution being adopted that declared the Cherokee Nation to be a sovereign and independent state.

The Cherokee Road to Removal

If any of the Cherokee had hoped that their adoption of settler ways and creation of nationhood would lead to a more emollient or conciliatory approach from the settlers and the US government in general, they were sadly mistaken. Their land had been eyed covetously for many years and, in 1815, a Cherokee reservation had been created west of the Mississippi in Missouri Territory. Small numbers had agreed to move and became known as the 'Old Settlers' by the vast majority of Cherokee who stayed on their traditional lands.

When gold was discovered in Georgia and within Cherokee Territory in 1828, pressure on the US government to remove all Native Americans to the west intensified significantly. When the state of Georgia attempted to extend its authority to include all Cherokee lands within state boundaries in 1830, the Cherokee Nation sent a delegation to the Supreme Court in Washington.

In 1831, the Supreme Court ruled that the Cherokee Nation was indeed sovereign and that, as such, the state of Georgia had no right to enforce its laws in Cherokee Territory. But President Andrew Jackson refused to enforce the ruling and, combined with the passing of the Indian Removal Act in 1830, he paved the way for the forceful removal of all Cherokee from Georgia.

The re-election of Andrew Jackson in 1832 led many Cherokee to view their removal as inevitable. This led to the creation of a deep fissure among the Cherokee, with people joining either the pro- or anti-relocation factions. The pro-relocation faction was led by Kah-nung-da-tla-geh who was widely called Major Ridge. He was a personal friend of President Jackson and had fought on the side of the US Army and was subsequently awarded the title of Major.

Ridge signed the Treaty of New Echota which secured financial compensation to the Cherokee people in return for their move to the reservation in Indian Territory. It may have been signed by Ridge but it was not signed by a single member of the Cherokee National Council and Ridge did not enjoy widespread support. There can be no doubt that the majority of Cherokee viewed his actions as treacherous.

Regardless, the Treaty of New Echota was ratified by Congress and a deadline was set for the complete removal of the Cherokee people from Georgia by May 1838. Any hopes that a change of president might result in a change of policy from the American government were soon dashed. Jackson's successor, President Martin Van Buren, stated that 'A mixed occupancy of the same territory by the white and red man is incompatible with the safety or happiness of either.' This belief, whether accurate or not, was enough to make him enforce the Treaty of New Echota despite the extremely shaky legal ground on which it was based.

Roundup

As the deadline approached, and with only the pro-removal minority faction having moved to Indian Territory, President

Van Buren sent a force of 7,000 troops to Georgia under the command of General Winfield Scott. They were supported by the Georgia Guard and were ordered to use whatever force was necessary to transport to Cherokee to the reservation in the west.

It took them just three weeks to round up every Cherokee man, woman and child, most often at gunpoint, and place them in specially constructed holding camps to await removal. This often took place on very short notice and they were given no time to collect clothing or possessions. As a result, many were barefoot, inadequately dressed and owners of nothing but the clothes that they were wearing. Gangs of looters followed Scott's troops and ransacked the Cherokee homes while they were still in sight.

Conditions in the holding camps, which were overcrowded and rat-infested, allowed disease to thrive and large numbers of Cherokee died before they had even embarked on the 2,000-mile overland march. Around 1,000 managed to escape and flee into the wild mountains of North Carolina but most faced the appalling prospect of an unimaginably arduous journey.

Setting off in the boiling heat of August in 1838 and divided into groups of between 700 and 1,500, they marched through Tennessee, southwestern Kentucky, southern Illinois, across the Mississippi River into southern Missouri and northwest Arkansas before eventually arriving in Indian Territory. Many, of course, never arrived at their new reservation. The pace of the march was set by the US soldiers who guarded them and exhaustion and disease thinned the numbers with every day that passed. Exactly how many died on the journey is not known. The federal government admitted to 400 deaths, but a missionary doctor named Elizur Butler believed 2,000 died in the holding camps and a further 2,000 perished on the journey. Others put the total at over double that.

Whatever the exact number, there can be no doubting the scale of the suffering that took place; the forced removal of the Cherokee has become synonymous with the Trail of Tears. A US soldier, when recording his memoirs, wrote: 'Murder is murder and somebody must answer. Somebody must explain the streams of blood that flowed in the Indian country in the summer of 1838. Let the historian of a future day tell the sad story with all its sighs, its tears and dying groans.'

Major Ridge and Retribution

When those who survived reached the end of their terrible journey, they found Major Ridge and his pro-relocation supporters already well-established on the reservation. The burning resentment felt by those who had been turned out of their homes, lost all of their possessions and forced to march for 116 days turned into a desire for revenge. On 22 June 1839, Major Ridge was ambushed and shot from his horse. His death triggered a low-level civil war between the pro- and anti-relocation factions that rumbled on for several years.

The Remaining Cherokee of the Southwest

Those individuals who managed to escape from the holding camps in 1838 ensured that a Cherokee presence was always maintained. Their descendants now number in the several thousand and continue to live in western North Carolina. Across the whole of the United States, around 730,000 individuals identify as being of Cherokee descent.

'THE FIVE CIVILIZED TRIBES'

For a period of time, the Cherokee, Choctaw, Chickasaw, Creek and Seminole nations were commonly referred to as the 'Five Civilized Tribes'. This reflected the perception of these groups' ability and willingness to adapt to white culture in comparison to other groups of indigenous people. Whether this was accurate or not, it was certainly patronizing and did nothing to spare them from the full horror of what contact with European settlers entailed.

If the movement of these 70,000 to 100,000 people across five states, in many cases at the point of a gun, were to happen today, there can be little doubt it would be called ethnic cleansing. Even when it was well-resourced and planned, such as when the Chickasaw were removed. The fact remains that it was an officially sanctioned racist act, and one that had scant regard for the lives and welfare of the people being moved and severed from their lands, cultures and ways of life.

THE SOUTHEAST

THE GREAT PLAINS

The Great Plains cover a truly vast area. They stretch from Subarctic Canada down to the blisteringly hot Rio Grande in modern-day Texas. They are over 1,000 miles wide, bounded on the east by the Mississippi River and on the west by the Rocky Mountains. Much of this area experiences hot summers and cold winters. Before development by Euro-American settlers, the landscape in the east was one of rolling tallgrass prairies that were kept watered by frequent downpours of rain and heavy winter snowfalls. In the west, a comparative lack of precipitation led to shorter grasses. However, both east and west were buffeted by almost constant winds. These blew almost uninterrupted across the Plains. The occasional tree-lined valley provided the only break in what could seem a featureless landscape.

For many people, the image of a brave, replete with warpaint and feather headdress, sitting astride a horse on the Great Plains is one that immediately springs to mind when Native Americans are mentioned. It has become the visual shorthand for all the indigenous peoples of North America and, to some, represents a 'typical' Native American, as if there was such a thing. Not only is this only far from typical, it is an image that would never have existed without the impact of the Europeans. It was the arrival of the Europeans that, both directly and indirectly, caused many nations to move on to the Plains. After the Euro-Americans took their lands in the east, indigenous people moved on to the Plains in search of a new home. And the horse, of course, was not present anywhere in the Americas before the arrival of the Spanish. Their introduction to the Plains was to have a profound impact on how life was lived there.

PEOPLE ON THE PLAINS

Humans have only been populating the Plains for a relatively short time. For most of the years that people have been present in North America, the Plains were too arid to support the wildlife that could in turn support a human population. However, around 800 years ago, climatic conditions on the Plains grew warmer and wetter. This meant large areas became suitable for cultivating crops. It also led to grasses carpeting much of the landscape. This provided the perfect pasture for bison who subsequently moved on to the Plains and thrived.

Over the centuries that followed, people moved on to the Plains, in both what is today Canada and the United States, in order to hunt these bison herds. It soon became apparent that the bison provided not only food, but almost all of the materials to make the tools, shelter and clothing necessary to survive on the Plains.

Surviving on Bison

The liver was commonly eaten raw and was considered a great delicacy. The flesh that couldn't be eaten at the time of the hunt was cut into strips and stretched over racks to be dried by the near-constant Plains winds. This jerky would keep for long periods and could be easily carried. The hides were either tanned and turned into clothing, moccasins, saddles, tepee covers, bags and bedding or left as rawhide and used to make harnesses, snowshoes, shields and sheaths. Sinew was used as bowstrings and thread for sewing and bones were used as arrowheads, knives, needles, jewellery, clubs and dice. The intestines and bladder were used as buckets and food containers. Even the dung was used as fuel for fires once it had dried. In most cases, the heart was practically the only part of the bison that was not utilized. It would be cut from the body and left on the hunting ground to give new life to the herd.

Hunting bison was both a hazardous and difficult pursuit, particularly before the arrival of horses on to the Plains. One method involved silently creeping among a scattered herd while they were feeding and attempting to pick off individual animals without spooking the other animals that were eating just metres away.

Another method that was particularly effective at killing large numbers of bison involved driving them off a precipice. This was achieved by draping a bison hide over a member of the tribe and positioning him at the head of the herd. He would then attempt to lead the animals towards the cliff edge. Once they were close enough, other members of the tribe would shout, scream and wave their robes in an attempt to spread terror among the animals and cause them to gallop over the edge where they would fall to their deaths or suffer serious injuries. At the bottom of the drop, yet more members of the tribe would be waiting to dispatch the injured bison with spears and clubs.

The Arrival of Horses

The Spanish introduced horses to the Southeast and, soon after, to the Great Plains between 1650 and 1750. It meant hunting bison, although still extremely dangerous, could be done more effectively and resulted in far greater numbers of bison being killed. Riding on horseback meant the hunters could keep pace with the stampeding herd and shoot the bison from close range with bows and arrows. Once rifles were acquired through trade with Euro-Americans, the method of hunting became even more effective.

The effect of this was to make bison the predominant food source for Plains tribes. It also meant that other tribes, whose territories had been encroached on by either settler or rival indigenous groups, moved to the Plains and started to support themselves by living nomadically and following the bison herds.

As a result, the Plains became home to speakers of a bewildering array of languages. By the eighteenth century several variations of Siouan, Algonquian, Athabaskan, Michif, Uto-Aztecan, Caddoan and Kiowa-Tanoan were all present. In order to facilitate communication between speakers of so many languages, a universal sign language was developed that enabled people to express a desire to trade or enquire after bison.

Spirituality on the Plains

As in most Native North American societies, those who existed on the Plains tended to believe that spirit beings inhabited all animals and plants as well as the sun, moon and stars. The most important religious ceremony for many different groups on the Plains, both sedentary and nomadic, was the Sun Dance. This took place during the summer and, although it would witness the gathering of the entire community, only a few volunteers or pledges were directly involved in the ritual.

These individuals would undertake a special spiritual preparation over the course of weeks or even months. A central pole was erected in the camp or village and, after a few days of dancing and praying to obtain the required spiritual strength, the volunteers' back or chest was pierced with wooden skewers. These skewers were then tied to the central pole and the pledge would lean back until the piercings were torn out under his body weight. It was believed that this act of endurance and self-sacrifice would result in good fortune for both the individual and his community.

NATIONS OF THE PLAINS

THE MANDAN

The Mandan speak a form of Siouan and had at some point lived in northeastern North America. However, by the eighteenth century, they lived in semipermanent villages along the Missouri River in modern-day North Dakota. They cultivated corn, beans, sunflowers and pumpkins as well as tobacco, and supplemented this with fishing, hunting bison and trading with nomadic tribes.

They lived in villages that contained anywhere between a dozen and a hundred dome-shaped earth lodges and were surrounded by palisades. Every village had a chief for war, a chief for peace and a chief for day-to-day matters. In 1750, there were at least nine sizeable and well-established Mandan villages but they were all but eradicated by smallpox epidemics. By 1837, there were fewer than 150 members of the Mandan still alive. These joined with members of the Hidatsa and Arikara tribes, who had suffered an identically appalling fate, to form what became known as the Three Affiliated Tribes.

The descendants of these tribes lived on their reservation until much of their land became submerged due to the construction of the Garrison Dam in central North Dakota in the mid-twentieth century. By the start of the twenty-first century, it was estimated that there were around 1,300 Mandan descendants living in the United States.

THE HIDATSA

Like the Mandan, the Hidatsa are also a Siouan-speaking people who live on the banks of the Missouri River and whose traditional existence was dependent on agriculture. It is believed they are the tribe from which the Crow originated before the latter abandoned the sedentary lifestyle in favour of becoming nomadic equestrians. The two tribes speak an almost identical language and had close ties that extended to both trade and marriage.

However, when the Hidatsa numbers were drastically reduced through a combination of smallpox and war with the Sioux, it was to the Mandan that they turned for an alliance. Such were the similarities in lifestyle, it is probably more accurate to describe it as a merger rather than an alliance and they successfully shared a reservation until the flooding caused by the Garrison Dam removed their best farmland. There are believed to be around 1,500 people living today who are descended from the Hidatsa.

THE ARIKARA

The Arikara were the third and final members of the Three Affiliated Tribes who shared a reservation at Fort Berthold in western North Dakota from the 1860s onwards. Unlike the other two tribes, the Arikara speak a form of Caddoan rather than Siouan and their roots lie in the mound-building societies of the Southeast rather than the Northeast. However, in the years that immediately preceded the arrival of the Europeans, like the Mandan and the Hidatsa, they lived in earth lodges along the Missouri River where they raised crops. They also followed similar religious practices and held sun dances every summer.

The position of their villages between the Cannonball and Cheyenne tributaries of the Missouri River were seen as an obstacle to the expansion of the fur trade by settlers. This led to the first ever campaign by the US Army against a tribe of the Plains and saw the Arikara abandon both their villages and their lifestyle in the 1820s in favour of pursuing the herds of bison.

At the end of the eighteenth century, the Arikara had a population of around 4,000. The impact of epidemics, war and community displacement saw this number dwindle drastically. In the 1860s, those who survived joined with the Mandan and Hidatsa tribes on the Fort Berthold reservation in North Dakota.

THE DAWNEE

From sometime before the sixteenth century until the end of the nineteenth century, the Pawnee lived along the Platte River in modern-day Nebraska. The Pawnee speak a version of the Caddoan language and, for many centuries, were comprised of several semi-autonomous bands that each occupied numerous villages.

Like nearly all Plains people before the arrival of horses, for most of the year they lived in dome-shaped earth lodges that were in close proximity to their crops. In the summer, while on bison hunts, they would live in portable, cone-shaped tents called tepees. These were made by stretching bison skins over wooden poles and were usually between five and nine metres (fifteen and thirty feet) in diameter and four to six metres (thirteen to twenty feet) high. They could be quickly and easily taken down, transported by being dragged by dogs and, later on, horses on devices called *travois*, and put back up again. This made them ideal when pursuing herds of bison and they were each large enough to provide shelter for an entire three-generation family.

Several facets of Pawnee spiritual life made them distinct from other Plains peoples. They believe the stars to be gods and traditionally used astronomy to inform their decisions such as when to plant corn or go on a bison hunt. Their religion also included the ritual sacrifice of adolescent girls who had been captured from other tribes, until this practice was abandoned in the 1800s.

Unlike many tribes on the Plains, relations with settlers and the US government were peaceful. Many members of the Pawnee served in the US Army as scouts when they launched campaigns against other tribes. The Pawnee signed several treaties with the government that gradually ceded its Nebraska territories. In 1876, the last of its land on the Plains was handed over and the Pawnee moved to a reservation in Oklahoma where they remain to this day. It is estimated that there are around 4,500 people of Pawnee descent who are alive today.

THE OMAHA

At some point, and for reasons that have been lost to history, the Siouan-speaking Omaha moved from the present-day Carolinas and Virginia on to the Plains in what is today western Missouri. From there, they moved to present-day Minnesota where they stayed until the seventeenth century. Then, the migrating Dakota Sioux drove them yet further west, where they settled in modern-day Nebraska.

The Omaha were organized patrilinially, and there was a fairly rigid class system that divided them based on inherited social status. This status could be enhanced, as it could in many Plains tribes, through exploits in battle. Touching an enemy during a battle or touching the body of a dead member of an enemy tribe while in the presence of their tribesmen were acts that carried great prestige. They were considered both courageous and honourable – much more so than killing a member of an enemy tribe – and were called 'counting coup'. Eagle feathers were often the reward for these daring acts.

In 1854, as they came under increasing pressure from ever greater numbers of settlers, the Omaha sold most of their land in Nebraska to the government. In 1882, they were allotted land in Nebraska that prevented their wholesale removal to Oklahoma and ensured their continuing presence on the Plains.

THE CROW

Having split from the Hidatsa in the mid-seventeenth century, the Crow adopted the archetypal nomadic

Plains lifestyle that centred around horses and bison. Their comparatively early adoption of this way of life saw them emerge as middlemen between settlers and other tribes in the trade of both horses and hides in exchange for guns, metal goods and blankets.

The displacement of the Blackfoot and Dakota Sioux by encroaching settlers led to them moving on to Crow territories. This caused intertribal conflict in which the Crow suffered heavy losses. As a result, they sided with the US Army in the Plains Wars of the second half of the nineteenth century and, in 1868, they accepted a reservation on lands in southern Montana. There are estimated to be around 15,000 people of Crow descent currently alive today.

THE SIOUX

The Sioux is a very broad and catch-all term for a loose alliance of indigenous people who all spoke varieties of the Siouan language family. The word Sioux itself is actually a contraction of the Algonquian term 'Nadouessioux' which means 'adders' or 'enemies'. It is therefore a pejorative term and was used by members of the Ojibwa to describe their great rivals.

There were three main branches of the Sioux based on the dialect they spoke. The Santee, sometimes known as the Eastern Sioux, spoke Dakota Siouan and were comprised of the Mdewkanton, Wahpeton, Sisseton and Wahpekute. The Yankton Sioux, who spoke Nakota Siouan, had just two divisions: the Yanktonai and the Yankton. The Teton Sioux, also known as the Western Sioux, spoke Lakota Siouan and were made up of seven divisions. These were the Blackfoot, the Hunkpapa, Brulé, Miniconjou, Sans Arcs, Oglala and Oohenonpa.

Sioux Spiritualism

The Sioux believed that four powers held sway over the universe. Reflecting its importance to their way of life, the bison featured prominently in all Sioux religious festivals. Much like many other Plains societies, the Sun Dance in particular and vision quests in general were important to the Sioux. This often involved praying, fasting and making vows until they were in receipt of visions that gave them special powers. Bear power, for example, was believed to enable people to cure others or lead to protection being granted either in war or on a hunt.

The Move to the Plains

Before the mid-1650s, the Santee Sioux inhabited the land around Lake Superior where they hunted bison and deer and foraged wild rice. War with the Ojibwa drove the Santee into lands occupied by the Teton and Yankton. The knock-on effect of this was the movement of the Teton and Yankton on to the Plains – where horses had recently been introduced. This caused them to abandon any form of agriculture and fully embrace the nomadic lifestyle of other indigenous tribes on the Plains. It also brought them into conflict with the Pawnee, Mandan, Hidatsa and Arikara whose villages were frequently raided by the Sioux. These intertribal conflicts go a long way to explain why the sedentary, agriculture-based tribes were quick to reach an agreement with, and even become allies with, the US government.

Conversely, having fought the Ojibwa and lost their former territory to them, the Sioux were wary when it came to incursions on their new territory. This was a vast area that encompassed land in the modern-day states of Wyoming, Colorado, Nebraska, South Dakota, North Dakota and Montana. Attempting to maintain territorial integrity over such a large area in the face of an expanding United States and millions of its gold-crazed citizens, as will soon become apparent, was to have terrible and tragic consequences.

THE CHEYENNE

The Cheyenne, who refer to themselves as Tsitsistas (meaning 'the people') are an Algonquian language-speaking group who originally lived in the Great Lakes region in parts of present-day Minnesota and Illinois. As Euro-American settlers pushed ever further west, the Cheyenne relocated to the Plains in what is today North Dakota, South Dakota and Nebraska. As with many other tribes, the move to the Plains led to a move away from farming and an increased dependence on horses and bison.

War with the Ojibwa and the Dakota Sioux led to the Cheyenne spreading further across the Plains and, in 1832, a large segment became established along the Arkansas River. From that point on, the Cheyenne were recognized as having a northern and southern branch – a fact recognized by the Fort Laramie Treaty of 1851.

Cheyenne Spirituality

The Cheyenne form of Sun Dance was extremely elaborate and involved. They believe in two major gods or deities; the wise one above called 'Maheo' and a god who lives below ground. Through the Sun Dance, they believe that particular objects, such as hats, become blessed or engendered with special powers. These hats can then be worn into battle and provide their wearer with special protection.

The Cheyenne at War

The Cheyenne fought against the Comanche, Apache and Kiowa tribes and, from 1857 to 1879, the US Army. Responses to Cheyenne raids on settlers and trading posts were brutal and extensive. When the Northern Cheyenne attacked General Custer at the Battle of the Little Big Horn, it provided a textbook example of a Pyrrhic victory (see below for details). From the late 1800s onwards, the Cheyenne have resided on their assigned reservation in Oklahoma. According to the latest census, there are just over 10,000 Cheyenne alive today with half of them living on reservations.

THE COMANCHE

The Comanche are an Uto-Aztecan-speaking tribe who had previously occupied territories in Wyoming but who had gradually moved south. By 1800, the Comanche were very powerful and, through a combination of aggression and ambition, had driven all other tribes, most notably the Apache, from the southern Plains. The name Comanche comes from a Ute word meaning 'enemy' or 'other' and the Comanche called themselves Numunuu.

By heading so far south, the Comanche were one of the first tribes to acquire horses from the Spanish and to breed them in significant numbers. The Comanche became skilled riders and their mastery of the horse enabled them to set out the blueprint for nomadic equestrianism that so many tribes were to follow and that has become synonymous with all Native Americans.

The bison was central to their survival and, by the second half of the nineteenth century, encroachment by settlers on to the Plains and the rapidly diminishing bison herds meant that this way of life was no longer sustainable. Initially, the northern branch of the Comanche attempted to struggle on after the southern branch had agreed to settle on a reservation in Oklahoma. This led to a series of conflicts, often triggered by a failure by the United States to abide by terms they had agreed to in treaties. Eventually, in 1867, the northern Comanche also agreed to move to a reservation in Oklahoma. Recent population estimates put the number of people of Comanche descent alive today at around 20,000.

THE ARAPAHO

The evidence of the oral traditions of the Arapaho points to them abandoning their permanent settlements and fields of crops in the woodlands of the east to move on to the Plains. Once there, this Algonquian-speaking people adopted the nomadic life of tepees, horses and bison hunting. Their diet was augmented by trading with other tribes, especially the Mandan, for corn, squash and beans. In return, the Arapaho supplied bison hides and other bison-derived products. From around 1830 onwards, they lived in two distinct groups that occupied territory in the north and south of the Plains.

The reasons for the move on to the Plains are not known but, if it was to avoid war, it was a failure. A state of almost continuous conflict existed between the Arapaho and the Pawnee as well as the Shoshone and the Ute. On the southern Plains, however, the Cheyenne became longstanding allies and the Arapaho joined the Cheyenne forces that wiped out Custer's troops at the Battle of the Little Bighorn.

Perhaps as a result of this alliance, the Southern Arapaho were assigned the same Oklahoma reservation as the Cheyenne as part of the terms of the Treaty of Medicine Lodge in 1867. The Northern Arapaho were moved to a reservation in Wyoming. At the start of the twenty-first century, it was estimated that there were around 15,000 people of Arapaho descent living in the United States.

THE KIOWA

There is archaeological evidence that the Kiowa originated in what is today the Kootenay Region of British Columbia in Canada. They moved to present-day Montana but continued to move until they arrived in what is now Nebraska, Kansas, Oklahoma and Texas. They then migrated to the Black Hills in around 1650 where they lived with the Crow tribe. It was the Crow who taught these speakers of the Kiowa-Tanoan language how to live and survive on the Plains with horses that were acquired from the Spanish.

They soon adopted the typical nomadic lifestyle and became notorious for long-distance raids. The targets of these raids ranged from people as far south as Mexico and as far north as Canada. The Kiowa were pushed further south by Cheyennes and Sioux who had themselves been forced to move from their territories near the Great Lakes by the invading Ojibwa. Once the Kiowa reached the Arkansas River, they went to war with the Comanche who already occupied the territory.

In around 1790, the fighting came to an end and the two groups formed a deep and lasting peace that grew into an alliance as the threat from new arrivals to their lands – people who were themselves fleeing a combination of Euro-American settlers and the US Army. This intertribal warfare led to the American Army intervening and the Medicine Lodge Treaty being signed in 1867. As part of the terms, the Kiowa were assigned a reservation in Oklahoma. Moving there did not lead to peace and they frequently fought with settlers who moved into the vicinity.

In 1901, the Kiowa reservation in Oklahoma was effectively dissolved and split into individual plots or homesteads of 160 acres and assigned to the head of each household. This broke the influence of the tribe and opened up land that was not specifically assigned to an individual to new settlers.

Our understanding and knowledge of this period have been greatly enhanced and enriched by a cultural feature of the Kiowa. Between 1832 and 1939 they had a tradition of creating pictorial histories to record each six-month period. The first was created by a Chief called Little Bluff who, worried that the Kiowa would forget their North Country roots after their move to Oklahoma, decided to chronicle their history from 1832 until his death in 1866. This started a tradition that was taken up by others and, although initially drawn on to animal skins, they were later drawn on to paper. These pictorial histories are not only invaluable to historians but are key to allowing Kiowas today to understand what they have survived and what it means to be Kiowa.

HOW THE PLAINS WERE LOST

At the time that Andrew Jackson's Indian Removal Act was being passed in 1830, the land to the west of the Mississippi was not viewed favourably by most people in the United States. It was the land where Native Americans were removed to so that Euro-American settlers could occupy the 'good' land they vacated. The lands to the east could then be put to use for maximum profit.

When the US government passed the Indian Trade and Intercourse Act in 1834, it seemed to confirm this view. As well as setting out laws regarding trade between US citizens and Native Americans, it created what was in effect a border between the United States and 'Indian Country'. This so-called Permanent Indian Frontier was placed on the western side of the Mississippi River. Any land to the east of it belonged to the United States of America. The land to the west of it was seen by many American citizens as treeless, waterless and useless. In fact, *Carey and Lee's Atlas* of 1827 labelled the Plains as the 'Great American Desert'.

Over the next few decades, attitudes changed dramatically. The people living on the Plains were soon to discover that it was no longer considered Indian Country, and the frontier was anything but permanent.

The Mexican-American War, 1846–48

The United States went to war with Mexico over America's annexation of Texas in 1845. When the United States emerged victorious in 1848, it was in possession of enormous amounts of territory that had previously belonged to Mexico. This included the land on the Pacific Coast that would soon become the American states of California and Mexico. The Native people who were living on the Plains suddenly found themselves sandwiched between states to both the east and west. And if American citizens wanted to travel between their east and west coasts, the most direct route was to trespass through 'Indian Country'.

Gold Fever

When a man named John Sutter began constructing a watermill in 1848 near present-day Sacramento, he inadvertently created a reason for hundreds of thousands of people to travel to California. He discovered gold. News of his discovery spread like wildfire and, by the end of the following year, 80,000 people had arrived in California. And the mass migration did not stop with these 'Forty-niners'. By 1852, the population of the once sleepy town of San Francisco had exploded to 225,000. Some of these migrants had arrived via the Pacific Ocean, including 20,000 Chinese. But the vast majority had travelled overland from the east.

The Oregon Trail

The route that was established to take these 'pioneers' across the Plains was known as the Oregon Trail. It departed from the town of Independence, Missouri which was situated on the frontier and ran west for over 2,300 miles. A typical journey lasted around eight months and was extremely arduous. It is estimated that around 34,000 men, women and children died while travelling west in the wagon trains between 1848 and 1860.

Conflict on the Plains

The dramatic increase in settlers travelling through the Plains after 1848 had immediate consequences for the Native Americans who lived on them. First, the wagon trains disrupted the movements of the great herds of bison. They also scared away or depleted the numbers of other wildlife that the indigenous people hunted for food. The shortage of game and bison led to tribes raiding each other's camps for their food and resources.

The sight of war parties, perhaps unsurprisingly, caused the wagon trains to panic and their instinct, assuming they were themselves about to be attacked, was to fire upon the Natives. Before long, both Natives and settlers were attacking each other on sight. As a result, both sides appealed to the government to intervene.

The Indian Appropriations Act of 1851

The Native Americans wanted the government to step in to stop the settlers trespassing on their land, disrupting the wildlife on which they depended, and to protect them from the violence that all too often resulted from contact between settlers and indigenous people. The settlers wanted the government to intervene to ensure their protection while they migrated across the Plains.

The government's response was to pass the Indian Appropriations Act in 1851. This set aside large sums of money to be used to relocate tribes from their current territories and marked an end to thinking of the Plains as 'Indian Country'. From this point on, it was the US government who would have the decisive say in who lived where on the Plains.

The Fort Laramie Treaty of 1851

One of the first consequences of the Indian Appropriation Act was the first Fort Laramie Treaty. Representatives of some Sioux, Crow, Cheyenne and Arapaho tribes gathered at Fort Laramie to hear what the government intended to do about the encroachment on their land. The government proposed a treaty where they would give the indigenous nations an annuity of $50,000 in food and goods for the next 50 years. Each nation would also be given its own territory, or reservation, on the Plains that the treaty promised would belong to them permanently.

In return, the Native nations had to agree to stay on their assigned reservation, therefore avoiding contact with both other tribes and settlers. This, it was believed, would reduce the amount of bloodshed on the Plains. They also had to agree to allow the army to build forts and patrol along the Oregon Trail and to afford safe access to the Plains to railroad surveyors.

Many Native people knew nothing of the treaty being signed at Fort Laramie and certainly did not agree to it. With no Native equivalent of the American president, disputes over any treaty with 'indigenous people' in general were inevitable. In this case, there were not just disputes. Many Native people simply refused to accept that the terms that had been agreed upon applied to them since they had not personally signed the treaty. As a result, large numbers of Natives acted as if the Fort Laramie Treaty did not exist, and they certainly did not stay in the land that had been assigned to them.

Reservation life was not compatible with the kind of nomadic equestrianism that most tribes on the Plains had built their societies around. However, if they were caught hunting outside of their reservations by the US Army, it was used as proof of their failure to meet their treaty obligations. As punishment, their annuity could be withheld and starvation became a real possibility.

The American government was not as quick to act when settlers broke the terms by trespassing or even building settlements and mines on reservation land, despite what they had promised when signing the treaty. Caught in a seemingly impossible trap, the leaders of more and more indigenous Plains groups began to advocate war as the only solution.

The Impact of the American Civil War, 1861–65

The North took advantage of the southern states' decision to secede from the Union to break the political deadlock that had grown around the issue of how to settle and develop the West. Before the war, the South had wanted to copy the southern model and see the West settled by enormous plantations that were worked by enslaved people. By the 1850s, much of the East Coast was crisscrossed by thousands of miles of railroads. There was a desire to extend the tracks west and build a transcontinental railroad to knit both coasts of the United States together. But the location of its starting and ending points was a matter of great contention – whether it went through the southern or northern part of the continent. The construction of the railroad was sure to bring enormous economic benefits along its route and vying interests in the North and South had resulted in deadlock. The outbreak of war meant the North was free to build a railroad in a location of its choosing. But wherever the railroad started and ended, it was going to cut straight through the Plains.

Homesteaders

In 1862, the government passed two acts that were to have a profound impact on the Native nations of the Plains. The Homestead Act enabled people to purchase 160 acres of Plains land from the government for just $10. The offer was open to any person over the age of twenty-one, or younger if they were the head of a family, including women, newly arrived immigrants and formerly enslaved people. The only people not able to purchase a homestead were soldiers of the Confederate South and, cruelly, bafflingly and appallingly, Native Americans.

The Homestead Act caused thousands of Europeans to cross the Atlantic to try to carve their own piece of paradise out of the wilderness. Thousands more Americans fled the overcrowded cities of the east to build their own farms. By 1876, six million acres of Plains had been developed by homesteaders. By 1930, an incredible eighty million acres of Plains land was under the ploughs of these small farms. And once land is farmed and fenced off, it is no longer suitable pasture for bison.

The Completion of the Railroad

The Transcontinental Railroad was finally completed when the two sets of tracks met at Promontory Summit, Utah in 1869. Such were the sums involved in building the railroad that stretched for over 1,900 miles that the two companies engaged to do it were heavily subsidized by the government. In addition to the $16,000 they received for every mile of track laid ($48,000 per mile in mountainous regions), they were also given millions of acres of land that ran alongside the railroad to sell to future settlers.

The railroad companies sent agents to Europe and ran very effective advertising campaigns to encourage people to 'go west'. By 1880, they had sold over 200 million acres of Plains land to settlers and new towns had mushroomed around wherever the train came to a stop.

The Impact of the Railroads on Bison

The tracks ran in an unbroken line right across the Plains, and were fenced off in many places. This interrupted the movement and migration of the bison far more than the Oregon Trail ever did. The bison also provided a cheap and convenient source of food for the thousands of men who had been employed to build the railroad. One of the men employed by the railway company to kill the bison was William Cody, who was later to become internationally famous as Buffalo Bill. He was paid $500 a month and kept a record of the number of carcasses he provided to the railroad company. In one seventeen-month period, he personally killed 4,280 bison.

Once the tracks had been completed, special 'Hunting Trains' were run that allowed tourists to shoot thousands of bison from the safety of open-topped carriages. The impact of all this was to greatly reduce the tribes' ability to support themselves and make them yet more reliant on the annuities promised in the Fort Laramie Treaty.

The Arrival of the Cowboys on the Plains

Despite their name, cowboys are probably more associated with Native Americans, horses and the wide-open Plains than they are with cows. But it was developments in the cattle industry in the second half of the nineteenth century that brought them on to the Plains and caused further disruption to the lives of the indigenous peoples who lived there.

During the Civil War, many ranchers in Texas had abandoned their herds to go and fight in the Confederate Army. When they returned, they found the herds had expanded beyond all recognition. This oversupply caused the price per head of cattle to plummet in Texas. There was, however, great demand for beef in the big cities of the north and east and a cow that would raise $5 in the Lone Star State would sell for over $20 in New York.

With the arrival of the railroad on the Plains, the ranchers realized that they only needed to drive their cattle to the nearest station for them to be transported to the lucrative markets in the east. This still involved getting cowboys to move the cattle hundreds of miles along trails that were blazed north across the Plains. The market exploded and, in 1870, over 300,000 cattle were driven down the Chisholm Trail alone. Often, the trails cut through indigenous reservations and caused both damage to pasturelands and disruption to wildlife. In some cases, the Natives charged a toll for every head of cattle that passed through their territory. In other cases, they attacked the cowboys. Disruption to commerce was not tolerated by the government and the US Army frequently retaliated on the cowboys' behalf.

Ranching on the Plains

It was the development of the 'open range' that caused the greatest threat to the indigenous peoples' way of life on the Plains. In 1861, a man called John Iliff discovered that cattle could not only survive the harsh Plains winters, but they could thrive on the pasture that grew there. There was no need to breed the cattle in Texas and drive them hundreds of miles across the Plains. Instead, they could be born and raised close to the railroad and then simply put into carriages when ready for market. The grass that the cattle ate cost nothing and they simply had to be branded to prove ownership and rounded up once a year. The potential for enormous profits attracted wealthy and powerful investors who started to flood the Plains with enormous herds.

These 'cattle barons', as they became known, increased the number of cattle on the Plains from 130,000 in 1860 to four-and-a-half million by 1880. Even in an area the size of the Plains, there is only so much pasture to go around – and the four-and-a-half million cattle ate the same thing as the bison. Without adequate pasture to sustain them, the bison population began to decline. The impact of this on societies that depended on the bison for their very existence is obvious. Either the government came to their aid or they starved to death.

Gold on the Plains

When gold was discovered near present-day Denver in the Rocky Mountains, it triggered what is sometimes known as the Pikes Peak gold rush. Around 100,000 fortune seekers descended on the area, trespassing through reservations and, in some cases, building camps and digging mines on land that had been promised to tribes in the Fort Laramie Treaty. Sometimes, the prospectors attacked the Natives. Some tribes, particularly the Cheyenne and the Arapaho, raided the miners' settlements and fought the US military that was sent to restore order.

After years of sporadic fighting in which many Cheyenne and Arapaho came close to starvation, their chiefs appealed to the US government to make peace. The result was the Fort Wise Treaty of 1861. This assigned six Cheyenne and four Arapaho tribes new reservations – including at a territory called Sand Creek. Many Cheyenne rejected the treaty from the outset because they did not trust the government to keep its word. Even more rejected it when it became apparent that the land at Sand Creek was unsuitable for raising crops and they faced starvation once again.

Raids by Cheyenne and Arapaho continued for three years before a Cheyenne chief named Black Kettle opened peace negotiations with the government once more. The talks failed, but Black Kettle was given the impression that he had secured protection for his people. He was instructed to remain close by so he could receive supplies and resume talks. Black Kettle and his band of around 750 mostly women and children established a camp in the bend of the Big Sandy Creek.

The Sand Creek Massacre

At dawn on 29 November 1864, Colonel John Chivington and around 1,000 soldiers and cavalrymen surrounded Black Kettle's camp. The surprise attack met with no resistance. Black Kettle managed to escape but, over the course of the next eight hours, around 230 Cheyenne and Arapaho were massacred. Nearly all were women and children or elderly and their bodies horrifically mutilated.

News of the massacre spread and united the Cheyenne, Arapaho and Lakota Sioux in a desire for retribution. For the next four years, they fought a full-scale war against both settlers and the US Army. A government committee ruled that Chivington had 'deliberately planned and executed a foul and dastardly massacre', but the government struggled to bring the uprising under control.

Eventually, the ending of the Civil War meant more full-time, professional soldiers could be brought to fight on the Plains. The twin strategies of targeting the Natives' means of support by destroying their sources of food and waging relentless winter campaigns led to an eventual defeat of the tribes in 1865. The fighting ended and the Cheyenne, Arapaho and Lakota were assigned new reservations.

The Bozeman Trail

When gold deposits were discovered in Montana in 1863, many of the prospectors who had been unsuccessful in the Pikes Peak gold rush immediately decided to leave Colorado. The most direct route from Colorado to Montana took them straight through Lakota Sioux lands. This route, known as the Bozeman Trail, directly broke the terms of the Fort Laramie Treaty but the government took no action to enforce it. It did not take long for the Lakota to take matters into their own hands and start attacking the gold-hunting trespassers.

After three years, the government entered into peace talks with the Lakota. However, they had simultaneously ordered the construction of army forts along the Bozeman Trail and on Lakota land. When the Lakota chief, Red Cloud, learned of this he broke off talks and ordered attacks on the US Army.

The Lakota were not able to capture the forts, but they were able to surround them and prevent any soldiers from leaving or reinforcements from arriving. They also prevented any prospectors from using the Bozeman Trail. At Fort Phil Kearny, a detachment of eighty soldiers were tricked into leaving the safety of the fortress to pursue some Lakota warriors. The soldiers were under the command of Captain William Fetterman and he unwittingly led them into an ambush. All eighty were killed in what became known as 'Fetterman's Trap'.

Red Cloud managed to garner the support of the Arapaho and the Cheyenne and they helped to continue the fight throughout the winter months. In 1868, the US government was finally forced to admit defeat. As part of the second Fort Laramie Treaty of 1868, they agreed to abandon the forts along the Bozeman Trail and assign new territories for the Lakota known as the Great Sioux Reservation.

Red Cloud promised to never lead his men in attacks against settlers ever again. He kept his promise. However, as soon as the forts on the Bozeman Trail were abandoned, they were burnt to the ground. Red Cloud's War, as it became known, was a rare but clear defeat for the US government in the conflict with the Natives of the Plains.

Little Crow's War

The Lakota weren't the only members of the Sioux who became involved in armed conflict with the government during the American Civil War. As part of the first Fort Laramie Treaty, the Santee Nation had moved to a reservation near Minnesota. Living on such a comparatively small reservation meant that a lifestyle of nomadic bison hunting was not possible so they tried to raise crops. When these crops failed, they were entirely dependent on the annuities from the government that had been promised as part of the treaty.

The American Civil War meant that the government's priorities were elsewhere and, in 1862, there was a delay in paying the Santee. The government agency store that was located on the reservation refused to supply any more food on credit and the Santee faced starvation.

When four young Santee braves were returning from an unsuccessful hunt, they happened across some settlers. Frustrated and angry, they attacked the settlers and killed five of them. The leader of the Santee, Little Crow, knew there would be terrible reprisals as a consequence of these killings and decided to go on the offensive. He led an attack on the government agency store that had refused to provide his starving people with food. Twenty men and ten women and children were killed in the raid.

When a troop of forty-five soldiers arrived on the reservation, they were ambushed and twenty-one were left dead. From there,

Little Crow launched a series of raids on settler villages and army forts, killing over 700 people. But Little Crow was unable to rally other Native groups to join his uprising and, with huge numbers of army reinforcements flooding the area, he headed west with some of his followers.

Those Santee who remained on the reservation either surrendered, or were captured and a military court sentenced 303 of them to death. President Abraham Lincoln commuted most of these sentences, but thirty-eight men were still sent to the gallows. On 26 December 1862, in front of a crowd of 4,000 spectators, they were executed on a scaffold that had been specially constructed to enable a simultaneous hanging. It was the largest mass execution in US history and all thirty-eight men were left dangling for half an hour after the traps had been released.

The surviving Santee were relocated to another reservation that had no soil suitable for farming and contaminated water that was unfit to drink. Over 400 died of sickness and starvation in the first winter on their new reservation.

Little Crow was shot and killed on 3 July 1863 by two settlers who scalped him before handing his mutilated body over to the state. They were paid a $500 reward and the scalp was purchased for a further $75. Little Crow's body was put on public display before being buried. It was later exhumed and displayed once more – this time at the Minnesota State Capitol. The corpse was eventually removed in 1915, upon the request of Little Crow's grandson, but only returned to the family for burial in 1971.

President Ulysses S. Grant's Peace Policy

The wars that had raged on the Plains between the indigenous peoples and the US government had proven that the current policy was not working. When Ulysses S. Grant was elected president in 1869, he decided to embark on a different approach. It had become clear that the Natives could no longer survive by hunting when confined to their reservations. It was also clear that they resented being held to ransom with money and supplies that the government was duty-bound to give them. The problem of trespassers and prospectors encroaching on reservation land also had to be addressed.

Grant's solution was to spend $2 million on an education programme that would teach the indigenous peoples of the Plains how to read, write, do simple maths and be able to assimilate with the rest of US society. He also placed devout Christians in charge of the government stores that were responsible for supplying the annuities. Grant believed committed Christians were less likely to be corrupt and would adopt a more tolerant and understanding approach to the Native peoples. The army was instructed to take a more proactive stance with trespassers who encroached on reservation land.

Many Native Americans perceived Grant's peace policy as an attempt to destroy their culture and wipe out their way of life. Big Eagle, a Lakota chief, said: 'The whites were always trying to make the Indians give up their life and live like white men, go to farming, work hard and do as they did. And the Indians did not know how to do that, and did not want to anyway.'

The policy also meant that any Native American found away from their assigned reservation was officially classified as 'hostile' and would be treated accordingly. But whatever its merits or ambitions, Grant's policy did not achieve its stated aim and bring peace to the Plains.

The Battle of the Little Bighorn

One result of Red Cloud's War was the signing of the second Fort Laramie Treaty in 1868. This assigned the Lakota Sioux a new reservation that encompassed the Black Hills of Montana. Having already suffered encroachment and attacks from prospectors along the Bozeman Trail, the Lakota ensured that the second Fort Laramie Treaty explicitly stated that no settlers were allowed to move on to their new reservation.

Less than ten years after the treaty was signed, gold was discovered in the Black Hills. The US government offered the Lakota $6 million or $400,000 a year to allow the Black Hills to be mined. This was refused and the Lakota, Cheyenne, Arapaho and other allied tribes began to get ready for war. Government troops were dispatched to Montana but an ambitious officer named George Armstrong Custer was already in the area. He had been protecting railroad surveyors and had taken the opportunity to look for gold. But it was fame rather than riches that he was truly after.

When Custer spotted the camp of a Lakota chief named Crazy Horse by the Little Bighorn River, he deliberately ignored direct orders and decided to launch an assault. Desperate for glory, he supposedly said: 'The largest Indian Camp on the North American continent is ahead and I am going to attack it.' On 25 June 1876, Custer split his force of around 600 men into three and personally led a group of 260 across the river and towards the camp.

Custer's Last Stand

Precisely what happened next is a matter of some debate as the only surviving member of Custer's party was a Crow scout who disguised himself as a Lakota warrior and was able to escape alive. What is clear is that Custer became cut off from the other two parts of his force and was heavily outnumbered. They were overwhelmed by perhaps as many as 2,000 Natives led by Crazy Horse, most of whom were armed with Winchester repeating rifles compared to the single shot Springfields of Custer's men.

Two hundred and sixty-four US soldiers were killed, including Custer. Around sixty Natives were killed with about the same number wounded. It was a rout. The defeat of the US Army was total, undeniable and humiliating. This was to have terrible consequences for the indigenous peoples of the Plains.

A Desire for Revenge

Public opinion among US citizens, many of whom had been sympathetic to the plight of the Native peoples, suddenly hardened upon hearing of the destruction of Custer's force. Rather than being seen as an impetuous, arrogant fool who had led his men to an easily avoidable disaster, he was being treated as a hero. 'Custer's last stand' almost immediately became the stuff of legend. His death, it was demanded, must be avenged and the 'savage' Natives taught a lesson once and for all.

New forts were built on the Plains. From these bases, the Lakota and Cheyenne were pursued relentlessly until they had returned to their reservations. The Lakota were forced to give up their weapons and their horses and, despite what was stipulated in the second Fort Laramie Treaty, the Black Hills were taken from them. Crazy Horse was arrested in 1877 and was bayoneted in the back while manacled. He died of his wounds shortly after.

The Wounded Knee Massacre

By 1890, the majority of indigenous peoples on the Plains were living in desperate and pitiful conditions. It was in this atmosphere of all-pervasive despair that belief in salvation through the Ghost Dance took hold.

A medicine man named Wokova, who came from the Paiute tribe of the Great Basin, had a vision. In it, he saw that a Native American Messiah was coming and that, if the indigenous people remained peaceful and danced the Ghost Dance, a great flood would remove all of the settlers. The waters would then recede and the great herds of bison would return alongside all of the indigenous people's dead ancestors.

News of this vision reached Chief Sitting Bull on the Great Sioux Reservation. Although he had concerns that it would provoke the soldiers, it had great appeal among his desperate people. Soon the Ghost Dance was being performed across every Sioux reservation.

As Sitting Bull predicted, this alarmed the agents and reservation police and orders were issued to arrest those chiefs who were encouraging the Ghost Dance. Sitting Bull was among those to be arrested but, when the police moved in, they quickly became surrounded by Ghost Dancers. In the confusion, shots started to ring out. When the shooting stopped, Sitting Bull lay dead alongside several other of his fellow Sioux and six policemen.

Yet the violence did not spread, and the Sioux continued to dance. Another Lakota chief, Big Foot, decided to seek safety in numbers in such a charged atmosphere and move his people to the Pine Ridge Reservation. On the way there, they were intercepted by members of the Seventh Cavalry. All 120 men and 230 women and children were taken to Wounded Knee Creek where they were closely guarded and ordered to camp.

The next morning, the Lakota were ordered to hand over their weapons. When one young warrior refused to part with his rifle, a struggle ensued and a shot was fired. The disarmed Sioux fought with whatever they could and the soldiers turned their guns on them. Soon, more than 300 Lakota Sioux lay dead or dying. Over half of them were women and children. Big Foot and his people were buried in a mass grave.

It was the last act of armed resistance by the Native peoples of the Plains.

THE EXTERMINATION OF THE BISON

No amount of armed resistance could have prevented the destruction of the ways of life of the Native Americans who lived on the Plains. In truth, it was the destruction of the herds of bison that irretrievably sealed their fate. In 1840, there were thought to be between thirty and sixty million bison living on the Plains. By 1889 there were just 512. There are several reasons for this astonishing slaughter.

As we have already seen, the bison were killed in the thousands to both feed the workers constructing the railroads and as a leisure pursuit for tourists. From 1871, this process was supercharged by the discovery of a new technique that could turn bison hides into high-quality leather. Almost overnight, the price of bison hides rocketed and the Plains were flooded with hunters.

These were armed with high-powered, long-range rifles and they soon developed a hunting method known as 'the stand'. This involved shooting individual animals from a long distance so that, if the animal was killed instantly, it did not spook the rest of the herd. The hunter could stay in position and gradually pick off bison after bison.

By the end of 1875, the southern herd was completely destroyed. The hunting of the northern herd did not start until after the Sioux had been defeated and the Northern Pacific Railroad was completed in 1880. It took just three years to wipe out the entire northern herd.

The Native Americans did try to stop the hunters from annihilating the herds, notably in the summer of 1874 when around 700 Comanches, Cheyenne, Arapaho and Kiowa attacked the bison hunters' base near Adobe Walls. But, much like the bison they were trying to protect, they were picked off a distance with rifles that often had telescopic sights.

A Deliberate Act?

Some have argued that the destruction of the herds was a deliberate government policy and there is some evidence to support this. General Philip Sheridan told the Texas legislature in 1873: 'These bison hunters have done more in the last two years to settle the vexed Indian question than the entire regular army has done in the last thirty years. They are destroying the Indians' food supply.... Send them powder and lead if you will, but for the sake of a lasting peace, let them kill, skin and sell until the last bison are exterminated.'

If it wasn't deliberate, it was certainly incredibly convenient. More than anything else, it enabled the Plains to become settled, developed and part of the United States of America.

PLAINS CULTURE TODAY

Many tribes from the Plains, like those from the Southeast before them, were relocated to reservations in Oklahoma. Others were moved to reservations in North Dakota and South Dakota. Without the bison, they were unable to maintain their ways of life but they have worked hard to keep their cultures, languages and dialects alive.

In recent years, there have been attempts to restore and conserve the grasslands that are needed to support the bison. From the brink of extinction, there is an approximate population of around 45,000 bison in North America at the start of the twenty-first century. Over half of these are in herds managed by Native nations.

THE SOUTHWEST

The Southwest region lies to the west of the Rocky Mountains and stretches to the Sierra Madre in what is now Mexico. It encompasses territory that is today part of Arizona, New Mexico, Utah, Colorado and California as well as northern Mexico. It is a very arid region with many areas experiencing less than ten centimetres (four inches) of rainfall per year. Where water is present, however, the soil is often fertile and able to support crops.

THE PUEBLO PEOPLE

Parts of the Southwest have been continuously populated for thousands of years. The Pueblo people are the direct descendants of some of the very first people to live in North America. On their journey south from Beringia (the former land bridge between Siberia and Alaska), their ancestors decided to stop and settle in an environment that would have been quite different from today. It was cooler, wetter and glaciers were still present on the top of nearby mountains. They would have encountered and hunted mammoths and sabre-toothed tigers and foraged for plants and seeds. The need to find new sources of food meant they would have moved their camps often and travelled over long distances.

Over time, the climate changed and, around 8,000 or 9,000 years ago, animals such as the mammoth died off. Rabbits, deer and antelope were still hunted but plants and seeds began to form a much greater proportion of the diet than they had done before. With no large game animals to hunt, there was less need to travel long distances in search of them and, around 5,000 years ago, the first rudimentary dwellings started to appear. These were not much more than dugouts in the sand covered with roofs made of brush, but it was proof of a more sedentary lifestyle being adopted.

Adopting Agriculture

It was around 2,500 years ago that the really significant development occurred and the Pueblo people, as they were to become known, began to focus on agriculture. Farming, primarily of corn, required them to stay in one place and, as a result, led to the development of the first villages. These appeared along the banks of what were later to be known as the Rio Grande and Rio Puerco and took advantage of the silt-enriched soils that the flood waters left behind every year. The dwellings that made up these first villages were pit houses and literally dug into the ground. Entrance and exit was gained through ramps and the domed roofs were covered with mud and brush and held up by support posts. Each pit house had a central fireplace for cooking and heating, while a hole in the roof allowed the smoke to escape.

Pueblo Pottery

Fire also played a key role in another important development by the Pueblo people of this period – pottery. The development of the technology that enabled them to create clay vessels around 2,000 years ago was one of the key reasons that the Pueblo people were able to thrive. It meant food and water could be stored easily and effectively. The black sooty residue that has been found by archaeologists on some pots provides evidence that they were also used for cooking. The ability to boil or stew foods rather than simply roast them opened many new possibilities when it came to potential foodstuffs. Not everything can be barbecued or eaten raw.

It was the women of the villages who were usually the potters. Pottery was only able to be developed in the Southwest because of the existence of the necessary raw materials. Reflecting the widely held belief shared among Native North Americans of the importance of living in balance with the natural world, a prayer of thanks would be said as the clay was removed from the ground. The clay was dried in the sun and then rehydrated over several days to create a solution that was passed through a sieve to remove debris. It was then tempered with volcanic ash to help prevent cracks during firing before being left to rest for several days.

The pots were created by coiling a long thin piece of clay into a spiral to make the base. More coils were then added to create the walls of the pot and the whole thing was then smoothed to a flat finish using pieces of wood. They were then typically decorated by applying pigments made out of plants or ground rocks, such as haematite, that contained iron. This was used to create the black-on-white pottery that is typical of prehistoric Pueblo pottery that normally features geometric patterns. Only serving and storage vessels such as mugs, bowls and pots were patterned. Those used for cooking were left plain. The process was completed by placing the vessels in a roaring bonfire to fire.

Housing

Pit houses remained in use until around 1000 CE when the population density in the Rio Grande Valley increased considerably. This may have been due to droughts causing people to move from areas that experienced seasonal rainfall to an area with a more permanent water source. The result of this population increase was the development of the type of housing that the Pueblo people have become synonymous with. The very name by which they are known is derived from their remarkable dwellings.

These homes, built in river valleys or high on rocky plateaus, are made from stone and sun-dried clay called *adobe*. They are several storeys high and have multiple rooms with separate, dedicated purposes, much like homes built today. The remains of over forty of these villages have been found, and there are thought to have been more than seventy in total, with each village containing houses comprising many hundreds of rooms. The largest settlement had over 1,000 rooms and was probably home to several thousand inhabitants. The rooms on the ground floor had no doors or windows, to keep enemies and intruders out, and access to the home was provided by ladders. Special underground rooms called kivas, perhaps an echo of their ancestors' way of life, were used exclusively for religious purposes.

When Spanish explorers first arrived in the 1500s and saw these huge communal buildings, they called them *pueblos*, from the Spanish word for village. Before long, and indicative of the unique nature of their architecture, the term was being used to describe their inhabitants too.

Another highly unusual if not unique aspect of Pueblo culture among Native North Americans was their cultivation of cotton for clothing purposes. This began around 700 CE and cotton cloth was soon being used to make long dresses for women and breechcloths and kilts for men.

Southwest Spirituality

Like most Native Americans, the religion of the Pueblo people and other inhabitants of the Southwest features spirit beings and shamans. According to their beliefs, the sun, moon, lightning, thunder, rain, plants and animals are all possessed of a spirit that can be angered or placated. Shamans are key figures in the interactions with these spirits and are valued for their ability to treat both physical and spiritual ailments.

Kachinas

Central to the religious beliefs of the Pueblo people are *kachinas*, or *katsinim* (sg: *katsina*) in Hopi culture. These are divine spirit beings, often believed to incorporate ancestors, that live with and interact with humans. The Pueblo people believe the kachinas will allow themselves to be seen if a traditional dance or ritual is performed by a man of the village while wearing a mask. As it is performed, the spirit being is believed to literally be present within the masked dancer, temporarily transforming him into the kachina.

Kachinas are also depicted in small wooden dolls which are used to help teach the identities of the more than 500 spirit beings to children. These are traditionally made by the men of the tribe and presented as gifts to the girls. Once a doll has been created, it is considered sacred.

PUEBLO DIVERSITY

There was, and remains, considerable linguistic and cultural diversity among the Pueblo people. Those in the east, in what is modern-day New Mexico, are speakers of the Tanoan and Keresan languages. Tanoan is thought to be distantly related to Uto-Aztecan, but Keresan appears to be unrelated to any known languages. To the west, in what is now northern Arizona and western New Mexico, the Hopi and Zuni languages feature predominantly alongside Keresan.

The Zuni

The Zuni group of Pueblo people are from an area of what is now on the border between Arizona and west-central New Mexico. Their dialect, a form of Penutian language, is known simply as Zuni. According to their oral histories, the Zuni are descended from people who emerged from underground before settling in their current location.

They are a deeply religious people and their society has been built on the farming of corn, squash and beans. They are organized matrilineally and divided into clans. Since the early nineteenth century, the Zuni have become renowned for their skills in making jewellery from turquoise and silver, as well as for their skills in pottery and basketry. There are some 10,000 Zuni Pueblo living today.

The Hopi

Of all the Pueblo people, the Hopi are located the furthest west in what is now northeastern Arizona. They speak a language of the Uto-Aztecan family and, although their precise origin is unknown, they are believed to descend directly from the people who settled in the region many thousands of years ago. The Hopi call these people the *Hisatsinom* or 'Ancient People' and archaeological evidence at abandoned pueblos in Awatovi and Sikyatki indicates there has been an unbroken presence in the area since their first arrival.

For many centuries, they have supported themselves through cultivating corn as well as beans, squash and melons. Their society is organized matrilineally and new husbands move into their mother-in-law's home. Monogamy is something that is greatly prized and emphasized in Hopi culture.

Religious ceremonies, such as initiation ceremonies and winter and summer solstices, are usually performed by men. The most famous – or infamous – of the Hopi ceremonies is the snake dance. This involves dancing with live snakes both in the performers' mouths and wrapped around their necks. The snakes used might include sidewinders and rattlesnakes, but also non-venomous species. This biennial ritual is held to ensure there is sufficient rainfall to cause the flooding and fertilizing of the land.

Like many Pueblo people, the Hopi both adapted to the arrival of the Spanish and adopted many of their ways. They have still managed to maintain a vibrant independent culture and kept many of their traditions alive. It is estimated that there are around 15,000 individuals of Hopi descent living today.

PUEBLO PEOPLE'S FIRST CONTACT WITH EUROPEANS

By the 1530s, Spain had established a vast and lucrative empire in Central and South America. Tails of cities of gold had incentivized conquistadors like Hernán Cortéz and Francisco Pizarro to conquer and explore Mexico and Peru, respectively. Tales of unimaginable riches were so tantalizing to Spanish ears that the many expeditions that ended in failure did little to dampen enthusiasm when new reports of El Dorado – the fabled city of gold – were received.

This is exactly what happened in 1536 when four survivors of a shipwrecked expedition made it back to Mexico City after eight years of wandering through the American Southwest. They told of seven 'large cities, with streets lined with goldsmith shops, houses of many stories and doorways studded with emeralds and turquoise'. It was enough for the viceroy of New Spain to send an expedition to determine its truth. A Franciscan friar named Marcos de Niza claimed the Pueblo region for Spain but returned within a year with inconclusive reports. His reference to the 'Seven Cities of Cibola' was enough to maintain interest in the region.

In 1540, a more comprehensive expedition was dispatched, this time headed by Francisco Vásquez de Coronado. He had arrived in Mexico in 1535 and had quickly established himself as a man of importance, rising to become governor of New Galicia. But he was an extremely ambitious man and desperate to emulate the conquests of Cortéz and Pizarro. Before embarking, however, he was warned that he was to lead a missionary expedition – not a military one.

The Coronado Expedition 1540–42

In February 1540, Coronado set off, accompanied by six priests, 300 Spanish soldiers, several hundred Mexican Natives, 1,000 horses and hundreds of pack animals. In June, they reached the first of the fabled 'Seven Cities' when they arrived at the Zuni settlement of Hawikuh. It was a dispiriting and disappointing discovery for the Spanish. Instead of gold, they were met with rock and adobe as well as Natives who were prepared to fight to defend their homes.

Repeated Spanish attacks eventually led to the Zuni abandoning their houses and Coronado made Hawikuh his headquarters. He may not have found gold, but there were much-needed stores to sustain his expedition as he prepared his next steps. Reconnaissance parties travelled as far west as the Grand Canyon and as far east as modern-day Santa Fe. It was during these fact-finding missions that they came across a Native American from the Plains whom they simply called 'The Turk'. He astounded the Spaniards with tales of unbelievable riches in a land to the east that was known as 'Quivira'.

Coronado decided to wait until spring before departing for Quivira. During the winter, open hostilities broke out between his party and the local Natives and numerous battles were fought that led to several Pueblo villages being abandoned and at least one having all of its inhabitants massacred.

The Quest for Quivira

Coronado led his entire expedition, guided by 'The Turk', out from their winter quarters in April 1541. After a gruelling forty days of marching, they finally arrived at

Quivira in modern-day Kansas. They were shocked and appalled at what lay before them. Instead of a glittering city of gold, they had arrived at a village of grass huts. When asked to explain himself, 'The Turk' said that it had all been a plan by the Pueblo people to lure them away from their villages and it was hoped that the Spanish would get lost and die of starvation.

'The Turk' was immediately executed by the furious and humiliated Spanish. They then began the long journey back to Mexico City, finally arriving in the spring of the following year. The expedition was seen as a failure, and Coronado died in relative obscurity. It was far from being the end of Spanish involvement in the Southwest region, however.

A Permanent Spanish Presence

In 1598, conquistador Juan de Oñate set off with missionaries, Mexican Natives and 400 soldiers from what was then New Spain to colonize the area around the Rio Grande. He established a settlement but, due to his failure to establish control and quell uprisings by the Pueblo people, he was officially replaced as governor in 1610.

The new governor, Pedro de Peralta, moved the settlers and established the city of Santa Fe. After Saint Augustine, Florida, and Jamestown, Virginia, this is the third-oldest permanent European settlement in the United States. By 1630, it was home to 250 Spaniards, 750 indigenous people and around twenty-five priests.

The lack of gold or silver in the region meant the only thing of value that the Spanish could extract was manual labour. The indigenous people were exploited from the very outset and forced into working as farm labourers, sheepherders, blacksmiths and domestic servants.

The Pueblo Revolt

This forced labour, combined with the destruction of their kivas, masks, kachinas and other sacred objects by Franciscan friars, fomented a feeling of great resentment among the Pueblo people. This boiled over in 1680 in what has become known as the Pueblo Revolt.

The revolt of 1680 was led by a medicine man named Popé of the San Juan Pueblo. There had been revolts before, but this time almost all of the pueblos participated and the Spanish were forced to flee for their lives. Twenty-one of the thirty-three Franciscan friars were killed along with a further 401 Spanish settlers. The surviving 1,946 Spanish moved to what is now Ciudad Juárez on the banks of the Rio Grande.

The independent Pueblo Confederation, created after driving out the European invaders, lasted only until 1693 when the Spanish retook control of Sante Fe. A *presidio*, or fort, was built, complete with a garrison of 100 soldiers and, in 1695, New Mexico's second town of Santa Cruz de la Cañada was founded. In 1706, Albuquerque was established and the Catholic faith's presence was re-established through 21 missions. It lasted less than fifteen years, and was ultimately futile, but the Pueblo Revolt helped preserve much culture and heritage.

YUMAN

The Pueblo people may be descended from the very first people to occupy the Southwest, but they are not the only indigenous people to live in the region. 'Yuman' is an umbrella term used to describe Native tribes who are believed to be descended from the prehistoric Patayan. They speak languages from the Hokan family and inhabited parts of the Southwest, as well as areas of California and Baja California, from possibly as early as 700 CE.

The River Yumans traditionally inhabited the area where the Colorado River meets the Gila River, and include the Mojave, Cocopah, Maricopa and Quechan tribes. The Upland Yumans are comprised of the Hualapai, Havasupai, Yavapai, Kumeyaay, Kiliwa and Papa tribes and originally lived near the Grand Canyon.

Yuman people generally lived in small, autonomous tribes or settlements. The River Yumans farmed the fertile floodplain whereas the Upland Yumans lived a more hunter-gatherer type of existence. When the Spanish first encountered the Yuman, they were characterized as being tall, powerful and warlike. They were described by a Spanish explorer as being 'the tallest and the most robust that I have seen in all the provinces, and their nakedness the most complete'. The term 'naked' may have been an exaggeration, but the Yuman wore minimal clothing. This usually included sandals and a breechcloth in summer and robes made of deer or rabbit skin in the winter.

Their religious beliefs involve a supreme creator, and their myths and stories are passed on through songs and oral traditions. Their traditional society was marked by the lack of value attached to material objects. They had no concept of inheritance and the possessions of a fellow tribe member were usually destroyed when they died.

Yuman Contact with Europeans

The first contact took place in 1540 when a voyage sent to resupply Coronado's expedition sailed up the Colorado River. The encounter was peaceful and without incident and there was not to be another meeting of Yuman tribes and Spanish expeditions until 1605. Once again, the encounter was peaceful, and it was nearly a century before there was another meaningful meeting. This occurred when Eusebio Kino arrived in 1700 to explore the area to ascertain whether California was an island or a peninsula. This was the most extensive and involved meeting yet but also passed without bloodshed.

However, in 1779, the Franciscans decided the region was ready for missionaries and they built two mission churches on the west side of the Colorado River. Unlike mission churches in other parts of the Americas, they were not protected by an accompanying large presidio. Instead, they had a small garrison of soldiers. Less than two years later, all of the Spaniards, missionaries and soldiers were killed and the mission churches destroyed. A Spanish expedition was dispatched to punish those responsible and an unspecified number of River Yumans were killed in reprisal.

The Upland Yumans had even less contact with Europeans than their river-based counterparts. What contact there was, was peaceful and the Yumans' attitude towards the Spaniards was predominantly friendly and favourable. This could not be said about their attitude towards each other, however, and intertribal warfare raged throughout the eigthteenth and into the beginning of the nineteenth centuries.

Impact of the California Gold Rush

It took until the discovery of gold near Sacramento, California in 1848 for contact with Europeans to have profound consequences for the Yumans and the other Native people of the Southwestern region. Much of the territory was ceded to the US in 1848 in the wake of the Mexican-American War. Additional land became the property of the United States as part of the Gadsden Purchase in 1853. Fortune hunters headed for California via a southern route and crossed the Colorado River deep in Yuman country. Steamboats were soon paddling up and down the Colorado River and exploration parties sought routes both for railroads and for new deposits of gold.

Contact between indigenous people and settlers or miners from other US states all too often meant conflict. As a result, the US Army soon became a permanent presence in the Southwest and forts were built. Throughout the 1850s, 1860s and 1870s, sporadic fighting, both intertribal and against settlers and the army, erupted across the Southwest. But, unlike on the Plains and in the Southeast, there were no concerted campaigns by the Native tribes. By 1880, all of the Yuman tribes had moved on to reservations. Perhaps reflecting the relative desirability of the land in the arid Southwest, all but the Yavapais tribe were assigned reservations that incorporated land they already occupied. At the start of the twenty-first century, around 9,000 people described themselves as Yumans.

THE PIMA

The Pima live in the Sonoran Desert region along the banks of the Gila, Salt, Yaqui and Sonora Rivers. Traditionally, they lived in small villages made up of oval-shaped lodges covered in grass and mud, with a shared central kitchen area. They are the descendants of the prehistoric Hohokam culture and speak a language from the Uto-Aztecan family.

It was the Spaniards who gave them the name Pima in the seventeenth century. They refer to themselves as *Akimel O'odham*, meaning the 'River People', and the river was central to their means of survival. By digging many miles of irrigation canals, they turned dry, dusty desert into farmland on which they grew corn, beans, squash, tobacco and cotton. Hunting, gathering and trading with other tribes also helped supplement their diet.

Their chief was elected and, unusually for Native North American tribes, men did both the farming and wove the cotton on looms. The women of the tribe did turn the cloth into clothes, however, and also produced intricate baskets.

The Pima Revolt

Also known as the O'odham Uprising, this occurred in 1751 and was the result of over half a century of abuse at the hands of missionaries and Spanish settlers. The first contact of any consequence had taken place in the late seventeenth century with the Jesuit missionary Eusebio Kino. Kino had set out from Mexico City with the stated aim of converting the people he came across. Everywhere he went, he established missions. He also introduced new livestock, fruit trees, vegetables and European crops such as wheat.

As a result, the new arrivals were initially welcomed. However, a combination of the devastating impact of European disease, forced labour and brutal punishments led to a deep dissatisfaction among the Pima towards the Spanish. As more colonists continued to arrive, missionaries took to their work with extra zeal to increase the number of converts. This often took the form of forcing the Pima to work the land that they had taken from them, usually with the aid of a whip.

There were minor uprisings in 1732 and 1748 that helped create an atmosphere of unease and distrust among the two peoples. These grievances accumulated and, under the leadership of a chief named Luis Oacpicagigua, the Pima launched a bloody uprising in November 1751. The Spanish were caught completely unaware by the co-ordinated attacks on their missions and settlements. Over 1,000 Pima were involved in the attacks and they used fire and arrows to kill more than one hundred colonists and burn down churches.

Spanish soldiers were dispatched north to quell the uprising and 3,000 O'odham warriors assembled in the mountains to meet them. Oacpicagigua sent word that, if the leader of the hated Jesuits were sent away, he would surrender himself to the Spanish and conflict could be avoided. The Jesuit leader, Father Keller, was ordered to leave and Oacpicagigua was arrested. But instead of addressing the Pima's grievances, the Spanish constructed a presidio to ensure there could be no more uprisings. Oacpicagigua died in prison.

In 1767, Jesuit priests were expelled from New Spain and replaced by Franciscan friars. The lives of the indigenous people continued to be afflicted by forced labour, brutal abuse and frequent rapes. There were sporadic revolts and missions continued to be attacked. But disease inflicted more death and misery upon the Native people than the actions of any number of Spanish soldiers or missionaries. As in almost every other area of North America, measles, influenza and smallpox tore through the indigenous populations of the Southwest.

THE NAVAJO

The Pueblo people, the Yuman and the Pima may have had the longest continuous presence in the Southwest, but they were not always the biggest or most powerful Native nation in the region. By the 1800s, that title belonged to the Navajo, who were much more recent arrivals. The Navajo speak a language from the Athabaskan family which originates in an area that is now in Canada. It is believed that at some point between 1100 and 1500 CE, the Navajo left the Subarctic and made the long journey south to settle in the dry, dusty and scorching heat of the Southwest.

The early Navajo were primarily hunter-gatherers who lived in highly mobile, nomadic societies. However, life in the Southwest caused them to adopt many of the customs and practices of their new neighbours. Interactions with the Pueblo people in particular saw them adopt farming and move into more permanent settlements. The skills and technology necessary to make pottery were also learned, as well as weaving, which soon became something the Navajo are still greatly admired for today.

Navajo Society

Traditionally, Navajo society was organized along informal and decentralized lines. Bands adopted ways of life and made economic decisions based on the land where they lived. Different clans were bound together by ties of marriage, shared ancestry and proximity. Each band would have a nominal leader who led discussions and negotiations, and the group would often extend over several villages or hamlets.

The Navajo religion places great emphasis on the concept of *hozho*, which roughly translates as 'harmony' or 'balance'. Hozho can be disrupted by violence, evil and death, and rituals are undertaken to restore the balance. Each ritual has its basis in the myths that explain the origins of the moon, the sun and the mountains, and chanters devote their whole lives to learning the intricacies of certain ceremonies. Dry paintings made from pollen and flower petals are also often made as part of the rituals.

Social events usually accompany ceremonies and are often attended by hundreds or thousands of people. The Navajo have been particularly successful in maintaining their traditions and religious practices despite an extended period of conflict and interference from the US government.

Navajo Contact with Europeans

The Spanish incursions into the Southwest during the sixteenth and seventeenth centuries had limited impact on the lives of the Navajo. The Pueblo Revolt of 1680 and the subsequent reprisals by the Spanish led to many Pueblo people seeking refuge among the Navajo and undoubtedly led to greater convergence in the two nations' ways of life.

It was a different story after the Mexican-American War, when the Southwest became US Territory. The American government decided it wanted to reduce both the strength and autonomy of the region's most powerful Native nation in preparation for the Southwest's settlement and development. Various treaties had been signed to put an end to the raids and episodes of violence that erupted as a result of prospectors and other trespassers arriving on Navajo land. All were deemed to have failed and so, in 1863, a more drastic approach was adopted by the government.

The Long Walk

The decision was made to move the entire Navajo Nation from its territories in northwestern New Mexico, Arizona and southern Utah to a tiny reservation in eastern New Mexico that was at least a 300-mile walk away. The logic behind the move was explained in a letter by Brigadier General James Carleton who was in overall charge of the military operation to move the Navajo. He wrote: 'If the Navajo are placed far from the haunts and hills and hiding places of their country, they would acquire new habits, new ideas and new modes of life. The young ones will soon take their places without these longings and thus, little by little, they will become a happy, contented people.'

The man Carleton put in charge of executing this move certainly had unusual ideas about the best way to create 'happy, contented people'. Colonel Christopher (Kit) Carson implemented a scorched earth policy against the Navajos and ordered the burning of their fields, the destruction of the settlements and the poisoning of their wells. By 1863, nearly 8,000 Navajos had been rounded up into various army forts in New Mexico, Arizona and Utah. From there, they were forced to march to Fort Sumner on the tiny reservation of Bosque Redondo.

The Long Walk was a harrowing ordeal for the more than 10,000 men, women and children who were forced to complete it. Depending on where they departed from, some marched as much as 450 miles and many did not survive the journey. Those who made it were kept imprisoned and impoverished by the government for the next four years.

A new government in 1868 recognized that a hideous error had been made and the Navajos were assigned a new reservation on their previous homelands. The forced march of the Long Walk and the subsequent imprisonment claimed the lives of an estimated 2,000 Navajo through disease, malnutrition and murder. It also left a legacy of bitterness and distrust.

The Discovery of Oil

The US government may not have been so willing to allow the Navajo to return to their homelands if they had known of the oil, gas and coal deposits that lay beneath its surface. Its discovery in 1921, and the subsequent extraction that has taken place over the following decades, has led to friction between the US government and the Navajo people that continues to this day.

Fracking technology means that more of these natural resources can now be extracted but has also led to fears about the impact this might have on the sacred sights of many indigenous people of the Southwest. It is estimated that as much as ninety per cent of public land in northern New Mexico has been leased to oil and gas companies for drilling. This is despite the fact that it threatens many active archaeological sites, including some with UNESCO World Heritage status, and that they continue to be of enormous spiritual importance to the Navajo and Pueblo people.

Navajo Successes

In the context of other Native North American nations, the Navajo have survived and thrived the colonization of the Americas by Europeans. They are the most populous of all North American nations and there are over 300,000 people who identify as Navajo living today – many in their traditional homelands in New Mexico, Arizona and Utah. A large number continue to speak the Navajo language, practise their religion and live a predominantly traditional lifestyle.

Many thousands have moved away from their homelands and settled in considerable numbers in other parts of the United States and built successful communities. The Navajo also have a tradition of volunteering to serve in the US armed services that continues to this day. During World War II, Navajo Marines famously used their native language to prevent American communications from being intercepted by the Japanese.

THE APACHE

The name Apache looms large in the popular consciousness when it comes to the Natives of North America. Like the Navajo, the Apache are Athabaskan speakers whose roots lie far to the frozen north. They, too, migrated south at some point after 1100 CE and adopted semi-sedentary lifestyles as farmers both on the Plains and in the Southwest.

Apache is a broad umbrella term used to describe numerous Athabaskan-speaking tribes that inhabited land that stretched over a vast area. This included territory that is in present-day Arizona, Colorado, New Mexico, Texas and northern Mexico. Apache is also not a term that they ever used to describe themselves and most probably comes from the Zuñi word 'apachu' which means 'enemy'.

The arrival of horses on the Plains led to an increased number of raids on Apache villages by various tribes, but particularly by the Comanche. In around 1750, the last of the Apache tribes living on the Plains left and moved south and west. The various tribes that make up the Apache Nation can be broadly divided into two groups: the Eastern Apache and the

Western Apache, with the Rio Grande acting as an informal border between the two.

The Eastern Apache contain tribes such as the Mescalero, Jicarilla, Chiricahua, Lipan and Kiowa Apache. The Western Apache include the Cibecue, Mimbreño, Tonto and Coyotero tribes, among others. There was no centralized tribal organization. Instead, Apache tribes tended to operate as autonomous bands under the leadership of an informal chief who was appointed rather than inheriting the position.

Once they had abandoned their farms on the Plains, they sustained themselves in the Southwest through a combination of hunting and gathering, farming, trading with Pueblo people and raiding other villages. Exactly how much they did of each varied from tribe to tribe but, broadly speaking, the Western Apache appear to have taken up farming more than those to the east of the Rio Grande. However, the Chiricahua are perhaps the most infamous for their perceived aggression and predilection for raids which targeted villages in New Mexico, Arizona as well as Mexico itself.

Raiding for a specific purpose, such as stealing horses, food or taking captives, was viewed as being different and separate from warfare and usually only involved small raiding parties. The distinction was lost on the US government and, in an effort to control the Apache groups after the Mexican-American War of 1846, they established several forts and reservations.

The Apache Wars

There had been conflict between US soldiers and the Apache during the Mexican-American War, most notably involving the Chiricahua chief, Cochise. Upon entering into negotiations with the government, Cochise famously said: 'I do not think you will keep the peace. Once again you tell me we can stay in our mountains and valleys. That is all we wish, we do not wish to fight and kill whites, and we do not want the whites to fight and kill us. We want nothing but to live in peace. But I do not believe you will allow us to remain on the lands we love. I warn you, if you try to move us again, war will start once more; it will be a war without end in which every Apache will fight until he is dead.'

When Cochise's brother and nephews were killed while being held captive by US troops, it sparked a conflict that, although not quite without end, was to rage for decades.

Over the years, chiefs such as Cochise, Mangas Coloradas, Victorio, Delshay and, finally, Geronimo were able to gather armies of hundreds of men and take them into battle against both the US Army and settlers. The first US Army campaign that specifically targeted the Apache took place in 1849 and its last major battle against the Apache took place in 1886. The fighting was unrelentingly vicious and even continued throughout the Civil War.

The tide only began to turn for the army once it started to recruit Apache scouts into its ranks. The disparate and autonomous nature of the Apache meant that, even when bands reached settlements with the government and agreed to move to reservations, they were still perceived as a threat by troops and attacked. Some bands, of course, had sworn to fight on and the brutal and heavy-handed approach of some soldiers only served to increase the number of braves who joined them.

Geronimo

The most famous, and ultimately final, Apache chief to wage war against the US Army was Geronimo. He was born in 1829 in what is today Arizona, and was originally named Goyathlay (One Who Yawns). At the age of seventeen, he was married and soon became the father of three children. In the mid-1850s, while on a trading trip to Mexico, his mother, wife and three children were all murdered.

Traumatized and brutalized, he joined the Chiricahua and was soon taking part in raids in both northern Mexico and across the border into US Territory. His actions were enough to gain him a level of notoriety worthy of a nickname and his Mexican adversaries began to call him Geronimo – the Spanish equivalent of Jerome. According to legend, this is because the Mexican soldiers he was attacking prayed to Saint Jerome for help and Goyathlay gladly accepted his new name.

As traditional Apache homelands started to become colonized by settlers from the United States, the Chiricahua continued to launch raids in an attempt to stem the tide. Determined to put a stop to these raids once and for all, in 1876 the government decided to relocate the Chiricahua to the San Carlos Reservation. This barren wasteland in east-central Arizona became known as 'Hell's Forty Acres' and it wasn't long before hundreds fled the reservation and, spurred on by Geronimo, resumed their war with settlers and the Army.

Repeated Capture and Escape

After being relentlessly pursued, Geronimo surrendered in January 1884 but, after hearing stories of his impending hanging, he escaped accompanied by thirty-five braves and 109 Chiricahua tribe members. The US Army deployed 5,000 troops to ensure his recapture and, five months later and over 1,600 miles away, exhausted and outnumbered, he was tracked down in Mexico. He surrendered once again.

There was to be one more escape on the march back to US Territory before Geronimo agreed to hand himself over after securing promises that he and his followers would be able to return to Arizona after a period in exile. This promise was never kept, Geronimo was never to set foot in Arizona again and he would spend the rest of his life as a prisoner of the United States government. He was placed on a train and shipped to Florida to carry out his sentence of hard labour. Businessmen in Pensacola were quick to recognize the potential the 'bloodthirsty savage' had as a tourist attraction. Soon, hundreds of people were paying to look at him in his cell every day.

While Geronimo and his men were imprisoned in Florida, hundreds of Apache children were being relocated from Arizona to the Carlisle Indian Industrial School in Pennsylvania. Those who survived the rampant tuberculosis found themselves cut adrift from their loved ones, culture and way of life.

A Living Exhibit

In 1894, though still captive, Geronimo was moved to Oklahoma where he took up farming, joined the Dutch Reformed Church and attempted to assimilate with US society. In 1904, he was permitted to appear at the St. Louis World's Fair as part of a living museum piece. Under constant guard, he made bows and arrows in an 'Apache Village' while Pueblo women sat next to him and made pottery. The exhibit was billed as a 'monument to the progress of civilization'.

After the fair, Pawnee Bill's Wild West Show reached an agreement with the government to allow Geronimo to join them.

He appeared under the billing of being 'the Worst Indian That Ever Lived' and audiences watched as the 'savage' was 'tamed'. His job was to play the role of the archetypal 'lying, thieving, treacherous, murderous' Native American.

A Presidential Audience

Such was his fame that he was invited to President Theodore Roosevelt's inauguration. He appeared alongside five Native American chiefs in an inaugural parade that involved them riding horses down Pennsylvania Avenue while wearing feather headdresses and face paint. The intention was to create a public display that illustrated that the hatchet had been well and truly buried. What better way to symbolize and illustrate that peace now existed between the United States and the Native Americans?

Behind closed doors, the government wasn't quite as magnanimous. Geronimo's private audience with Roosevelt was cut short after he begged the president to allow him to return to Arizona. Roosevelt told him, through an interpreter, that Geronimo had 'killed many of my people, you burned villages and were not good Indians.' He was advised to put his appeal in writing.

Geronimo's Death

Geronimo returned to Oklahoma and wrote his memoirs. One night he fell from his horse and lay undiscovered until after dawn. A few days later, on 17 February 1909, he died from pneumonia. The *Chicago Daily Tribune* broke the news of his death with the headline 'Geronimo Now a Good Indian'. This was an allusion to the widely shared quote that was mistakenly attributed to General Phillip Sheridan about the only good Indians being dead Indians.

The Apache Nation Today

In 1913, members of the Chiricahua were finally given the opportunity to return to the Southwest and move on to the Mescalero Reservation. Around two-thirds accepted the offer with the rest remaining in Oklahoma. In total, there are thirteen formally recognized Apache tribes in the United States today living across Oklahoma, Arizona and New Mexico. It is estimated that their population totals around 100,000.

THE GREAT BASIN

Broadly speaking, water that falls or rises in North America goes one of two ways. If it is to the east of the Rocky Mountains, it will eventually flow into the Atlantic Ocean through the Gulf of Mexico. If it is to the west of the Rockies, it will find its way into the Pacific either directly or through the Gulf of California. That is unless it is in the Great Basin.

THE LAND

The Great Basin is a vast bowl-shaped area that includes land from the modern-day states of Nevada, Utah, Idaho, Wyoming, Oregon and California. It has no rivers running in or out of it. Any water that falls in the Great Basin either leaches into the ground via sinkholes or is lost to evaporation. The Great Basin is home to the Great Salt Lake, which was once an actual lake that was formed by water from the melting glaciers at the end of the Ice Age. Over the centuries, Lake Bonneville, as it was known, evaporated into the dry lake beds and salt flats that we see today. The same thing happened to Utah Lake, Mono Lake, Pyramid Lake and various others.

Thousands of years ago, the presence of such large amounts of water meant it would have been a vastly different territory in terms of the plants and animals that lived there. Consequently, it could theoretically have been home to large numbers of humans. However, unlike in other parts of North America, archaeological evidence of ancient peoples living in the Great Basin has yet to be found.

Harsh and Unforgiving

In recent centuries, the Great Basin has been a complicated place for humans to survive. Summers are hot, winters are cold, food is scarce and much of the water is brackish. To survive in such an unforgiving land year round requires great skill, expertise and knowledge.

The Native tribes who were living in the Great Basin at the time of the European arrival certainly had this. Food was so hard to come by that they constantly moved to access what was available. The food that was either hunted or gathered was usually in such small quantities that people tended to travel in small groups of thirty to 100 people. The basis of these groups was the family unit and four to ten families might travel together and form a band either due to familial ties or convenience. The benefit of living and travelling in such small groups meant that, whenever food was found, there was usually enough to go around. They only ever took as much food as they required, and they alternated hunting and gathering sites to give the environment time to replenish. This was not only pragmatic and sensible, but it was also essential to ensure their survival.

Such was the scarcity of food and the difficulty of living in the Great Basin that the Native American population rarely exceeded a total of 40,000. This, in an area of around 51,000 square kilometres (20,000 square miles), meant the Great Basin was thinly populated and most groups led isolated lives.

Food of the Great Basin

Fruit such as the chokecherry, raspberry, gooseberry and buffalo berry were picked and eaten when they were in season. Roots and tubers were dug out of the ground with the help of a pointed stick that was usually around one metre (three feet) in length. It was the extraction of the roots of the sego lily, camas and yampa with these sticks that led to Natives being referred to by the pejorative term 'diggers' when Euro-Americans arrived in the region.

The prickly pear cactus was a highly valuable source of food. The flower and fruit were eaten either raw, boiled or roasted and the nutritious inner bark was also harvested both for food and medicinal purposes. Small game such as rabbits, rats, lizards and birds were hunted and grasshoppers were roasted and ground into flour.

Pottery was acquired through trade with the Pueblo people to the south, which enabled foods to be boiled or stewed, and they would also use earthen ovens to cook food. This involved digging a metre-deep (three-foot-deep) hole, lining it with stones and building a fire inside it. Food was then placed within layers of damp grass and stones before being covered with earth and left overnight.

Once the horse arrived in the Basin, bigger animals such as bison, sheep, elk and deer were hunted by many tribes. But by far the most important food source in the Great Basin was the *piñon*, or pine nut. These became ripe in September and the pine nut harvest was one of the few occasions when there would be large gatherings of people. Annual festivals that involve a pine nut blessing dance are still held to celebrate the harvest to this day.

Huts were built near the forest and men, women and children all worked together to collect and process the nuts, which provided a lifeline throughout the freezing winter. Pine nuts are a rich source of protein and, once shelled and dried, can be eaten raw or pounded into flour or mush and added to other foods.

Shelter and Clothing

The hunter-gatherer lifestyle of the people of the Great Basin lasted unchanged until the nineteenth century. Therefore, one of the main requirements they had for their homes was that they could be put up and taken down easily. The lack of large animal skins meant that domed frames of willow branches were covered with plant materials that varied depending on what was available and the time of year. In the summer, a light covering of sagebrush or grass would suffice. In the winter, bark and soil were added, with rocks often being piled around the base to provide extra insulation. These sturdier, winter homes were called *wickiups* and would have a central hole in the roof to allow the smoke from the fire to escape.

Temperatures were so high in the summer that men often did not wear clothes at all. Women usually wore loose aprons made of plants such as sagebrush and yucca that were held together with cords made from tree roots. Both men and women habitually went barefoot through the summer months. In the winter, robes made from rabbit skins were worn by both sexes and fur caps were common too. As walking was the almost exclusive method of transportation, snowshoes were worn in the winter to enable them to travel through the deep snow that fell on much of the region.

The people of the Great Basin took a practical and pragmatic attitude to clothing and its function was far more important than its form. In later years, after the arrival of the horse and increased contact with both tribes of the Plains and

Euro-Americans, the clothes became more ornate and were commonly decorated with feathers and beadwork.

THE PEOPLE OF THE GREAT BASIN

With such a paucity of archaeological evidence, exactly when people moved on to the Great Basin and where they moved from is incredibly difficult to identify. As is often the case, a commonality of language offers the greatest clues to shared ancestry and therefore possible origins. All but one of the tribes of the Great Basin are speakers of languages from the Uto-Aztecan family. The Washoe, however, speak a type of Hokan.

The Washoe

The fact that the Washoe are speakers of Hokan indicates that their ancestors travelled east over the Sierras before settling in the area surrounding Lake Tahoe. Experts believe that the degree of difference in the dialects of the Washoe and their linguistic 'siblings' in California means that this migration probably took place around 4,500 years ago.

The Washoe, or *Wašišiw* – meaning 'people from here' – believe Lake Tahoe to be sacred. It is thought to have healing powers and be the place that gave life to the land, plants, animals and people. The word for 'edge of lake' in the Washoe dialect is *Da ow aga* and it is from this term that the word 'Tahoe' is derived.

The traditional Washoe Territory incorporates two distinct ecosystems: the arid region in present-day Nevada and the forests on the Sierra Nevada Mountains that are today part of California. This, combined with the fish available in the lake itself, meant that the Washoe had access to a greater variety of food sources than other tribes of the Great Basin. In much the same way as their Californian ancestors, the Washoe harvested acorns from the woodland as well as pine nuts.

Rabbit drives were held in the autumn, shortly after the pine nut harvest, and took advantage of the large gathering of people. This involved herding hundreds of rabbits towards a large net made from the fibres of the sagebrush. People would spread out in a long line and gradually move towards the net, forcing the rabbits to flee in front of them. The rabbits would become entangled in the net where they would be clubbed to death by other tribe members who lay in wait.

The meat of the rabbits was usually roasted and eaten in great quantities after the drive. It was also dried on racks to be saved for winter when it would be rehydrated by being added to soups. The pelts were as important as the meat and they were cut into strips and woven together on a frame. These large rabbit skin blankets were double-sided so they were furry on both the inside and outside. They were vital in the winter and served as both outer cloaks and bedding.

The Ute

The modern state of Utah is named after the Ute people. According to their tribal tradition, the Ute have inhabited lands in what is now Utah, Colorado, Wyoming, eastern Nevada, northern New Mexico and Arizona since the beginning of time. While this could be disputed, the prevalence of the Uto-Aztecan language certainly provides evidence that the Utes share common ancestors with many inhabitants of the Great Basin. As people travelled to new areas, they became separated and splintered from their original people. Before long, they adopted and became known by different names. Those who moved to the north became known as the Shoshone, others became the Paiute and those who moved on to the southern Plains of the Southwest region became the Comanche.

The remaining Ute formed a loose confederation of bands who recognized each other's primacy in hunting and gathering in a particular geographical area. The Gouache band lived on the eastern slopes of the Rockies, the Caputa band in the San Luis Valley and the Weenuchiu occupied the San Juan River Valley. The White River Ute, also known as Parianuche and Yamparika, lived in the valleys of the White and Yampa river systems and the Uintah lived east of Utah Lake.

As some Ute tribes lived in the Southwest as well as the Great Basin, they became one of the first Native American peoples to use horses. Some historians date their access to horses to 1637, when they were stolen from the Spanish in Sante Fe, but Ute tribal histories give a date closer to 1580. Regardless, the arrival of horses among the Ute meant enormous changes to their way of life and soon led to them becoming big-game hunters. They travelled across the mountains to the east in search of bison which, before long, became a vital source of food, clothing and many other items.

The Paiute

The Paiute split from the Ute and then split again into two further distinct groups. These became known as the Northern and Southern Paiute. The Northern Paiute occupied lands in eastern Oregon, western Nevada and east-central California. The Southern Paiute lived in what is now southern Utah, southeastern California, northwestern Arizona and southern Nevada.

The Northern Paiute lived a traditional hunter-gatherer lifestyle that was typical of much of the Great Basin. Unlike many other tribes, they had access to large numbers of fish in the form of the Lahontan Cutthroat Trout. Its annual migration to Lake Tahoe was a major event in the Northern Paiute calendar. The Northern Paiute are probably best known for the actions of a medicine man named Wovoka. It was Wovoka who began performing the Ghost Dance in 1890, believing it would bring about the salvation of the Native peoples, bring back the bison herds and sweep away all of the Euro-Americans in a great flood. The Ghost Dance soon spread to other nations and, when soldiers tried to stop it, culminated in the massacre at Wounded Knee.

The Southern Paiute practised floodplain gardening by creating reservoirs and irrigation canals to capture the melting snow in the spring months. By doing so, they were able to cultivate corn, pumpkins and sunflowers. Details of this were recorded by the Spanish explorer Escalante in 1776 who commented on the 'well-dug irrigation ditches'. Once the planting was complete, the Southern Paiute travelled to the cool of the high country where they gathered plants and berries and hunted in the forests. They also collected agate, a type of rock that was extremely useful for making arrowheads, spearpoints and tools. Southern Paiutes became adept at weaving baskets which, when sealed with pine pitch, were used to carry water.

The Shoshone

The Shoshone are another Uto-Aztecan-speaking tribe who share the same ancestors as the Ute people. The Shoshone, sometimes referred to as the Snake, divided into three groups known as the Western, the Northern and the Eastern or Wind River. Shortly after horses arrived in the Great Basin, the Comanche broke away from the Wind River Shoshone and moved into what is now Texas.

Before the arrival of the Euro-Americans, the Western Shoshone were a very loosely affiliated group of bands and families that hunted and gathered in what is now southern Idaho, central Nevada and northwestern Utah. The bands that make up the Western Shoshone are often named after the food that was predominant in the area they occupied. For example, the Mahaguadüka literally means 'mentzelia seed eaters' and Tsaiduka translates to 'tule eaters'.

The Eastern or Wind River Shoshone heralded from what is now western Wyoming. In the nineteenth century, they camped in the Wind River Valley, which they called 'Warm Valley', in the winter before moving to the Fort Bridger area of Wyoming for the summer. It is believed that Sacagawea, who famously acted as an interpreter for the Lewis and Clark expedition in 1804–06, was a member of the Wind River Shoshone.

The Northern Shoshone traditionally occupied lands in northern Utah and Idaho. Much like the Ute, the Wind River Shoshone and the Comanche, once horses arrived in the Great Basin the North Shoshone became bison hunters and raiders and adopted many of the practices and ways of the tribes of the Plains. This included the use of tepees for shelter and placing great importance on the honour gained from raids on other tribes.

The Bannock

The Bannock tribe perhaps typify the complex and shifting nature of intertribal relations in the Great Basin. They are an offshoot of the Northern Paiute who, after the arrival of the horse, decided to move eastward to hunt bison. Before Euro-Americans began to settle in the Great Basin, the Bannock were only a small tribe whose numbers never exceeded more than 2,000 people. However, they forged close relations with the Western Shoshone and often camped alongside them. Intermarriage was common and the two cultures soon became blended. Before long, the tribes began to use the term Shoshone-Bannock and, after colonization, they shared the same reservation.

Although the Bannock were few in number, they exerted a great influence over their friends and neighbours in the Great Basin. It was the Bannock who encouraged and incited their fellow Natives to revolt against the increased encroachment of the Euro-Americans in the second half of the nineteenth century. This culminated in the Bannock War of 1878.

STRUCTURE OF SOCIETY

The nomadic nature of travelling between scant resources meant that the family unit was the most important societal structure in the Great Basin. A person was typically in a band made up of grandparents, parents, aunts, uncles, brothers, sisters, cousins, nieces and nephews. The small nature of these groups meant that there was sometimes a lack of suitable marriage partners and, in such cases, brothers often shared a wife.

Children were put to work gathering food as soon as they could walk and those who were too young were normally left under the supervision of the grandparents. Marriages were usually arranged although not exclusively so. The tradition among some Paiute was for a man to declare his intentions by sleeping at the feet of the woman he wanted to marry. Unmarried women slept next to their grandmothers and, if she did not want to marry him, the young woman would get up in the night and sleep next to her mother instead.

The marriage ceremony was informal and marriage was often marked with nothing more than the couple starting to live together. Similarly, divorce among the people of the Great Basin was informal and common.

Leadership

When bands were so small in size, a degree of informality was perhaps natural as all of the band members would be either relatives or as familiar with each other as relatives. When it came to choosing a leader, people tended to follow someone for as long as they were successful. In other words, for as long as they led them to sources of food.

The arrival of the horse brought changes to the nature of leadership for many groups in the Great Basin. They began to adopt many of the practices and structures of the Plains tribes and leadership roles became more regulated and formal. Many Ute tribes, for example, began appointing civil chiefs to rule over everyday affairs and war chiefs to make decisions over military matters.

Spirituality in the Great Basin

Like almost all Native North Americans, the people of the Great Basin believe in the existence of spirits in nature. This extends not only to people, animals and plants but also to the sun, rain, mountains and rivers. A spiritual leader or shaman helps to communicate with the spirit world.

The creation story shared by many people of the Great Basin involves the wolf and the coyote. The wolf is a powerful, wise and respected figure and his brother, the coyote, is a trickster. It is through their various struggles against each other that the world around us takes its form. The exact stories vary from people to people: some believe that the world was initially covered in water and that the wolf and coyote created the land from mud. Others believe that the wolf created the solar system but the coyote was responsible for spreading people throughout the Great Basin. In one Shoshone story, it is said that, after he had created them, the wolf did not want people to die but the coyote insisted on it. However, when the coyote's son died, he changed his mind and tried to stop death. The wolf would not let him and the Shoshone believe that death is the punishment for the coyote's tricks.

Rituals and Dances

The peoples of the Great Basin hold a variety of ceremonies and dances that have their own purpose and significance. Some, such as the Ute, would hold bear dances to imbue them with the strength, skill and luck necessary to successfully hunt bears. The Shoshone adopted the Sun Dance, which is so common among the people of the Plains, to help bring healing and harmony. The Ghost Dance that spread through so many Native nations in the latter years of the nineteenth century originated with the

Northern Paiute. One dance that all people of the Great Basin have in common is the Round Dance. This is a thanksgiving dance that involves holding hands and dancing around a pole or significant tree. Sometimes it is held in the autumn to give thanks for the pine nut harvest or the first rabbit drives and sometimes it is held in the spring to give thanks for new beginnings.

Rituals around death varied from group to group. The Washoe traditionally burned their dead and the deceased's home. The Shoshone dead were buried in rock-covered graves. The Ute were also buried but often had their belongings buried with them. For the Paiute, mourning was marked by the widow and close relatives of the deceased cutting their hair. Convention stated that a Paiute widow was not allowed to remarry until her hair had regrown.

Sickness was often attributed to spirits inhabiting the body and shamans and medicine men traditionally recited chants and performed rituals to remove the spirit from the body. Sacred carvings were also used in healing as they were believed to protect from spirits. There were also more pragmatic approaches to sickness through the use of herbal medicines that are still used today. Bear root, a plant that grows widely in the higher elevations of the Rockies, has antibacterial properties and is still used in teas, baths or ointments for a wide variety of ailments.

Rock Art

The Great Basin is renowned for the large number of pictures that have been carved and painted on to its rocks. Many are inside caves and rock shelters and depict a wide variety of subjects. Some resemble people and animals whereas others are more abstract and are made up of a series of dots and lines.

It is impossible to date rock art and its purpose is equally difficult to identify. Some are scratched into the surface of a rock to create a kind of relief. These are called petroglyphs and, other than when vandalized, are usually well preserved. Others are painted on to the surface and are known as pictographs. The fact that many pictographs remain today is a testament to the sophisticated paints that the various tribes were able to manufacture. The paints were comprised of a mineral to create the colour, red from haematite being very common, a binder such as egg, blood, seed oils or honey to make the pigment stick to the rock, and a fluid, such as juice, water or urine, to make the paint liquid and of the right viscosity.

Although the precise reasons for rock art have been lost, there was undoubtedly a spiritual motivation for many of them. Those pictures depicting battles or hunts may have been produced in the hope they would help lead to successful outcomes. Or they may have been created to give thanks for a great victory or successful hunt.

Hunting Tools

The Shoshone developed techniques for making extremely powerful bows from the horns of the bighorn sheep that lived in the Rocky Mountains. The horns were heated and straightened before being joined together by wrapping them with rawhide. They took around two months and a great deal of skill to make and, although they were at most only around eighty centimetres (thirty-one inches) in length, they were considerably more flexible than wood. This flexibility translated into power, and they were more than capable of firing an arrow all the way through a bison.

Bighorn sheep bows were highly prized when trading with other nations and tribes and found their way into the possession of tribes on the Plains and beyond. So highly were they prized that a single bighorn sheep bow could be traded for a horse or a rifle.

To help them in their hunts, the Northern Paiute created duck decoys out of tule reeds. These were floated on marshes and tricked ducks into thinking it was a safe place to land and feed. Hunters then shot them with bows and arrows.

THE ARRIVAL OF THE EUROPEANS

Although Spanish explorers first entered the Great Basin and made contact with the Ute in the early seventeenth century, most indigenous people of the region did not see any Euro-Americans until at least midway through the 1800s. Fur trappers and explorers entered the Basin after the Louisiana Purchase of 1803 but, such was the paucity of beavers and other fur-bearing animals in the region that they soon moved on. The inhospitable nature of the landscape and climate seemed to keep potential colonists away. Ironically, it was the very fact that the Great Basin seemed so unappealing to US citizens that caused the first Euro-Americans to settle there in large numbers.

The Mormons

The Church of Jesus Christ of Latter-day Saints was founded by Joseph Smith in Palmyra, New York in 1820. Smith believed that an angel visited him and told him of the existence of some ancient texts that were inscribed on gold plates. He believed that the angel told him how to find the plates and transcribe the texts which, Smith said, contained prophetic visions of Jesus Christ living and teaching in North America. He published these writings as the *Book of Mormon* and he soon had several hundred followers who were called Mormons.

Many residents of Palmyra saw Smith as a blasphemous fraud and the Mormons soon became the target of violent attacks. As a result, they moved first to Kirkland, Ohio and then to Independence, Missouri but violence, attacks and riots followed them wherever they went. At the same time, their numbers continued to grow and Smith led them to Commerce, Illinois. Through a combination of hard work and religious fervour they prospered, and the Mormons built a huge temple and renamed the town Nauvoo, from the Hebrew word for 'beautiful place'. By 1840, there were 35,000 Mormons in Nauvoo with more converts regularly arriving from other states and from Europe.

When Smith announced in 1844 that God had told him that Mormon men could take more than one wife it caused uproar both inside and outside the community. When he said he was planning on running to become president of the United States the uproar turned to anger. On 27 June 1845, Smith was shot and murdered by an angry mob and Mormons found themselves being hunted down all across the countryside.

Brigham Young

The new leader of the Mormons, Brigham Young, believed that wherever there were non-Mormons, persecution would soon follow. He said, 'If there is a place on this earth that nobody wants, that's the place I'm looking for.' This place, he decided, was on the banks of the Salt Lake in the Great Basin.

Many prospectors, settlers and colonists who moved on to Native American lands undoubtedly viewed the indigenous peoples as savages who had failed to utilize the land on which they lived properly. The Mormons had quite a different view, but this did not prevent their arrival from becoming a disaster for many of the Natives of the Great Basin.

According to the *Book of Mormon*, the indigenous people of the Americas are the descendants of ancient Israelites who migrated to the New World well before Columbus set sail. Therefore, rather than seeing them as worthless savages, the Mormons believed Natives to be 'chosen people' who would come to embrace the teachings of the Latter-day Saints Church and play a significant role in its future. With this undoubtedly in mind, Brigham Young emphasized a policy of kindness and accommodation towards Native Americans and extolled the virtues of a peaceful coexistence.

In practice, these good intentions were not compatible with reality. From the Natives' perspective, 16,000 Mormons suddenly appeared on the horizon in 1847 and immediately started to carve a city out of the wilderness. Once Salt Lake City had been established, the Mormons fanned out into the surrounding country and established satellite settlements. Thousands more continued to make the perilous journey across the Plains and over the Rockies to join them.

Water sources were diverted to irrigate crops, and livestock were left to graze on plants that the Paiute relied upon to survive. The arrival of so many Mormons with their European farming practices upset the delicate balance of the Paiute's existence. In just a few years, a way of life that had sustained the Paiute for centuries was no longer viable. The result was starvation. In response, the Mormons launched missionary expeditions to provide assistance and convert tribespeople to their faith.

The Mountain Meadows Massacre

One unintended and tragic consequence of these closer ties was the Mountains Meadows Massacre of 1857. At the time of the Mormons' arrival in the Great Basin, it belonged to Mexico. Victory in the Mexican-American War saw possession of the Utah Territory transfer to the US. This prompted fears among the Mormons that the persecution they had experienced in New York, Missouri and Illinois was about to be repeated if and when non-Mormons started settling in Utah.

Brigham Young was appointed to the position of territorial governor of Utah by the US government in 1850, but several non-Mormon officials were also sent to the territory. This led to friction and accusations by the government officials that they were being intimidated and prevented from fulfilling their duties. Tension rose to such an extent that preparations for war were made by both Brigham Young and the US government. One of the measures Young took was to encourage the Paiute to attack and harass any wagon trains that passed through the territory.

This was the fraught and febrile atmosphere that a group of settlers known as the Fancher party found when they entered Utah Territory on their way to California. They passed around 200 miles south of Salt Lake City and rumours spread among the Mormons that the migrants had an anti-Mormon agenda. It was enough for a local Mormon militia to enlist the help of some members of the Paiute and launch an attack on the wagon train.

The Fancher party proved to be more than capable of defending themselves and fended off assaults for several days. This posed an enormous problem for John Lee, the leader of the Mormon militia. As the Fancher party were sure to report that they had been attacked by Mormons, not just the Paiute, there would surely be reprisals by the US government.

Lee decided to offer the Fancher party safe passage out but lured them into a trap. A total of 120 people, including every man, woman and child over the age of seven, were then murdered in cold blood. Their deaths were blamed entirely on the Paiutes and a cover-up was attempted.

It still led to US soldiers being dispatched to Utah and, when they arrived in June 1858, they were allowed to march through Salt Lake City unopposed. Young accepted the new governor who was imposed upon Utah and a deal was struck that would see Lee face justice. In return for providing evidence that proved Lee's guilt, the prosecutor agreed not to pursue any other Mormons through the courts. Lee was convicted and executed at Mountain Meadows in 1877 but the murders left a stain on the reputations of both the Mormons and the Paiutes.

Gold

Shortly after the arrival of the Mormons at the Great Salt Lake, gold deposits were discovered in California. The steady number of migrants who had been passing through the Great Basin increased both suddenly and dramatically. In 1859, gold and silver were discovered within the basin itself leading to the creation of 'boomtowns' such as Virginia City and Washoe almost overnight. The influx of thousands of prospectors was a key factor in the admission of the state of Nevada to the Union in 1864. At its peak, around $36 million of silver was extracted from Nevada's mines every year. This was enough to justify the establishment of a branch of the US Mint in Carson City, Nevada.

The woodlands that were the source of the precious pine nuts were cut down in vast swathes to provide timber for mineshaft props, buildings for prospectors and even firewood. The sacred woodlands, which were also the habitat of the animals that were hunted, were soon barren, featureless hillsides.

Disease

Large numbers of Euro-American colonists, whether fleeing religious persecution, prospecting for gold or travelling for any other reason, were always accompanied by disease. As well as the smallpox, chicken pox, influenza and mumps that had devastated Native communities all over North America, the migrants arriving in the Great Basin also brought cholera with them.

Globally, the first cases of cholera were reported in India in 1817. By 1829, it had spread to Europe and it reached London in 1832. The first cases in North America were reported the very same year and its arrival spread panic as well as death. There were several reasons why it was so feared. Firstly, it struck suddenly and a person who was seemingly perfectly healthy could be dead just hours later. Secondly, the way in which people expired was particularly distressing. The onset of diarrhoea was so violent that a person could lose up to 20 litres (five gallons) of fluid in a single day. The dehydration this caused led to a thickening of the blood and the bursting of blood vessels. This often resulted in a blueish-grey pallor to the skin and, for this reason, cholera was commonly referred to as the 'blue death'. Once the blood reached a certain viscosity, major organs were unable to function and an agonizing death soon followed. This often took place in a pool of stinking excrement.

The final reason it was so feared was because its method of communication was completely unknown. Developments in Europe in the late nineteenth century finally established the link between water and cholera, but the Native American communities of the Great Basin had no idea that a water source had been contaminated by the diarrhoea of a cholera victim. As a result, they would have unwittingly ingested the bacteria. Once one member of a band was struck down, the copious volumes of diarrhoea involved meant that infection of friends or family was almost inevitable.

WARS IN THE GREAT BASIN

With resources and water sources at such a premium in the Great Basin, it is perhaps not surprising that they were the focus of the first conflicts between the encroaching Euro-Americans and the people who had occupied the lands for many centuries. The fencing off of water sources by mining communities and Pony Express mail stations created an atmosphere of burning resentment and meant that events could quickly escalate.

The Pyramid Lake War 1860

This conflict erupted after an attack on a Pony Express station and watering post. There are conflicting accounts about the motivation for the attack, but what is known is that five Euro-Americans were killed and the station, which also served as a store and saloon, was burned down. Some accounts claim it was due to an argument over the trade of a horse for a defective gun between a Paiute man and the proprietors of the station. Others claim it was due to the kidnapping of two Paiute boys who were discovered tied up in the cellar of the post. Another account claims that two Paiute girls were raped and held captive by the store owners, and it was the girls' father who burned it down with the owners and store customers trapped inside.

Whatever the exact reason, it was immediately apparent that the murders and destruction of the post would lead to reprisals. The Paiute chief Numaga had consistently advocated a peaceful approach to dealing with the Euro-American arrivals and the death and disruption they brought with them. When he heard of the deaths at the station, he said: 'There is no longer any use for counsel; we must prepare for war.'

A militia of around 100 men was quickly formed by the miners of Virginia City, Silver City and Carson City. They were poorly armed and poorly disciplined but determined to pursue those responsible for attacking the post. As they approached the south of Pyramid Lake, they saw a small band of Paiute and immediately attacked them. The Paiute retreated and the militia gave chase. When the Paiute entered a ravine, the militia followed them only to be confronted with a much larger group of Paiutes who blocked their escape and began to fire on them from all sides. Seventy-six members of the militia were killed and many others were injured. Just three Natives were killed in the fighting.

Another militia was formed, but it was the arrival of a US Army detachment of artillery and infantry from Fort Alcatraz that proved to be decisive. The Second Battle of Pyramid Lake was fought in the exact location of the first but with a wildly different outcome. Twenty-five Paiutes were reported killed with the rest scattered across the Great Basin. The construction of a fort at the southern edge of Pyramid Lake meant Federal forces became a permanent presence and, while there were still skirmishes, armed uprisings were suppressed. Although relatively few Paiute were killed in the actual fighting, food gathering was severely inhibited and starvation probably claimed more Paiute lives than bullets during the Pyramid Lake War.

Life on a knife edge was obviously not unique to the Paiute. Unable to sustain themselves due to the destruction of their food sources and with their numbers severely reduced by the ravages of disease, many indigenous people agreed to sign treaties. These involved them giving up their rights to land and moving on to reservations but did not rescue them from their plight in the way they hoped. Once there, desperate conditions and the failure of the government to fulfil their treaty obligations led to more wars between the Native peoples of the Great Basin and the US Army.

The Bannock War 1878

In 1869, 600 members of the Bannock, along with considerably more Shoshone, agreed to move on to the Fort Hall Reservation in Idaho. As part of the treaty, they were promised food supplies to sustain them as they transitioned from being hunter-gatherers to farmers. It became immediately apparent that the food supplied was not sufficient and many soon fled the reservation. Others travelled to a nearby prairie where camas plants grew in large numbers and the root was harvested in preparation for the coming winter.

Tension between the Natives on the reservation and nearby Euro-American settlers continued to simmer and occasionally boiled over into fights. This sometimes led to the army entering the reservation to arrest individuals or confiscate weapons, but the events of 1878 led to conflict on a much wider scale. When the Bannock and Shoshone left the reservation in the spring of that year to harvest the camas roots, they found that settlers had been grazing their livestock on the prairie and the camas had all been eaten.

Facing a winter of starvation, several hundred Bannocks, accompanied by Northern Paiute allies, banded together under Chief Buffalo Horn. They launched a large-scale raiding offensive all along the Snake River Valley designed to secure food and drive out Euro-American settlers from the area.

The response from the US Army was rapid and vigorous and the uprising was short-lived. Outnumbered and outgunned, the final fight took place at Charles' Ford in Wyoming where 140 Bannock men, women and children were killed. The surviving rebel Bannocks agreed to return to their reservation.

General George Crook, who fought wars against several indigenous nations and was described by General William Tecumseh Sherman as the 'greatest Indian fighter of them all' was in no doubt over who was to blame for the Bannock War. He wrote: 'It cannot be expected that they will stay on reservations where there is no possible way to get food and see their wives and children starve and die around them. We have taken their lands and deprived them of every means of living.'

The Meeker Incident or Meeker Massacre of 1879

In 1868, the leaders of six bands of Ute signed a treaty, known as the Ute Treaty, with the US government. As part of the deal, the Ute agreed to cede the land on the eastern side of the Rockies and live on a reservation on the Western Slope in what had become Colorado. Though much smaller than their traditional lands, the reservation was still large and required two 'Indian Agencies' to distribute the food and supplies that had been stipulated in the treaty. One of the agencies was known as the White River Agency due to its location near the river that formed the reservation's northern border.

Throughout the 1870s, shipments of food were frequently delayed or not delivered at all which led the Ute to become increasingly angry and desperate. In the face of starvation, they began leaving the reservation to both hunt and take supplies from Euro-American settlements. The situation around the White River Agency was already tense when a new agent named Nathan Meeker was put in charge in early 1878. Meeker was a zealous Christian with a mandate to introduce new farming techniques to the Utes. He was an uncompromising character and reacted to the refusal of the Utes to engage with cow milking or farming by withholding food and supplies.

When Meeker ordered the ploughing over of crops that were being grown to feed racehorses, it led to his assault. He immediately requested troops to come and protect the agency. The approaching troops were spotted by a Ute party and their presence was interpreted as a declaration of war. They sent away their women and children and began holding war dances.

On 29 September, as the soldiers crossed into the reservation, the Utes opened fire on them from higher ground. Fourteen soldiers were killed and the rest were pinned down by Ute fire for over a week. When the Ninth Cavalry arrived on 5 October, twenty-three Ute soon lay dead and the rest were forced to surrender.

News of the soldiers' arrival and the outbreak of fighting quickly spread in the reservation. The agency buildings were immediately set alight. Meeker and ten other Euro-American Agency employees and civilians were killed and their bodies mutilated. Meeker's wife and daughter, as well as the wife and children of another agency official, were captured and taken to a secret location.

News of Meeker's death caused outrage, and legislation was nearly passed in Colorado that would have put a twenty-five-dollar bounty on Ute scalps. By October, those holding the captives had been tracked down and the hostages were released unharmed. An investigation into the incident, which was widely reported as a massacre in the newspapers, failed to reach any kind of resolution because the Utes refused to either divulge the names of those responsible for the killings or deliver them to the authorities.

In the absence of individuals to punish, Congress approved a non-negotiable treaty that would collectively punish all of the White River Utes. In 1881, the Yampa, Parianuche and Tabeguache Ute bands were force-marched from the Colorado reservation to a much smaller reservation in Utah.

In 1950, the US government recognized that the forced removal of the Ute had been illegal. The White River Ute did not get their land back, but they did receive financial compensation. They remain on the Uintah-Ouray Reservation in Utah to this day.

THE TRIBES OF THE GREAT BASIN TODAY

The arrival of tens of thousands of Mormons and then successive gold and silver rushes utterly disrupted the delicate balance of the Native way of life in the Great Basin. With this in mind, it is perhaps not surprising that most Native peoples of the Great Basin were living on reservations by the end of the nineteenth century. Many began to work as labourers on the farms of the Euro-American settlers who had moved on to what was once indigenous land and their children were sent to boarding schools in a concerted attempt to force assimilation upon them.

Many Great Basin Natives still live on those reservations today but, perhaps counterintuitively, this has enabled them to fight to preserve their culture and languages. In 2013, a kindergarten was opened on the Fort Hall Reservation in which students were exclusively taught in the Shoshone dialect. Older students received daily Shoshone lessons and there are real hopes that their language, which forms so much of a people's identity, will survive and thrive.

Similarly, the Washoe hold annual gatherings around Lake Tahoe in late spring to celebrate their culture and heritage, and to help keep their language alive. Some nations have combined and share reservations. Shoshone and Bannock people live together on the Fort Hall Reservation and members of the Shoshone and the Paiute also share the Duck Valley Reservation in Idaho.

Using figures from the 2010 census, there are around 2,000 Washoe living in the United States. There are approximately 13,000 Shoshone, 14,000 Paiute and 12,000 Ute. In addition to this, there are around 6,000 who identify as Shoshone-Bannock and a further 4,000 who identify as Paiute-Shoshone.

CALIFORNIA

Of all the cultural areas that Native North America has been divided into, the area of California had the greatest population density before the arrival of Europeans. Encompassing the area of the modern state of California as well as Mexico's Baja Peninsula, it extends from the Sierra Nevada in the east to the Pacific Coast in the west. It is comparatively small in size when put against the Great Plains or the Subarctic region. However, it is an area of astonishing variety when it comes to natural features, and of incredible richness in terms of natural resources. There are mountains, coastlines, redwood and fir forests and southeast of the region contains the Mojave Desert.

This richness and variety is mirrored by its indigenous population. California is home to over 500 tribes who, between them, speak dialects belonging to over twenty language families. This makes it the most linguistically diverse area in all of North America. These language families include Penutian, Hokan, Uto-Aztecan, Athapascan, Yukian, Algonquian and Yuman. They diverge into a myriad of separate dialects, often simply named after the people who speak them. These include the Yana, Yurok, Pomo, Wintun, Hupa and Maidu. It is not without reason that Native California has often been described as being more linguistically diverse than all of Europe.

In terms of numbers, without reliable census data, historical population numbers are always going to be best estimates. The margin for error is extensive but scholars have put California's population before the arrival of Europeans somewhere between 300,000 and one million people. Even if the lower estimate is taken, it is still an extraordinary number for such a small geographical area (around 200,000 square miles or 320,000 square kilometres). What factors could have led to such population density and to so many different groups settling in California?

Somewhere between 5000 and 4000 BCE, the hunter-gatherers who inhabited the Pacific Coast began to exploit the resources they found both inland and at the water's edge. They began to gather shellfish, harpoon seals and catch fish. They gathered seeds, especially acorns, and hunted the animals of the forest. Sources of food were so plentiful that permanent and semipermanent villages began to appear and wholly nomadic lifestyles were abandoned. Villages helped create small tribes, or tribelets, that ranged from a few hundred to a few thousand people. Some tribelets included the people from just one village, whereas others included several villages, often with a main settlement and several outposts close by.

Permanent villages were further consolidated around 3000 BCE when a change in the Californian climate led to conditions that were more favourable for agriculture, particularly along the Colorado River. The planting, tending and harvesting of crops required a far higher degree of planning, organization and co-operation. The result of this was the development of hierarchical societies, often led by chiefs, who made decisions, allocated work and distributed resources. This increased the divergence between the groups and led to the development of distinct differences in identity, beliefs and ways of life.

THE HUPA (NORTHWEST)

A notable group located in the northwest of California is the Hupa. They originally spoke an Athabaskan dialect that came to be known as 'Hupa', and built their villages on the banks of what is now the Trinity River. Their dwellings were made of timber and dug into the ground with separate lodges for the men to sleep away from the women and children. There were often also sweat lodges and separate buildings for women to stay in during menstruation.

The climate around the lower Trinity River is extremely mild and there were ample resources to sustain the Hupa. They hunted elk and deer, caught salmon and, like many other Californian tribes and tribelets, gathered acorns in the forest. Acorns were a key reason why California was able to support such large populations.

Access to Acorns

There are fifteen species of oak tree in California, each providing acorns with varying degrees of yield, nutritional value and fat content. All acorns have a higher fat content than wheat or corn and this helped people survive the lean winters. But it was the fact that acorns could be stored and provide food all year round that made them so central to Native Californian existence. By placing the acorns in caches that were raised off the ground, groups such as the Hupa were protected from the perils of fluctuating yields and winter famines.

As a result, many Native Californian groups devoted months of every year almost exclusively to gathering and processing acorns. Men would climb vast oak trees and use sticks to knock the acorns to the ground. There, they were collected by the waiting women and children who had laid out blankets to help them in their task.

Once the baskets were full, they were carried to nearby granite rocks which served as milling stations.

To make acorns edible takes a considerable amount of work and co-operation. Initially, the caps and outer shells of the acorns were cracked and removed by skilled women using a rock pestle. The nutritious inners were then pounded against the granite to create a fine flour or meal. It took about an hour to grind one kilogram (a little over two pounds) of acorns and, once all of the harvest had been turned into meal, the women would bury their heavy pestle near the rocks in anticipation of next year's haul. The use of the same granite rocks as mortars was so regular and prolonged that deep depressions were often made in the rocks that are clearly visible today.

The acorns may have been shelled and ground into meal, but they were still inedible at this stage. Acorns contain large amounts of tannic acids which, if consumed, cause ulcers in the mouth and intestines and prevent the body from metabolizing protein. To remove the tannic acid, the acorn meal had to be repeatedly washed in water. Depending on the variety of oak from which the acorn came, this could take anywhere between four to six hours. Over time, people identified which varieties required the least washing and understood that hot water accelerated the process of leaching the tannic acid from the meal. Hot springs then became highly popular places to process acorns. Once the acorns were finally ready to eat, the women of a group would bake the acorn flour into bread, although it would also be added to soups.

Harvesting acorns blurred the lines between foraging and farming. There was undoubtedly a large element of husbandry in the way the Californian Natives managed and cared for the oak trees that they so heavily relied upon. They routinely built fires underneath their oak trees for several reasons. Firstly, it removed and killed insects and weeds at the base of the tree that could affect the yield of acorns. Secondly, it removed the undergrowth and made it easier to lay blankets flat against the ground so the acorns could be collected once they had been knocked from the branches. The burnt ground also stimulated the growth of mushrooms, another precious food source, and made travel through the forests easier. Any approaching enemies would find they had less cover and could be more easily spotted before they could launch a surprise attack.

Large supplies of acorns also meant that inland groups such as the Hupa could trade with coast-dwelling groups. In exchange, they might receive sea fish, shellfish or highly nutritious seaweed. They could also purchase dentalia (mollusc) shells which, along with woodpecker scalps, were great status symbols among the Hupa and other tribes.

THE MAIDU

Directly to the east of the Hupa, in the territory that extended from the Sierra Nevada to the Sacramento River, were the traditional lands of the Maidu people. Life in the mountains was considerably more difficult than in the valleys and the Maidu were not as prosperous as other Californian groups. The weather conditions they experienced were also more challenging than those faced by most of their fellow Californians.

Living on mountainous territory that was unsuitable for agriculture and not ideal for foraging meant that the Maidu relied on hunting to survive. Elk, deer, bears, rabbits, ducks and geese were all hunted in a variety of ways. Like most other indigenous American groups, they utilized bows and arrows, clubs, spears, slings, snares, nets, traps, pits and dogs to capture and kill their prey.

The housing of the Maidu often consisted of a simple lean-to that was made of brush and bark and built into the mountainside. Despite having perhaps the greatest need for warm and secure housing, the Maidu had the simplest of dwellings in all Native California. House types varied from group to group but the majority of Native Californian dwellings were substantial and dome-shaped. They had a central pole and were covered with whatever material was readily available, but grass and bark were most commonly used. Some groups, like the Hupa, built partially subterranean dwellings and had large ceremonial buildings that could hold several hundred people. These were used to host festivals and perform rituals and were common across California before the arrival of the Europeans. Many groups also built earth-covered sauna-type buildings called sweat lodges. Ritual purification through sweating before major hunts and religious ceremonies was common among Californian Natives and is still conducted by many Native Americans today.

The Maidu, like many of the indigenous peoples of northern California before contact with Europeans, followed the Kuksu religious belief system. Kuksu is sometimes referred to as a cult and its adherents would wear ceremonial clothes to impersonate spirits and perform elaborate narrative dances. In the majority of cases, it would be exclusively the men of the tribe who would undertake the rituals. Many villages had specially constructed underground dance rooms in which they would meet. The dances and rituals were performed to help ensure successful hunts, fertility, good health and bountiful harvests.

Further south, the Toloache religion was much more widely followed. Followers of Toloache would imbibe a drink made from the jimsonweed plant that would put them into a trance. They believed the trance would give them access to supernatural knowledge and insights into their futures.

All Native Californian groups shared a belief that the supernatural controlled events and could affect their lives. It was considered the cause of sickness, the weather and the size of the harvest. As a result, people who were believed to have supernatural powers were widely revered and enjoyed a high status. Most groups would have at least one shaman who would be called on to help the community. This could involve performing rituals, creating cave paintings and poetry or simply giving advice. Shamans could be men or women and they often earned considerable material wealth as well as respect because of their skills.

THE POMO

Towards the centre of California, where San Francisco now sits, lived a Hokan-speaking people called the Pomo. Pomo lands included coastlands as well as highlands in the interior. This gave them ready access to deer, fish and acorns, meaning that food was rarely in short supply.

One aspect of Pomo Territory also made them extremely wealthy compared to other Californian tribes. Large salt deposits meant they always had a highly sought-after and lucrative resource to trade with other tribes. Pomo lands were also rich in magnesite. This, when combined with ground-up shells, was made into beads that were often used as a de facto currency across California and beyond.

It wasn't just the Pomos' beads that were highly prized; their basketry was some of the finest produced in all of North America. They incorporated coloured feathers and beads and were woven so tightly that they could be used to hold water without leaking.

THE COCOPAH

The Cocopah tribe are based in the south of California and traditionally used the annual snowmelt from the Rocky Mountains to help sustain their agriculture-based lifestyle. Every spring, the Colorado River would burst its banks as it passed through Cocopah Territory. As the waters retreated, the land would be left rich in nutrients. The Cocopahs then planted corn, beans and squash, crops that had all been introduced from Central and southern America, in the newly enriched soil.

The work was divided along gender lines with men digging the holes and women planting the seeds and covering them with earth. Throughout August and September, the fields were weeded and in October the crops were harvested. Women were tasked with picking and husking the corn and men carried the produce back to the village for further processing and storage. The climate, like in most of California, meant that clothing was very simple and minimal for the Native Californian people, including the Cocopah. In the case of men, clothing was often non-existent. Women would typically wear short skirts made of bark fibres or thin animal skins, and robes were used by men and women to give protection from the rain and wind during storms. Sandals were worn by the Cocopah and most other tribes in the south with moccasins being worn in central and northern parts of California.

THE YUROK

The Yurok speak an Algic language that is believed to be related to Algonquian. They are renowned as great fishermen, eelers and canoe makers. Their traditional territories lay along the lower Klamath River and the Pacific Coast, and fish formed the majority of their diet – particularly salmon and sturgeon. With water being so central to their lives, it is perhaps not surprising that they developed great skill at creating dugout canoes from the redwoods that grew around them.

The basic approach to creating a dugout canoe might seem incredibly simple. Find a large redwood log, cut it in half lengthways and then carve out the inside wood to create a canoe-shaped vessel. In practice, it is a demanding process that takes such a high degree of skill that canoe building is considered a sacred art by the Yurok.

Canoe makers only used fallen trees and searched for wood that had the closest grain and was therefore the least permeable. They were hollowed out by burning small sections and chipping out the burnt sections with adzes. Once the required high-sided shape had been achieved, fire was utilized once again to bring out and melt the wood's natural resins and create a seal. A finished canoe, which might be over six metres long, took several months to build. Canoes are not only practical objects that enabled the Yurok to travel up and down the rivers and out into the ocean, they also have a spiritual element. To this day, they form a key part of dances such as the White Deerskin Dance and are used to ceremoniously transport the participants.

Compared to most Native American cultures, the Yurok were traditionally quite wealth orientated and that wealth was measured in dentalia shells. Dentalia are mollusc shells that are shaped like tiny elephant tusks. It was harvested from the ocean and worn in necklaces. It was also commonly used as a form of currency. Items were purchased, dowries were paid and debts were settled by using dentalia. Men commonly had tattoos on their arms that enabled them to measure the length, and therefore the value, of the shells. Other objects considered to be of great worth included canoes, blades made from obsidian, woodpecker scalps and albino, or white deerskins.

Like most Californian Native Americans, music and dance are vital parts of life for the Yurok. Dances are the most important spiritual, ceremonial and social events of the year and are held for a variety of reasons. There are dances to mark the seasons, heal the sick and pay homage to ancestors. The Yurok, much like the Hupa, hold world renewal ceremonies to help ensure that the salmon continue to swim and the food supply is guaranteed for future generations. Music for these dances is provided by a variety of instruments. Flutes are made from wood or the bones of birds, and whistles are made from bone. Rattles play a more prominent role than drums in Native Californian music and can be made from many materials.

THE CHUMASH

The Chumash was the name given to the people who were living in the central and southern coastal areas of California and who spoke a form of the Hokan language. There is evidence that indigenous people have been living in this area for around 13,000 years and it is believed that the Chumash are the descendants of these first inhabitants. Wherever a village was located within the territories, food was abundant, although the acorn formed the staple of their diet. Before the arrival of the Europeans, the Chumash lived in around one hundred and fifty independent villages of various sizes and had a total population of at least 25,000 people.

One of the most remarkable aspects about traditional Chumush culture was the type of canoes that they constructed. Unlike other tribes, such as the Yurok, they did not hollow out large logs but made the vessels out of planks. These vessels, known as 'tools', were made from redwood trees that drifted down the coast and were then hacked into planks. The planks were then lashed together using animal tendons and sinews before they were sealed using a tar-like substance called 'top'. This was a mixture of pine tar from trees and asphaltum, a naturally incurring oil-like substance that seeps up on to the earth's surface in parts of California.

Another notable aspect of Chumash culture was their rock paintings. These were probably made for religious reasons and we are left to guess at their exact meanings. Dating the images is similarly difficult, although most that have survived to the present day are probably less than 1,000 years old. The cave paintings remain sacred to the Chumash people and most are extremely fragile. For these reasons, other than notable and curated examples, the locations of rock paintings are not shared with the general public.

THE ARRIVAL OF EUROPEANS IN CALIFORNIA

The Chumash may have been the first people to inhabit California, but they were also unlucky enough to be the first to have contact with Europeans. The Spanish were the first Europeans to arrive in California. The region derives its name from a fictional island paradise populated entirely by beautiful women that featured in the book *Las Sergas de Esplandián*, which was enormously popular in sixteenth-century Spain. The Spanish, approaching from the south, initially believed they had discovered an enormous island and decided to name it after Garci Rodriguez de Montalvo's literary invention. It was only as they travelled further north that they realized it was attached to the mainland and not an island at all.

Contact was first made in the 1530s when Cortez's men arrived in what they called Baja. This peninsula is part of the Native cultural area but belongs to modern-day Mexico. In 1542, the Spanish arrived in Alta, or northern California, and, when Juan Rodríguez Cabrillo's expedition landed in what is now Santa Barbara, they laid claim to it.

For the next two centuries, Native Californian contact with Europeans was rare and intermittent. England's Francis Drake led an expedition there in the late sixteenth century with the primary aim of looting gold from the Spanish. He did, however, land in California and make contact with the Miwok people. With an arrogance typical of Europeans arriving in America, he named the land 'New Albion', nailed a brass plaque to a tree and claimed English sovereignty over the land. It may have impressed Elizabeth I upon his return to Old Albion, but England did nothing to follow up or secure Drake's claim.

Spanish Colonization of California

It took until 1769, and an increased British and Russian presence in the area as they searched for the Northwest Passage, before the Spanish attempted to colonize California in earnest. In that year, the Franciscan Priest Junípero Serra established a mission in San Diego. In 1770, Gaspar de Portolá set up a military outpost in Monterey and established an overland supply route with other

Spanish settlements in New Mexico and Arizona. The results were almost immediately and predictably catastrophic for the Native Californian populations.

Twenty-one missions were founded, with the intention of 'civilizing' and converting the local populations to Christianity. In addition to this, four fortified ports or presidios were built to enforce Spanish authority. The presidios were built in San Diego, Monterey, San Francisco and Santa Barbara, and Spanish citizens built pueblos or walled towns in Los Angeles, San José and Branciforte (later to become Santa Cruz).

The Spanish did not go out to the Natives to convert them. Instead, they removed them from their home communities and moved them into the missions. This was the fate that befell nearly all of the Chumash. Once there, they were baptized, stripped of their names and identities by being given Spanish names, separated from their families in single-sex dormitories and put to work on the mission's farms. All under the watchful eye of the fathers who ensured they lived according to the Catholic teachings they were given. Failure to live as ordained would often result in interventions that were both swift and brutal.

The introduction of European livestock and farming techniques also had a devastating impact on the Californian environment. Huge areas of forest were cleared to accommodate cows, sheep, goats and horses. These animals multiplied rapidly and were often turned loose to graze. Free-grazing animals ate the acorns and grasses on which the Natives and the indigenous wild animals relied. In a matter of months, economies and ecosystems that had lasted for thousands of years were critically undermined by domesticated livestock. To survive, many Californian Natives were forced to move on to the missions.

European Epidemics

Even more devastating than the ecological disaster brought by the Europeans was the introduction of disease. Congregating in the missions created the crowded, unhygienic and unhealthy conditions necessary for sickness to spread like wildfire. Between 1769 and 1810, missions recorded outbreaks of typhus, typhoid, pneumonia, diphtheria, pleurisy and measles.

Native women and children were disproportionately affected. Spanish soldiers and colonists spread the sexually transmitted diseases of syphilis and gonorrhoea which led to plummeting fertility rates and soaring infant mortality. The life expectancy of a Native Californian living on a mission was just twelve years.

In the thirty-one years between 1769 and 1800, the population of the Natives of California reduced by fifty per cent. Such catastrophic death rates naturally led to the population numbers of those living inside missions to fall through the floor. Most died and others fled before they became infected. This caused the Franciscan fathers to find new ways to bolster the number of converts and residents of their missions. They sent parties inland in search of new converts and to bring back those who had decided to escape the squalor and disease of the missions.

These parties were attacked which in turn caused reprisals by the Spanish soldiers and violent punishments both inside and outside the missions' walls. Indigenous people were routinely flogged for transgressions such as being too sick to work. They were placed in stocks or had their legs bound and many missions had prisons and underground dungeons. There can be no doubt that the Native Californians learned some very harsh lessons at the hands of Spanish Christians.

The Mexican Province of California

When Mexico won its war of independence against Spain in 1821, Alta (Northern) California became a Mexican province. The missions were secularized and the Mexicans established a ranching culture and encouraged Californians to trade with the merchants from Britain and the United States. California was viewed as something of a backwater by the newly independent Mexican government but, led by the trapper Jedediah Smith in 1826, it became an increasingly popular destination for US citizens.

By the 1840s, American immigrants outnumbered Mexican citizens and, in 1846, they revolted against the Mexican government and declared California an independent nation. At the same time American settlers were fighting for Californian autonomy, the United States was fighting the Mexican-American War. California was occupied by American soldiers and two years after the Treaty of Guadalupe Hidalgo was signed to end the war in 1848, it became America's thirty-first state.

The California Gold Rush

Agreements between nations were soon overtaken by developments in the ground and the rivers of California. On 24 January 1848, James Marshall discovered gold while constructing a sawmill near modern-day Sacramento. He had unknowingly fired the starting pistol on the California gold rush and started one of the biggest mass migrations in human history.

Prospectors flocked to California from other parts of the United States and all over the world. People from as far away as Australia and New Zealand felt the pull of riches beyond their wildest dreams. Thousands of Chinese decided to escape famine and seek their riches in America. Throughout the nineteenth century, almost all of America's Chinese immigrants lived in California where they learned that racial prejudice was not limited to the Natives.

In 1849 alone, more than 100,000 people moved to California. And the migration did not stop with the 'forty-niners'. Others realized they could become rich by selling services and equipment needed by those who were trying to get rich. San Francisco became utterly transformed and, by 1860, the population of California had tripled from its pre-gold rush levels to over 300,000.

The impact on the Natives was apocalyptic. The terms 'genocide' and 'ethnic cleansing' have been frequently employed by historians to describe the actions of the settlers. Although these are not terms that were used at the time, there can be no doubt that there was a concerted effort by some people to exterminate the indigenous population of California.

At the same time as the Californian constitution expressly forbade Native Americans from voting, the governor of the state authorized and funded militias to hunt down and kill indigenous people. When there were insufficient resources to pay for them, the federal government stepped in. During the 1850s and 1860s, the US government spent over $1 million footing the bill for what were described as 'pedagogic killings'. The survivors of these murders, they believed, had been taught a lesson.

With California law also forbidding the sale of firearms to Native Americans, the task of the militias and vigilantes was made that much easier. When laws were passed that prevented Native Californians from working as lawyers, serving on juries or even testifying against white people, they had literally no legal recourse to prevent their persecution.

When Natives took the law into their own hands, the response was often unimaginably brutal. In 1850, when members of the Pomo tribe rose up and killed two cattle ranchers who had enslaved, raped and murdered members of their tribe for over two years, they had no idea just how terrible the consequences of their actions would be.

The brother of one of the dead ranchers formed a posse and started indiscriminately killing Natives in revenge. Many Pomo fled and hid on an island where they had traditionally gathered every April to fish. Captain Nathaniel Lyon, of the First Dragoons of the US Cavalry, was given orders to find the members of the Pomo who had killed the ranchers and 'exterminate if possible'. He soon tracked them down.

In his own words, 'the island became a perfect slaughtering pen'. Those who swam ashore to escape the heavy artillery fire were met with bayonets. When the killing stopped, around two hundred members of the Pomo lay dead. The vast majority were women and children. The Pomo called the island Bo-No-Po-Ti. It is now called Bloody Island.

Sometimes the massacres involved hundreds of Natives, sometimes they were murdered in ones and twos. Between 1846 and 1873, between nine and 16,094 Californian Natives were killed at the hands of vigilantes, militias or the State of California. Countless others were enslaved. The 1850 Act for the Government and Protection of Indians empowered law enforcement to police indigenous people and enabled the indentured labour of Natives – including children.

In Los Angeles, employers were allowed by the law to purchase those who had been incarcerated. City officials would sweep the town for drunks on Saturday nights and display them by chaining them to the front of the city jail. Farmers would then bid for them on Monday morning and set them to work in their vineyards or ranches. At the end of the week, they were rewarded with enough highly alcoholic aguardiente to ensure their presence outside the city jail on Monday morning would be guaranteed.

It was not just murder and enslavement that befell the Natives, it was also ecological disaster. Individuals panning for gold were soon replaced by hydraulic mining technologies that tore entire mountains apart and clogged the rivers and streams. The introduction of vast cattle herds to provide the beef to feed the thousands and thousands of new arrivals meant the clearing of forests and the destruction of habitats.

The diseases introduced from Europe continued to take their toll and it is estimated that just 30,000 indigenous people survived in California after the perfect storm of the gold rush. These survivors lived an existence utterly removed from the ways of life that had existed just a generation or two before.

Coda

There is a particularly poignant coda to the Californian Native way of life. In 1911, a malnourished indigenous man wandered into the city of Oroville in northern California. He was unable to speak any English and his presence soon attracted the local newspapers who called him 'the last wild Indian'.

An anthropologist identified the language he spoke as Yahi and named the man *Ishi*, which is the Yahi word for man. It emerged that he was a member of the Yana band from northeastern California that was brutally attacked by groups of miners in the

1860s. Around fifty of the Yani were killed in the attacks and the surviving tribe members fled into the isolated canyons in the region.

Ishi was just a child at the time of the attacks and he spent the next half-century living in the wilderness as his fellow tribe members gradually died around him. By 1911, he was the last surviving member. Despite being initially jailed, Ishi was taken to the San Francisco Bay area where he shared his Yani stories and songs and demonstrated his toolmaking and hunting techniques to audiences. He died of tuberculosis in 1916.

NATIVE CALIFORNIANS IN THE TWENTY-FIRST CENTURY

Today, there are more than 100 federally recognized Californian nations and more indigenous people live in California than any other state. Over 140,000 Native Americans live in the Bay Area alone. They have endured centuries of turmoil, oppression and concerted attempts to completely remove them from the lands on which they have lived for thousands of years.

Reservations, or *rancherias* as they are known north of the city of Los Angeles, serve as both homes and repositories for many Native nations. They are places where they can welcome tourists, educate them and earn dollars by selling their art and their crafts. But the nations are not historical artefacts trapped in a kind of aspic. They are living, breathing communities that continue to hold and uphold the ceremonies, rituals and values of their forefathers. The Maidu hold an annual Bear Dance and the Yurok continue the White Deerskin Dance of their ancestors. In 2014, the Wiyot Nation held its first World Renewal Ceremony since

1860. Nations also work to preserve and protect their ancient lands. The Hupa, who have always caught salmon, now own hatcheries and release their fish into streams and rivers. The Yurok work in similar ways to protect fish stocks on the Klamath River.

The picture is not universally rosy, and ecological issues continue to impact indigenous people. Widely used pesticides mean basket making is no longer possible in many parts of California: The weavers run the grasses through their mouths as the basket is constructed and the presence of hazardous chemicals in such high quantities means this process is now unsafe. The vast majority of indigenous people in California live in urban areas and most are cut off from their people, history and culture, many struggle to get by. The percentage of Native Americans who live in poverty in California is almost double that of White Americans.

C A L I F O R N I A

THE NORTHWEST

The Northwest region is a narrow strip of land, just 240 kilometres (150 miles) wide, that stretches from the southern border of Alaska down to northern California. Its western border is the Pacific Ocean and the extent of its land to the east is marked by the mountains of the Coast Range and the Cascades. It incorporates land that is now in Alaska, British Columbia in Canada, Washington, Oregon and California.

The region enjoys mild temperatures and ample rain. Before the nineteenth century, this created a landscape covered in dense forests and bursting with animal life. In addition to this, the coasts and rivers provided seemingly limitless sources of food, including fish, shellfish, whales, seals and porpoises. As a result, when Europeans first entered the region in the 1700s, they found it to be comparatively densely populated with over thirty nations calling it home. Some spoke Athabaskan, others a type of Salishan known as Coast Salish and there were also speakers of Tshimshianic too. Some languages, such as Chinookan and Haida, appear to be unique to their respective nations.

Sources of food were so plentiful and so comparatively easily accessed that the people of the Northwest were able to spend more time on cultural and social activities. This meant that, when compared to some other areas, their possessions were more decorated and their social conventions and rituals more elaborate.

PLENTIFUL FOOD

Of all the sources of food available, salmon was probably the most important and certainly the most revered. For many nations in the Northwest, the salmon is a supernatural being that sacrifices itself for the benefit of mankind every year. But, unlike nations in the Plateau, for example, they were not solely dependent on the salmon. Shellfish were gathered in enormous numbers and the candlefish was also highly prized.

The candlefish, or eulachon, was given its name by Euro-American settlers because of the large amount of fat in its body during spawning. Fat can make up to fifteen per cent of its body weight and, if it is dried and strung on a wick, it can serve the purpose of a candle and was used for precisely this purpose by early explorers. The name eulachon is from the Chinookan language. Some people believe the state of Oregon derives its name from the corruption of this word by Euro-American settlers as they travelled along the 'Eulachon Trail'. The fat from candlefish was also used by Native nations to help preserve the large amount of salmon that was caught during the annual run.

Coastal nations, such as the Haida, fished for halibut in the ocean. This was a precarious business as the halibut can weigh up to 180 kilograms (400 pounds) and habitually swim along the ocean floor. Catching them involved dropping large, V-shaped hooks into the water from canoes and then quickly paddling to shore before the giant fish either escaped from the hook or overturned the boat.

Sea mammals such as whales, seals and porpoises were also hunted by coastal tribes. This would take place in canoes and involved harpooning the animals and attaching floats or buoys made from inflated seal skins. Once a whale had been killed, usually through a fatal blow with a harpoon to its heart, its mouth would be sewn shut to prevent it from taking on water and sinking on the journey back to land.

Terrestrial animals, such as deer, elk, bears, lynx, rabbits and mountain goats were also hunted in the woods and forests of the region. Roots, bulbs and tubers were dug from underground, and berries, nuts and seeds were gathered. On the coasts, marine algae known as red laver or Porphyra abbottiae was gathered and eaten in large quantities. At least one Tsimshian coastal community held a 'seaweed camp' for the entire month of May where they would harvest and dry the seaweed on the sunbaked rocks on the shore.

NORTHWESTERN SHELTER

It was not just food that was in plentiful supply in the Northwest. There was also ample timber with which they could make their homes. Most nations of the Northwest used cedar to create large rectangular homes called plank houses. They were built by creating a frame out of logs. Planks were then attached to this to create the floor, walls and roof with a central hole to let the smoke from the fire pit escape.

Plank houses ranged in size from six metres (twenty feet) wide and nine metres (thirty feet) long to eighteen metres (sixty feet) wide and thirty metres (100 feet) long. Inside, mats hung from the ceilings to create partitions and provide a degree of privacy as several families were normally housed within each dwelling. Wooden platforms built off the walls also created spaces for sleeping and storage. These were their permanent homes and, in a land that offered so much in terms of food, it was not necessary to vacate them for long periods while the village went in search of resources.

Villages were comprised of several plank houses that were normally built in a row, on a bed of sand or gravel, and facing water. It was common for the front of the house to be painted. The village chief would normally decide on where each family would live within the houses available and which family's head was placed in charge of affairs within each plank house. When this person died, it was the usual practice for his family to move out of the house or for the plank house to be burned down so as not to disturb the deceased's spirit.

NORTHWESTERN CLOTHING

The temperatures that were typically experienced in summer meant that men did not normally wear clothes. In the winter, it was to the cedar tree that they turned once again to provide protection from the elements. Cedar bark was split or shredded into fibres that were woven into knee-length tunics. Women wore aprons and skirts made from woven cedar bark but also deerskin. For those in the north of the region or who lived in the mountains, robes made from the fur of bears, bobcats, seals, sea otters and racoons were popular. Robes were also woven from the hair of dogs and mountain goats. In the winter, moccasins were worn by both sexes and snowshoes were also worn when necessary.

Both men and women enhanced their appearance through jewellery made from shells, bones, antlers, teeth and copper. This was worn in the form of necklaces, bracelets, anklets and piercings in the ears, nose and lips. Face painting was also common and afforded protection from the wind and sun as well as altering their appearance. Tattoos were another tradition in which both men and women partook. Certain designs became family traditions and others were a sign of status.

NORTHWESTERN SPIRITUALITY

The religious beliefs of the nations of the Northwest share several common features. One such belief is that the salmon are supernatural beings who take the form of fish each year and swim up the river in order to sacrifice themselves and sustain humankind. Once landed, the spirit beings leave the bodies of the fish and return to the sea. Their reincarnation and return to the river the next year can be ensured if the bones and guts are returned to the water. If they are not, it is believed that the spirit beings will be greatly offended and refuse to return. As in other areas, such as the Plateau, the arrival of the first salmon of the run is marked with a ceremony.

THE POTLATCH

The most important ceremonial festival in the Northwest is known as the potlatch. Births, deaths, marriages and changes in social status were all celebrated with several days of feasting and gift-giving to the assembled guests. The term potlatch comes from the Nuu-chah-nulth word *patshatl* which means 'sharing'.

Copious amounts of food such as salmon, venison and seal were prepared and laid out for invited guests to share. Whatever was not eaten at the potlatch was taken home by attendees.

The most important aspect of a potlatch was the gift-giving – with the gifts both offered and received being indicative of the social status of the respective parties. The highest-ranking guests might receive copper items such as shields or plaques, whereas lower-ranking guests might be given a blanket.

Recently born children were often given their official names at potlatches, in much the same way as some Christians name their children at baptisms. Names were important in Native Northwest societies and were often passed down through families. Names also conveyed social status so when someone was given an ancestor's name, they also took on their position within the nation.

SPIRITS

The spirit world is incredibly important to the Native peoples of the Northwest, as it is to nearly all the indigenous peoples in North America. The onset of adolescence is seen as a particularly important time in a person's life, a time when contact can be made and relationships established with specific spirits. Vision quests are normally embarked upon during adolescence and girls and boys spend several days alone, sometimes on a mountain, where they fast and pray and contact their guardian spirit being. It is believed that special skills, such as basket making, wood carving, healing, hunting or fishing, are gifted by the spirit guardian during these quests. Upon reaching adolescence, each girl and boy would also be given their own song and dance. This personal dance is then performed throughout their lives during ceremonies and spirit dances.

Shamans feature strongly in the traditional spiritual lives of the people of the Northwest. They are believed to be able to heal the sick through supernatural means as well as being able to cause illness. Sickness is often attributed to spirits or the malicious use of witchcraft.

WOOD CARVING

Skill with wood is what the Native peoples of the Northwest are most famous for. Stone chisels, drills and adzes were used to create everyday objects such as spoons, bowls and boxes of unsurpassed beauty. Shark skin was used to sand and polish the wood and items were often elaborately carved and painted. Families in the Northwest had their own animal or symbol and this was carved into their ladles, bowls, etc.

Functional items were often elevated to being works of art through the skill and ornamentation involved in their manufacture. Wood was steamed and bent to make boxes that were used to store food for the winter. Others were used to cook food and they would be filled with water before having hot stones placed inside them. Other carved wooden items that could be found in plank houses included chamber pots, fish hooks and animal traps.

Logs were hollowed out with the help of strategically placed fires to make canoes. The burnt wood was removed with a stone adze and, once hollowed out, the logs could be steamed to create a flatter bottom and wider centre.

Smaller canoes were used to paddle up and down streams and larger ones were taken to sea for halibut fishing and whale hunting expeditions.

Woodworkers also used their skills to create ceremonial masks and instruments. During dances, masks and rattles were required by shamans and spiritual leaders to help them represent birds, fish and other animals. Transformation masks, which changed faces when a string was pulled, took great skill to make and often took years to complete. They were key for spiritual leaders when telling myths, as they enabled them to illustrate how supernatural beings changed form.

Natural copper deposits in the Northwest meant that craftsmen also had copper to work with. Arrowheads, knives and shields were made from it and engraved plaques known as 'coppers' served the purpose of banknotes.

SOCIETY

The cultures of the Northwest were entirely based on hunting and gathering. However, unlike most other hunter-gatherer societies, they enjoyed such plentiful supplies of food that there were often surpluses. They also did not have to devote as much time as other hunter-gatherer societies to collecting and processing food. As a result, they developed stratified social hierarchies similar to those in the Southeast farming societies before the arrival of the Europeans.

In fact, the Northwestern class system of ruling elites, commoners and slaves was unique among societies that did not raise crops. Typically, tribes were divided into groups or 'houses' that numbered somewhere between thirty and 100 people who belonged to the same extended family. The members of each house lived together and shared the same hunting, fishing and foraging sites.

Within each house group, individual members had their own social rank that was determined by the social status of their ancestors. The highest in rank was normally the son of previous leaders or 'chiefs'. In theory, these leaders had great autocratic powers and could single-handedly determine what happened on a day-to-day basis. In practice, as all property was jointly held, chiefs would lead by consensus and co-operation.

Slaves, on the other hand, had no rights and no influence on the decisions made by the house. In many cases, they had been captured from other tribes in childhood and taken, either by the people who captured them or by a tribe who traded them, many miles from their original homes. They were considered the property of their owners and, like any other object they owned, could be sold, given away or destroyed at their owner's discretion. Most houses had some slaves but not often more than ten in total.

Another interesting and possibly unique aspect of Northwest culture was the formal education of children by their elders to prepare them for their future role within society. Those born to high status would begin their education while still in their infancy and would learn the social etiquette of everyday life as well as special rituals, prayers and songs.

TOTEM POLES

Totem poles are one of the most widely known aspects of all Native North American culture and yet it is only the people of the Northwest who make them. Totem poles encapsulate three key aspects of Native Northwestern life: skill at wood carving, spirituality and social stratification. They usually stand between three and eighteen metres (ten to sixty feet) tall and were traditionally placed in front of a family's home and faced the water.

Building a totem pole was the work of many months and great care was taken when choosing the cedar from which it would be made. Many nations performed ceremonies of thanks before cutting a tree down and transporting it back to the village. Men traditionally carved and painted the pole and the faces represented on them often symbolized a mythical family ancestor. Some more elaborate poles had many animal images, and each carried its own esoteric meaning. The sequence of the figures combined to tell a story that would be well-known and understood by family members.

A totem pole was also a visual representation of its owner's wealth and power. The bigger and more elaborately carved the pole, the richer and more powerful the owner. Other poles, known as mortuary poles, were built on top of graves and acted as a type of headstone. The moist Pacific climate of the Northwest means that cedar poles have a lifespan of between 60 and 70 years before they begin to rot and fall so there are none remaining from antiquity. However, they do continue to be built, and shame poles in particular have been used as a form of protest against the loss of land. A shame pole that was built in response to the environmental disaster caused by an oil spill in Alaska in 1989 still stands to this day.

NATIONS OF THE NORTHWEST

The Northwest region has a great diversity of microenvironments such as mountains, coasts, forests, grasslands and wetlands.

This translates into a great diversity of people in terms of the way they lived, and live, their lives.

The Tlingit

Of all the nations in the Northwest region, the Tlingit were the northernmost, traditionally inhabiting the lands from Yakutat Bay to Cape Fox. They speak an Athabaskan dialect known as Tlingit and, according to their oral traditions, are the descendants of migrants who travelled from the Canadian interior and from California to the south.

Traditionally, the Tlingit economy and lifestyle were based around the annual salmon run, but they also hunted sea mammals such as seals, porpoises and whales. Their skill with wood meant they lived in large, permanent plank houses, erected totem poles and built canoes.

The Haida

Although they share many other cultural similarities with their Tlingit neighbours, the Haida speak a completely different and seemingly unique language. Their traditional territories in present-day British Columbia, Canada, centred around the Queen Charlotte Islands and the south of Prince of Wales Island. Fish, in the form of salmon, halibut and cod, were available in large numbers and required relatively little effort to catch. As a result, they had time to pursue artistic, architectural and cultural pursuits. Wooden objects, from totem poles to spoons, were highly decorated with depictions of both natural and supernatural beings and the Haida developed a distinctive style to their carving. Potlatches became the key ceremonial, spiritual and social aspect of Haida life.

The Makah

The Makah once occupied a vast area of both inland and coastal territory. Their motif of a thunderbird perched atop a whale gives a clear indication of the importance that hunting whales has played, and continues to play, in the lives of the Makah. At the time of the first contact with Europeans, somewhere between 2,000 and 4,000 Makah were living in five permanent villages comprised of numerous plank houses. In the summer, many moved to camps closer to the coast to take advantage of all that the sea had to offer.

The Makah were highly skilled mariners who used various types of canoes to navigate the turbulent Pacific Ocean. There were specific canoes for fighting wars, whaling, fishing for halibut, fishing for salmon and hunting for seals. Makah fitted sails to their canoes so they could harness the wind and travel great distances in pursuit of their prey.

Today, the Makah are a federally recognized tribe and many members still live on their 27,000-acre reservation in Washington State. However, in contrast to the vast majority of Native North American nations, historians have gained a greater insight into the pre-European contact lives of the Makah thanks to an incredible archaeological discovery made in 1970.

The Site at Ozette

An ocean storm uncovered a coastal village that had been buried by a mudslide and trapped in time since around 1700 CE. The thick mud, which was probably caused to slide by a catastrophic seismic event, completely sealed off the organic matter from the air. This meant that thousands of items that would, under normal circumstances, have rotted away as the years passed were miraculously preserved. Baskets made from the fibres of cedar bark, blankets made from dog hair, four-metre-long whaling harpoons and sealskin buoys were among the items that were painstakingly unearthed over an eleven-year period.

In total, over 55,000 artefacts from six cedar plank houses were unearthed and, while the excavation took over a decade to complete, the suddenness of its submersion in mud was both catastrophic and miraculous. The exceptional levels of preservation and the overriding feeling of there being a moment frozen in time have led to the site at Ozette being called the 'western Pompeii'. So complete was the seal created by the mud that, as fire hoses removed it, bright green 300-year-old leaves were suddenly exposed. They began to blacken within seconds of exposure to oxygen but, for a few brief moments, the workers excavating the site gazed upon the same verdant leaves that the Makah were looking at somewhere around the year 1700.

While most of the material discovered is from around 1700, it appears that this was just the latest in a series of mudslides that have struck Ozette over the centuries. Other layers of well-preserved material have been discovered that have been radiocarbon dated as being 800 years old. The oldest finds have been dated to 2,000 years, and there is the potential to find items that are older still.

A Tribal Excavation

Another aspect of the archaeological site at Ozette that is special and perhaps even unique is that the dig has been led by tribe members. Outside academic specialists were brought in but, unlike at other excavations, the discoveries have been kept by the tribe and are displayed at the Makah Cultural and Research Center that opened in 1979. Tribal elders also worked with the archaeologists, each bringing their specific knowledge and expertise, to help create a more complete understanding of the past.

The Tsimshian

The Tsimshian speak three separate dialects, Niska, Kitksan and coastal Tsimshian from the Penutian language family. They traditionally occupied territories in what is today Alaska and British Columbia and had an economy built on fishing. The summer months were spent catching, processing and preserving the migrating salmon and candlefish, or eulachon and tribal diets were supplemented with the land animals hunted in the winter months. Potlatches, ornate wood carvings and highly decorated plank houses were key features of traditional Tsimshian culture before the arrival of the Europeans.

Like many other nations in the Northwest, it was a highly stratified society with a strict social hierarchy. The Niska and the coastal Tsimshian were split into four major clans and the Kitksan were divided into three. These were then further divided into family lineages, with each having its own place in the social pecking order. The head of the highest-ranked lineage was recognized as the chief of the clan.

The Kwakiutl

The Kwakiutl traditionally inhabited the waterways between Vancouver Island and the mainland in what is now British Columbia, Canada. They speak three dialects, Haisla, Heiltsuq and southern Kwakiutl, which are all derived from the Wakashan language family. Its culture shares many similarities with other tribes of the Northwest Coast: they subsist mainly on the plentiful fish, their society is stratified by rank and they excel at woodworking. Potlatches are also a key feature of Kwakiutl life.

The Coast Salish

As the name implies, the Coast Salish are a Salish-speaking people who traditionally inhabited what is now most of Washington State as well as the Strait of Georgia, southern Vancouver Island and Puget Sound. At some point, their ancestors migrated to the coast from inland where other Salish speakers remained.

Living next to the sea, it is perhaps not surprising that fish formed the majority of their diet, although those who lived along the upper reaches of the rivers probably relied more on hunting terrestrial animals. The Coast Salish lived in plank houses that were part of permanent villages during the winter months. In the summer, they usually scattered in pursuit of fish, animals, nuts and berries.

The Bella Coola

The Bella Coola, also known as the Nuxalk, are also Salish speakers who are thought to have descended from the main body of Salish. At some point, their ancestors migrated north and settled on what is now the central British Columbia Coast in Canada. Traditionally, life was organized on a village level, with the villages built along the lower parts of the Bella Coola Valley and the Dean and Burke Channels.

There was no overarching Bella Coola government that connected these villages, but their inhabitants shared a familial sense of unity based on a commonality of language, culture and origin. Their traditional social structure was complex and consisted of chiefs, an aristocracy, commoners and slaves, as well as shamans. The Bella Coola suffered particularly badly during the smallpox epidemics and were reduced to living in a single village by the late nineteenth century.

The Nuu-chah-nulth

Also known as the Nootka, the Nuu-chah-nulth traditionally inhabit the Southwest Coast of what is now Vancouver Island in Canada. They speak a language from the Wakashan family and are closely related culturally to the Kwakiutl people. There is evidence that points to ancient connections or roots with the Inuit and Aleut cultures in the frozen north. Central to these is whale hunting, which was the basis of the Nuu-chah-nulth subsistence and economy.

The whale harpooner, who stood at the head of the large dugout canoe, was a person of high social rank who usually inherited the position. Families would pass down practical, ceremonial and supernatural insights and secrets that were believed to help ensure the success of a whale hunt.

The most important aspect of the Nuu-chah-nulth's spiritual year is the shaman's dance. This defines and reinforces every individual's social rank and involves the reenactment of ancient struggles between ancestors and supernatural beings. The performance normally ends with a potlatch and the distribution of property based on the social hierarchy.

The Chinook

The Chinook traditionally occupied lands that are now part of Washington and Oregon and stretched from the mouth of the Columbia to the Dalles River. Their geographical location was ideal for establishing and maintaining contact with Native nations to the north, south and east into the interior as far as the Plains. As a result, they became famous as a trading people.

The salmon that arrived in their rivers in such ample numbers every year were caught and preserved and formed the basis of both their diet and trading empire. They were exchanged for dentalia (tooth) shells – which were highly prized for their decorative purposes by almost all Native peoples; slaves from California; canoes from the Nuu-chah-nulth and a whole host of other items.

The Chinook language is apparently unique to them but Chinook Jargon, a simplified combination of Chinook, Wakashan and several other dialects, became the universal trade language of the Northwest. After the arrival of Europeans, English and French words were incorporated into Chinook Jargon and it was used to facilitate trade from California to Alaska.

CONTACT WITH EUROPEANS

The physical location of the Northwest region meant it was one of the last to be reached and colonized by Europeans. The first European to make contact with the people who lived there was a Russian explorer named Alexei Chirikov who met with the Tlingit in 1741 as he journeyed south from the Subarctic region. As was so often the case with Europeans exploring North America, it was the pursuit of furs that motivated Chirikov's arrival in the Northwest.

Sea otter fur was particularly highly prized and, as the people of the Northwest valued material wealth and linked it to social status, they enthusiastically engaged in trade with the Europeans. The Russian contact was looked on suspiciously by the Spanish who controlled so much land to the south and were, according to the Pope's Treaty of Tordesillas, the rightful owners of the land in the Northwest. As a result, in 1744, they dispatched a trading and spying mission and explorer Juan José Pérez Hernández made land in what are now the Queen Charlotte Islands. Once there, he erected a large wooden cross and buried a glass bottle at its base containing documents that claimed the lands as the property of Spain. Contact was then made with the Haida who traded sea otter pelts, blankets and clothing made from cedar bark fibres in exchange for metal goods.

Captain Cook

When Captain James Cook arrived on the Northwest Coast in 1778 in search of the fabled Northwest Passage, it proved to be a major turning point in the history of the region. Cook stopped at the Nootka Sound to source fresh water and food and was met by the Nuu-chah-nulth people. They soon engaged in trade and among the items that Cook's men received were sea otter pelts that they immediately put to use as bedding.

When Cook arrived in China on the next stage of his voyage, his men were greatly surprised to discover how much the sea otter furs were desired by Chinese women and by the enormous sums they were willing to pay for them. Many of Cook's men wanted to immediately set sail and return to the Northwest Coast to collect more sea otter pelts and a mutiny was only narrowly avoided. News of the enormous profits that could be secured from sea otter pelts soon spread, however, and another British sailor named James Hanna made his fortune from their trade.

Hanna traded iron bars for pelts with the Nuu-chah-nulth and then transported them to Macau where they sold for eye-watering prices. Hanna then filled his holds with silks, tea and spices and set sail for Europe where more enormous mark-ups awaited him. Other merchants soon followed suit and, before long, vessels from Britain, Spain, France, Russia, Portugal and the newly formed United States were dropping anchor off the Northwest Coast.

In the 1790s, the struggle over who controlled the maritime sea otter pelt trade, and specifically Nootka Sound, almost directly led to Britain and Spain going to war. In the end, the Nootka Controversy, as it has been called, did not result in open warfare and the maritime fur trade was soon superseded by trappers approaching overland from the north and the east.

The Overland Fur Trade

Unlike traders who arrived by ship, overland fur traders often settled and put down roots. Although the fur trade continued to be mostly peaceful and perceived to be beneficial by both Natives and Euro-Americans, it meant that settlers established permanent footholds in the region. The presence of Euro-American colonizers invariably attracted others and, once the Oregon Trail was established in the 1840s, life for Natives in the Northwest was irrevocably changed.

The 1857 Gold Rush

The steady arrival of Euro-Americans to the region was supercharged by the discovery of gold in the Fraser River in British Columbia in 1857. In February of that year, the head of the Hudson Bay Company in British Columbia shipped a small amount of gold that had been discovered in the Fraser River Valley to the San Francisco Mint to be assessed and processed. News of the discovery swept through California, where the 1849 gold rush was just petering out, like wildfire. By April, hundreds of these Californians had uprooted and arrived in Victoria, British Columbia. And they were just the first few. It is estimated that 40,000 Californians eventually moved north in the hope of having better luck in new surroundings.

The new surroundings were markedly different from what they had left in California, and many timed their arrival particularly badly. Panning for gold in the Fraser required the waters to recede to expose land, and gold, that was normally submerged by the river. The prospectors who arrived in May, June and July found that the waters were too high and thousands were forced to sit around and wait.

The lands of indigenous people were suddenly invaded by large numbers of miners who began digging without consulting the local tribes. When challenged, the miners threatened violence and there were incidents when Native women were sexually assaulted. The rivers were the focal point of the prospectors' activities and also the source of the salmon that so many Native people relied upon. The miners diverted rivers, occupied fishing sites and ruined crucial spawning grounds. The result was the Fraser Canyon War of 1858 when numerous indigenous tribes, including the Coastal Salish, rose up in armed revolt against the miners. The resistance proved futile, however, and when a truce was called in August 1858, the miners continued to access whatever territories and resources they wished.

Smallpox Epidemics

Devastating as the disruption to the vital spawning grounds was, it was nothing compared to the apocalyptic impact of the arrival of smallpox in the Northwest. As the region was one of the last to be colonized by Euro-Americans, it was one of the last to be exposed to the disease. This did not in any way lessen its appalling effects, and it has been estimated that between sixty-five and ninety-five per cent of the entire indigenous population of the Northwest was wiped out by successive smallpox epidemics. This is a far higher mortality rate than even the Black Death of 1348, which is estimated to have killed between thirty and forty per cent of the people of medieval Europe and Asia.

Today, thanks in large part to the discovery of the first vaccination by Edward Jenner, smallpox stands alone as the only disease that humankind has successfully eradicated. While it was present, it was a highly infectious disease. The most common form of transmission was through coughing and sneezing, known as 'droplet infection', although physical contact with an infected person or corpse could also lead to the disease being spread. There are accounts of smallpox being weaponized and gifts of blankets being deliberately contaminated in an attempt to cause an outbreak of the disease, particularly during the French and Indian War in the 1760s. There is no evidence that, even if this tactic was ever employed, it worked successfully.

Mortality rates varied from epidemic to epidemic but the horror of smallpox meant that survivors often bore the scars of the pus-filled blisters that covered their bodies. When blisters covered the eyes or entered the inner ears, the infected person was often left blind or deaf. The period from initial infection to death or recovery was normally around a month, and during the first two weeks of infection the individual was asymptomatic but infectious. Those who survived emerged from the sickness with a lifelong immunity to later epidemics. One of the reasons that smallpox was so devastating to Native North American populations was because they represented 'virgin soil' for the disease.

The first smallpox epidemic to occur in the New World took place as early as 1519 and arrived with Cortés. At that point, every single indigenous individual had the potential to become infected and carry the disease further. Non-immune populations who tended to live in close proximity to each other and share communal, multigenerational dwellings meant that infection rates were extremely high. Recent research indicates that populations that lack genetic diversity, such as the indigenous people of the Americas, also offer less resistance to viral infection.

Throughout the Americas, smallpox wreaked havoc wherever it appeared but, in the Northwest region, the epidemics of 1836–38 and 1862–63 precipitated what has been described as a population collapse. Whole villages, bands and tribes were wiped out and it is estimated that the indigenous population of the Northwest fell from around 500,000 in 1750 to somewhere around 100,000 just 100 years later. At the same time as the Native population was declining at such a catastrophic rate, Euro-Americans continued to arrive and stay in ever greater numbers.

Reservations, Reserves and Oppression

It was in this context of death, disease and enormous disruption to their lives that most nations in the Northwest were forced to sign treaties. These invariably involved handing over vast swathes of their traditional territories to the government. The sheer number of Euro-Americans who settled in the Northwest and the disruption that they brought to the ecosystems with huge enterprises such as salmon canning plants meant that continuing their traditional ways of life simply was not possible.

Other aspects of Native life disappeared because of legislation. The potlatch, which was central to the cultural life of so many Northwestern nations, was banned in Canada in 1885. Although the potlatch ban was often ignored or circumvented, people were imprisoned for breaking the ban that remained part of Canadian law for nearly seventy years. Several justifications were given for its outlawing, such as the risks to health posed by large gatherings, the barrier to assimilation with wider Canadian society and the widely held belief that potlatches were fundamentally incompatible with the values of a 'Christian capitalist society'.

RENAISSANCE

To survive, many Natives became guides for those looking for gold. Others gained employment on farms and in the salmon canneries. Some individuals started their own businesses which excelled, especially in the fishing industry where their expert knowledge of the waters and the fish that lived in them could be put to good use. Several Natives became wealthy from such enterprises and their businesses helped provide employment opportunities for other indigenous people.

By the start of the twentieth century, some Northwestern Natives had started to organize and fight back against their treatment by the governments on both sides of the border. The Alaska Native Brotherhood, and similar organizations in Canada, began to put pressure on their respective governments to protect their rights and improve the way they were treated. In the 1950s, the Affiliated Tribes of Northwest Indians (ATNI) was founded. This fought to establish fishing and hunting rights on their ancestral lands and to re-establish autonomy when it came to tribal governance. After years of being refused access to rivers where their forefathers had fished for generations, and being arrested when they attempted to, the ATNI began to co-ordinate protests in the form of fish-ins. Several decades of struggle later, a federal judge ruled in 1974 that the original nineteenth-century treaties were unfair and that the indigenous nations were legally entitled to half of the salmon caught in Washington waters every year.

In 1971, forty-four million acres of land was returned to Alaskan Natives along with almost $1 billion. Shortly after, people from the Tsimshian, Haida and Tlingit nations formed the Sealaska Corporation to help preserve the cultures, land and natural resources of the Northwest region. In Canada, the right to hold potlatches was won in 1951 and, in the decades that followed, the British Columbia government created the First Citizens Fund that helps support and sustain the culture and economy of its Native or First Nation populations.

Despite the ravages of smallpox, the precipitous decline in population and the existential threats to their culture that the Native peoples of the Northwest endured for much of the nineteenth and twentieth centuries, they have survived. Many nations still hold their traditional ceremonies and celebrations, including potlatches, and their cultures and languages continue to be taught to younger generations. Road signs in some parts of British Columbia are written in both English and the language of the Nuu-chah-nulth.

Populations have recovered from their perilously low numbers and, according to the latest census figures, there are over 20,000 Coast Salish, 25,000 Tlingit and Haida, 8,000 Nuu-chah-nulth, 4,000 Tsimshian and nearly 2,000 Makah living in the United States and Canada today.

THE NORTHWEST

THE PLATEAU

The Plateau Region is a huge area that is comprised of land from the modern-day US states of Washington, Oregon, Idaho, Montana and California. It also extends north of the border and includes much of Canada's British Columbia. It is a region that is surrounded by mountains. The Rocky Mountains and the Lewis Range serve to form its respective northern and eastern borders. To the south and west, the parameters are marked by the Blue Mountains and the Cascade Range.

It is also a region of varied landscapes and contains rolling hills, broad flatlands, steep gorges and rugged mountains. There are extensive wooded areas but also vast expanses of grassland and desert. In winter, temperatures can plummet as low as minus thirty-four degrees Celsius (minus twenty-nine degrees Fahrenheit) and reach a scorching thirty-eight degrees Celsius (100 degrees Fahrenheit) in the summer. Precipitation is mostly low apart from in the mountains where it often falls as snow.

This lack of rainfall means that human presence in the region, which dates back over 10,000 years, has centred around its two major rivers and their tributaries. The Fraser River is situated in the north of the region and the Columbia River is located further south.

EARLY INHABITANTS

Our knowledge and understanding of the first people to inhabit the region mostly comes from archaeological evidence found in what has become known as the Marmes Rockshelter. Named after Roland Marmes, a farmer who owned the land on which it was found, it was first excavated in 1962 and eventually provided archaeologists with thousands of well-preserved items that helped shine a light on the lives of the first humans to live in the area.

The rock-shelter is an alcove measuring around fifteen metres (forty-nine feet) wide and eight metres (twenty-six feet) deep underneath an overhanging ledge of basalt. Once discovered by humans, shortly after the great Ice Age floods, it remained in constant use for thousands of years. The first excavations found storage pits containing the remains of grass mat linings, animal bones and traces of plants. Shortly after, the skeletons of eleven humans were found. Radiocarbon dating of shells and organic material found next to them indicated that the bodies were 8,000 years old.

Subsequent excavations in 1968 found human remains that were over 10,000 years old. Bone needles with eyes of similar diameters to modern needles were discovered, indicating intricate and delicate work was undertaken. The major discovery was the unearthing of a cremation hearth that was used as part of ritualistic burial practices. The remains of a total of thirty-eight individuals were identified along with shell beads, an infant's cradleboard, tools, weapons, ornaments, bear teeth and the detritus of thousands of years of human habitation. Work on the excavation site was far from complete when, tragically, it was very probably lost for ever.

The Loss of the Marmes Rock-shelter

Work on the construction of the Lower Monumental Dam on the Snake River had already commenced at the time of the rock-shelter's discovery by modern archaeologists. By 1968, the dam was nearing completion and would soon create a reservoir that would immerse the rock-shelter unrsder fifteen metres (forty-nine feet) of water. There were frantic appeals and attempts to convey the importance of the site. The creation of the reservoir was delayed and President Lyndon B. Johnson agreed to provide $750,000 to build a dam around it to prevent it from becoming submerged. The sub-dam stood at 150 metres (500 feet) high and 600 metres (2,000 feet) wide – and was utterly futile. The water simply seeped through the glacial gravel on which it was built at a rate of 170,000 litres (45,000 gallons) a minute. Archaeologists worked around the clock to cover the existing trenches with plastic sheeting and sand. Who knows what might be found by archaeologists in the future? Or what has been lost for ever?

Silt and Salmon

The lack of fish bones excavated with the human skeletons in the Marmes Rockshelter can probably be explained by the amount of silt that would have been present in the rivers so soon after the end of the Ice Age. Combined with warmer temperatures, these fine particles of grit would have prevented salmon from migrating up rivers. As a result, the earliest inhabitants would have had to rely on hunting terrestrial animals and gathering plants to survive.

Cooling Climate

Between 6000 and 2000 BCE, the climate and rivers of the Plateau region began to cool. The rivers also began to clear themselves of the glacial deposits that had prevented the salmon from venturing too far upstream. The increased number of fish and the increased distance which they travelled along the rivers had implications for people who lived in the region. They began to build semipermanent settlements along riverbanks to take advantage of the nutritious food source that could be easily harvested. New methods of preserving fish were also developed to help sustain them through the winter months, but villages were often left when the fish were not running in order to hunt game.

A wide variety of animals were hunted but deer and rabbits were greatly valued for both their meat and hides. Pine nuts, huckleberries, blueberries and roots such as parsnips and wild carrots were also gathered, and the cultivation of corn spread up from Mexico during this period. However, scientists estimate that as much as forty per cent of Plateau people's diet was made up of fish at this time.

The houses that were initially built alongside rivers bore a great similarity to the pithouses that were dug out of the ground in the Southwest region. They were round or oval in shape and ranged from three metres (ten feet) to ten metres (thirty-three feet) in diameter. The pit was then covered by a roof of woven mats that were supported by a wooden frame.

The rivers also acted as conduits for trade. Items of jewellery made from seashells have been found in sites far upriver that are many hundreds of miles from the sea. Pipes made from types of stone that are not found in the area also point to trade taking place over considerable distances – perhaps even across the Rockies or with the people of the Subarctic.

Population Growth

Between 2000 BCE and the modern era, the climate of the Plateau region continued to cool. This meant the rivers remained cooler, evaporated less and maintained a higher flow of water. This, in turn, greatly increased the number of fish that swam upstream every year. The growth in fish numbers led to a corresponding growth in population and number of settlements. On the lower reaches of the major rivers, where the fish numbers were highest, villages of 100 or more houses became common.

Larger settlements meant an increased sense of identity and a growth in conflict between groups. Archaeological evidence from this time points to villages being increasingly built on islands because of the protection the water afforded from would-be attackers. By 1000 CE, the tribal groupings that were present when the Europeans arrived had started to emerge.

The increase in hostility did not prevent trade, however, and technology and ideas as well as goods travelled up and down the major rivers of the region. The bow and arrow arrived in the Plateau region in around 400 CE and soon became the primary weapon used for both hunting and warfare.

More important even than the bow and arrow was the arrival of horses. Historians believe they first arrived on the Plateau somewhere around 1720 and the grass plains made for an ideal environment to raise horses. The increased mobility they provided quickly led to significant changes in Plateau culture and its people soon became renowned as accomplished riders and breeders.

By the middle of the nineteenth century, travellers from the US estimated that the tribes of the Plateau had more than 20,000 horses. They had developed the skills and knowledge necessary to make saddles, bridles, stirrups and all the other tack required to ride them effectively. These were often elaborately decorated and became, along with the horses themselves, symbols of wealth and status.

SALISHIAN-SPEAKING TRIBES OF THE PLATEAU

Salishian is a language that was commonly spoken by tribes who traditionally inhabited the upper basins of the Columbia and Fraser Rivers. This linguistic family is sometimes referred to by the umbrella term of Salish, which comprises scores of different tribes. These include the Coeur d'Alene, Wenatchee, Spokane, Sanpoil, Shuswap, Kalispel, Lake, Cowlitz, Nespelem, Okanagon, Thompson and Flathead.

The Flathead

Of all these tribes, the Flathead are probably the best known. Despite the impression given by their name, they were called Flathead by Europeans because they did not partake in the practice of intentionally changing the shape of their skulls. This was common among other Salish tribes and was achieved by securing an infant's head in a cradleboard and applying consistent pressure to the forehead through the binding cloth. The effect was to create an elongated, cone-shaped skull that did not appear to have any impact on mental capabilities.

The Flathead were traditionally located furthest east of all the Salish groups and had regular contact with indigenous tribes on the Plains. With the arrival of horses, the Flathead became bison hunters and warriors who raided other tribes. Bison hides were a great asset when it came to trading with other Plateau tribes due to the cold winters.

Clothing and Baskets

Clothing on the Plateau was usually made from the fibres of plants and tule reeds that were woven together. Deer hides, or buckskins, were also widely used and, depending on the temperature, worn as breechcloths or leggings by men. Women dressed in buckskin tunics and both sexes wore moccasins.

The beavers that lived in the rivers and streams of the Plateau were always highly prized by hunters even before the arrival of Europeans. Not only was their thick fur useful for winter clothing, but their sharp and strong front teeth were inserted into wooden handles to make extremely effective knives.

Plant fibres and fine tree roots were also used to make baskets that served a variety of purposes, such as fish traps and food storage. Plateau basket makers were some of the most skilled of all indigenous people and they often incorporated geometric patterns by weaving dyed materials into the weft and warp.

The Bow and Arrow

Deer hides became more commonly used for clothing after the adoption of the bow and arrow from around 400 CE. Various types of bows were used and the simplest, usually called the longbow, was made out of a single piece of tapered wood. Shorter bows were given extra power by glueing layers of deer sinew to the outer curve which gave increased strength and elasticity to the wood. Other bows were fashioned from the rib bones of bison or elk and were used to shoot targets at close range. Grooved stones were used to make straight wooden arrow shafts and three feathers were attached to help the arrows remain stable in flight. Different heads were attached depending on the intended use. Arrows used for rabbits or birds had no heads, but bigger animals were attacked using stone heads of various shapes that were attached with hemp string.

Salishian Spirituality

Like many Native North Americans, the religion of tribes on the Plateau centred around guardian spirits and vision quests. An individual's health and good fortune are believed to depend on their relationship with spirits, and shamans are often used to heal people both physically and spiritually. After death, it is believed that good souls journey to an upper world governed by the deity Amo'tken, whereas bad souls are consigned to an underworld ruled by Amte'p.

First foods, such as the arrival of the first salmon, were marked with religious ceremonies. The first salmon to be caught each year was ritually dismembered with parts of it being distributed throughout the tribe. The remains of the carcass would then be returned to the water while prayers of thanks were given. Some Salish tribes had specially appointed 'salmon chiefs' who organized and presided over the ceremonies.

Winter Spirit Dances were also commonly held. Some groups held them during the winter solstice in late December, and others waited until January or February. For many, the dance would take place over a set period, whereas other groups kept the dance going until the snow on nearby mountains started to melt. The Winter Spirit Dance provided opportunities for individuals to reconnect with spirits they had established relationships with during vision quests. It was also a time of thanksgiving and a celebration of the start of a new year.

PENUTIAN-SPEAKING TRIBES OF THE PLATEAU

Plateau tribes that spoke Penutian include the Nez Percé, the Yakama, the Walla Walla and the Umatilla. Before the arrival of the Europeans, the survival of these tribes depended to a large degree on fish – particularly salmon. Hemp was vital as its long fibres could be twisted into nets of enormous proportions. Examples have been found of nets that are two metres (six-and-a-half feet) high and 100 metres (328 feet) wide. These were stretched across the entire width of rivers and anchored to the riverbed with rocks.

The annual salmon run was the most important event of the spring and probably the whole year. The exact timing of the run depended on the group's location along the river, with those positioned further downstream seeing more fish and seeing them earlier. Nets placed across the river, spears, traps and hooks were all used to catch the migrating salmon, but the most efficient method was probably the dip net. This technique involved standing on rocks or a wooden platform that had been specially constructed to catch the fish in a bag-shaped net on the end of a long pole. Sometimes weirs were built to narrow the space that the fish had to swim through and make the task of catching them easier. A skilled and experienced operator could catch up to 500 fish a day with a dip net.

Salmon Feasts

With such plentiful food, salmon feasts were held by many Plateau tribes. These took the form of fish-based harvest festivals and everyone was free to eat as much as they could, enjoy themselves and give thanks for the return of the run. Depending on their location, some groups experienced runs throughout the summer and even into autumn. Different species spawn at different times and, as a result, run up the river at different times. In the rivers of the Plateau, there are five species of sea-run salmon: sockeye, pink, chum, coho and chinook. Of all the varieties of salmon present on the Plateau, the chinook is the biggest and can weigh as much as thirty-five kilograms (seventy-seven pounds). In addition to these species of salmon, steelhead trout also enter the Plateau river systems. These are a type of rainbow trout that spends its life in the sea but spawns in freshwater.

Preserving Fish

Plentiful as the fish were for most tribes, especially those downstream, they were not available year-round and, once caught, quickly became inedible if not processed. Heads were usually removed and cooked to be eaten immediately and the roe from the female fish was extracted and dried or smoked. The body of the fish was then gutted, skinned and spread open so it too could dry in the sun or over a fire. Salmon flour was often then made from the meat. This required the fish to be completely dehydrated of all moisture and oil before being pounded into a fine powder. This was then wrapped in dried fish skins and pressed into baskets where it could be removed and added to soups throughout the winter. Salmon flour not only helped preserve the fish, but by dehydrating it, sixty per cent of the weight was lost which made it far easier to transport.

INFLUENCE OF EUROPEANS

The Plateau region was among the last in North America to be visited or settled by Europeans. However, the

Europeans' presence was felt on the Plateau long before their physical arrival.

First Contact

The Spanish colonization of the Southwest in the seventeenth century meant that groups who traded with tribes on the Plateau were in frequent contact with Europeans. The Apache, Navajo and Ute all raided Spanish settlements, and it is probably through these tribes that horses first arrived in the region.

Fur traders to the north also established trading relationships with tribes in modern-day Canada. These tribes, in turn, traded with those on the Plateau and this is the way metal knives, axes and traps first found their way into the region. And wherever European livestock and technology went, they were always accompanied by European diseases. Measles, mumps and smallpox spread along the rivers and became endemic. Tribes that did not contain a single member who had set eyes upon a European were utterly ravaged by these new illnesses. By the start of the 1800s, it is estimated that the indigenous population of the Plateau had been reduced by half.

Some groups disappeared altogether. Others amalgamated in a desperate attempt to survive. Initially, the tribes in the centre of the region suffered less than those who bordered areas that had been colonized. However, the arrival of the horse led to increased mobility of both people and pathogens and, in 1780, a devastating smallpox epidemic that raged through the Plains crossed the Rocky Mountains and spread across the Plateau.

The Impact of Horses

The arrival of the horse altered almost every facet of the existence of some tribes. The lives of the Nez Percé in particular were almost unrecognizable after the horse. The speed and distance they could now travel meant they were able to mount expeditions across the Rockies where they hunted bison and built relationships with tribes on the Plains. The Nez Percé, named after the French term for 'pierced nose', began to adopt many of the customs of the Plains tribes such as the tepee and war dances. The villages built on the banks of the rivers and lifestyles dependent on salmon were abandoned in favour of a life built around mobility and the horse.

Almost uniquely for Native American tribes, they established a selective breeding programme and were instrumental in creating the spotted horse that became known as the Appaloosa. Possibly named after the Palouse River where the Nez Percé lived, it is now recognized as a specific breed and continues to be raised today. The tribe's vast herds and skills as both horsemen and warriors enabled the Nez Percé to rise to a position of dominance over other tribes of the Plateau.

The Lewis and Clark Expedition

The direct influence of Europeans and Euro-Americans increased dramatically from the start of the 1800s. The Louisiana Purchase of 1803 meant that all land that had previously been claimed by France between the Mississippi River and the Rocky Mountains now transferred to the United States. Curious to know what lay to the west of the Rockies and in preparation for making a claim to it, President Thomas Jefferson dispatched an expedition in 1804.

Headed by Captain Meriwether Lewis and Lieutenant William Clark, they left St. Louis, Missouri, and travelled up the Missouri River into present-day North Dakota. There, they hired a French Canadian fur trapper named Toussaint Charbonneau to act as a guide. He persuaded them to allow his wife Sacajawea (or Sacagewea) with them to act as an interpreter. Some reports state that Charbonneau had won his Native American wife in a gambling game and others claim he purchased her. Whatever the truth, in April 1805 she joined the expedition with her two-month-old son.

When they were short of food, it was her knowledge and expertise of local plants and roots that prevented starvation. When they came into contact with local tribes, she ensured they could communicate with them. They successfully crossed the Rockies and made it on to the Plateau where Sacajawea was able to communicate with the Nez Percé through sign language. There, they built a small outpost which they named Fort Clasp near present-day Astoria, Oregon.

The expedition returned to St. Louis in 1807 and received a hero's welcome. What happened to Sacajawea is unknown. It is believed she and Charbonneau attempted to take up farming in St. Louis, but some accounts state they soon left for a life on the Plains, leaving their son, known as Pomp, in the care of William Clark. Some claim she died of disease in 1812 while at a fur-trading post called Fort Manuel in what is now South Dakota. Others claim she travelled around the Plains for many years and lived to be 100 years old.

The Arrival of the Fur Traders

The Lewis and Clark Expedition opened the region to increased interference by settlers. As was so often the case, the first to establish a presence were the fur traders. In 1807, the North West Company, which was in fierce competition with the

Hudson Bay Company in Canada, established a trading post in the north of the Plateau region. In 1811, they opened one near the mouth of the Columbia River and another one the following year among the Nez Percé.

The hunting of animals for their fur soon became the focus of many tribes on the Plateau. The Nez Percé, however, had already made the switch to an equestrian way of life and were not interested in becoming trappers. Instead, they continued to breed horses that they either directly traded for goods with the posts or traded for furs with other tribes, which they then traded for goods.

Such was the desire for pelts that fur-bearing animals became all but extinct on the Plateau within a couple of decades. But by the 1840s, the Native North Americans of the Plateau were facing a new, much greater threat.

The Oregon Trail

In 1842, nineteen wagons carrying one hundred and fourteen US citizens arrived at what would soon become Oregon City. The route down which they had travelled was soon to become known as the Oregon Trail and, over the next eight years alone, 11,000 US settlers were to follow in their wake. In 1846, Great Britain and the United States reached an agreement over ownership of the Plateau region and settled on a boundary line that ran along the forty-ninth-degree line of latitude. Everything above the line was British and the southern part of the Plateau became an official territory of the United States.

Settlers no longer rushed through the Plateau, they began to settle on it in large numbers and soon outnumbered the indigenous tribes. As they started taking ever more land that tribes had considered theirs for generations, conflict inevitably arose. As a result, the US government stepped in.

The Walla Walla Treaties

Washington Territory, soon to be Washington State, was created by the US Congress in 1853. Its new governor, Isaac I. Stevens, called together tribal leaders in the hope he could get them to agree to move on to reservations and lessen their contact with US settlers. In return for recognition of US sovereignty over the territory and for moving on to reservations where new settlers would be prohibited from entering, Stevens offered the tribe leaders half of the fish of the region in perpetuity alongside annual payments of cash and goods.

Many of the tribal leaders were extremely reluctant to accept these terms but most were eventually worn down by Stevens' persistence. It took the United States Senate a further four years to ratify the treaties, however, and, in the meantime, gold was discovered in Yakama Territory. News of the discovery spread far and wide and there was soon an influx of ruthlessly ambitious prospectors trespassing over lands that had just been defined as inviolably Native American Territory.

THE YAKAMA WAR

It was the actions of some of these prospectors that led to events spiralling out of control and the eruption of what has gone down in the history books as the Yakima War. The difference in spelling is because, in the mid-1990s, the Yakima Nation renamed itself to Yakama to better reflect the pronunciation in its Penutian dialect. Despite Stevens' promises that settlement by US citizens on tribal lands would be prohibited, the prospectors roamed freely and regularly assaulted indigenous people.

In 1855, a Yakama woman was travelling with her daughter and baby when they came across a group of miners. Both women were sexually assaulted and all three were murdered by the miners. The husband and father of the women tracked down the murderers, ambushed them and killed all of them in revenge. News of the miners' deaths reached the Bureau of Indian Affairs and they sent an agent named Andrew Bolon to investigate. He came across a group of Yakama and, while travelling with them, explained that the deaths of the miners were going to be investigated and those responsible would be punished. This greatly angered some of the Yakama and, after a debate among themselves, Bolon was stabbed in the throat and killed.

The Yakama knew there would be retaliation for the murder of a government official and prepared for war. Sure enough, when an expeditionary column was sent out from Fort Dalles, it was met by a large group of Yakama warriors. The troops were routed in what became known as the Battle of Toppenish Creek.

Immediate Escalation

The defeat threw the settlers of Washington Territory into a panic but, emboldened, the Yakama and their ranks were swelled by new bands joining the fight. Fears of a general Native uprising were seemingly confirmed when the White River settlements were attacked and nine men and women were killed. A shortage of troops in the area meant that many settlers fled until sufficient numbers of soldiers could be assembled.

Progress in subduing the uprising was hindered by infighting among the leaders of the US forces over the best way to proceed. The decision to launch unprovoked and pre-emptive attacks against the Walla Walla and Palouse on the assumption that they would eventually join the war on the Yakama's side escalated the war even further.

The year 1856 began with a 6,000-strong army made up of warriors from the Yakama, Walla Walla and other tribes descending on the town of Seattle. The residents evacuated and relentless fire from the large guns aboard the USS Decatur led to the attack being abandoned. Martial law was declared in the spring, but it did not prevent fourteen settlers and three US soldiers from being killed in an attack in the Cascades Rapids.

In the summer of 1856, the arrival of large numbers of Federal troops and the construction of Fort Simcoe turned the tide of the war against the Yakama and their allies. Fighting dragged on for another two years but, at the Battle of Four Lakes in September 1858, the Native forces suffered a decisive defeat. Under the terms of the treaty, the tribes – including the Yakama – moved on to reservations. The killers of Andrew Bolon were tracked down and hanged.

THE NEZ PERCÉ WAR

When the United States began to exert its influence, the Nez Percé stayed neutral or even helped the US in its conflicts with Plateau tribes by supplying horses. That was to change as the century entered its final decades. In 1873, President Ulysses

S. Grant promised the Nez Percé that they would be able to retain their territory in western Oregon. Just a few short years later, in the face of lobbying from the Oregon government and settlers in the area, he changed his mind in dramatic fashion.

In May 1877, General Oliver O. Howard summoned the leaders of the Nez Percé and informed them that all members of their tribe must vacate the lands they currently occupied and move to a reservation. They had thirty days to make the move.

As it was spring, the rivers were swollen by the melting snow and many young horses and calves drowned while trying to cross them. There was a general air of anger and desolation as the tribe made the journey to the reservation and, when they happened across a group of settlers who had killed members of their tribe, some young warriors could not resist the opportunity to exact revenge.

A raid was launched and four settlers were killed. With echoes of the relatively minor incident that triggered the Yakima War two decades earlier, this was the event that was to cause conflict to return to the Plateau in what became known as the Nez Percé War.

White Bird Canyon

Chief Joseph of the Wallowa band argued that a peaceful solution should be sought and an attempt made to placate the US. His fellow chiefs, many of whom were deeply unhappy at being forced to move to the reservation, argued that they should take the opportunity to change the cards they had been dealt. The deaths of these settlers meant that war was coming anyway. They argued they should prepare for it and attempt to force a better outcome than they were currently facing.

The fighting began in earnest when, on 17 June 1877, 100 soldiers approached a Nez Percé camp at White Bird Canyon in Idaho. The Nez Percé dispatched an envoy under a white flag to meet the soldiers and he was shot dead. The Nez Percé immediately fired back and, in the battle that ensued, thirty-four US soldiers were killed, sixty-three guns and large numbers of horses and ammunition were captured. None of the Nez Percé lost their lives and only two were injured.

The Battle of Clearwater River

The camp that had been attacked at White Bird Canyon contained around fifty warriors and many more women and children. As they moved west after the battle, other members of their tribe joined them and, by July, their numbers had swollen to 150 braves and over 500 women and children. The group was caught unaware at their camp near the Clearwater River when General Howard launched an attack with artillery and his 400 soldiers.

Despite being unprepared, the Nez Percé managed to fight their way out at a cost of four dead warriors and another six wounded. When the shooting stopped, there were thirteen dead US soldiers and another forty who were wounded. The Nez Percé had been forced to abandon many of their tepees and supplies of food, however. Chief Joseph decided to take the group east in the hope that they could evade more troops and forge an alliance with their longstanding friends from the Plains – the Crow.

The Battle at Big Hole

More troops were placed at General Howard's disposal and, despite their best efforts, the noose began to tighten around the

Nez Percé. By the start of August, they had replenished their stores, constructed new tepees and travelled over 300 kilometres (200 miles) east. At 3:30 am on 9 August 1877, Howard launched another surprise attack. This time, the Nez Percé were caught completely unaware and many were killed while sleeping in their beds. Eighty-nine Nez Percé were killed, of whom only twelve were warriors. Many of the survivors claimed that a Gatling gun, a type of early machine gun, was used in the attack and aimed low at the tepees.

Despite the initial slaughter of the attack, the Nez Percé quickly rallied and cut off a portion of Howard's troops. An artillery piece was captured and so was a pack mule that was carrying over 2,000 rounds of ammunition. The Nez Percé had sustained terrible losses and suffering but they ended the battle better armed than when they started it. Years later, Chief Joseph's nephew, Yellow Wolf, revisited the site and recalled: 'Wounded children screaming with pain, women and men crying, wailing for their dead. The air was heavy with sorrow. I would not want to hear, I would not want to see again.'

Ten days later, the Nez Percé went on the offensive and launched a raid on the army's main camp at Camas Meadows. They made off with 200 army pack animals, which both increased their stores and severely disrupted the army's plans to pursue them. This bought Chief Joseph time and he used it to lead his people through the newly created Yellowstone Park before turning north into Montana to try to make contact with the Crow.

The Dash for Canada

It soon became apparent that the Crow were not willing to join the Nez Percé uprising. With the army relentlessly pursuing them, they made the decision to head for Canada, just as some of the Sioux had done in the aftermath of the Battle of the Little Bighorn the previous year. At Canyon Creek, on the Yellow River, they were attacked once again and, as before, the Nez Percé managed to escape.

Chief Joseph, wary from previous incidents of being caught by surprise, used scouts to keep a careful watch on who was following on the trail behind them. When they reached Cow Island, just eighty kilometres (fifty miles) from the Canadian border, he knew that his pursuers were far behind him so made the decision to stop and rest. What he did not and could not know was that the army was using the telegraph system to communicate the location of the Nez Percé. General Howard and his forces may have been pursuing them, but Colonel Nelson A. Miles was positioned ahead of them with fresh troops and waiting to intercept.

At the foot of the Bear Paw Mountain, Miles surrounded the Nez Percé and waited for the arrival of General Howard. When he caught up with them on 4 October, Chief Joseph decided it was time to surrender.

'I Will Fight No More For Ever'

The Nez Percé camp had dwindled down to just eighty warriors and around three hundred and fifty women and children. Many had died in battles or succumbed to the appalling conditions and bitter cold. Many others had decided to disappear into the tribes of the Plains or sneak across the Canadian border in small groups.

On the afternoon of 5 October, in a howling gale and after enduring days of being shelled by artillery, Chief Joseph walked out through snow that lay five inches deep to meet Howard and Miles and offer his rifle in surrender. On a bitterly cold day and over 1,300 miles from home, the words he spoke are some of the most famous spoken by a Native North American Chief: 'I am tired of fighting. Our chiefs are killed. The old men are all dead. It is the young men who say yes or no. He who led on the young men is dead. It is cold, and we have no blankets. The little children are freezing to death. My people, some of them, have run away into the hills and have no blankets, no food. No one knows where they are – perhaps freezing to death. I want time to look for my children and see how many I can find. Maybe I shall find them among the dead. Hear me, my chiefs. I am tired. My heart is sick and sad. From where the sun now stands, I will fight no more for ever.'

AFTERMATH

Despite gaining personal assurances from General Howard, Chief Joseph was never allowed to return to his homeland on the Plateau. After their surrender, the Nez Percé were sent first to Kansas and then to Oklahoma. When the Nez Percé were allowed to go home, it was under the terms of the General Allotment Act, or Dawes Act, of 1887. This meant that, rather than returning to a tribal reservation, they were allocated individual plots.

An extensive census was undertaken by the US government and 2,278 members of the Nez Percé tribe were identified. Every man, woman and child was given eighty acres alongside a further 30,000 of common tribal land. This totalled 212,240 acres – leaving 542,064 acres of what was termed 'surplus land'. The Nez Percé were given no other option other than to sell this 'surplus land' to the government at $3 an acre. Each member of the tribe was given around $600 with a further $1 million being placed in a tribal trust fund.

Struggles on the Farms

The Nez Percé had been horse breeders, not farmers, and they had no experience, expertise or enthusiasm for raising crops. The terms on which they received the land also led to great problems. The original owners were unable to either sell their land or leave it to an individual when they died. This meant that plots got divided among relatives who often had no interest in farming it. In many cases, the land was simply rented out to settlers to farm and the Nez Percé tried to live off the money they received. By the start of the twentieth century, Native Americans living on the Plateau were statistically among the poorest people of the region.

Water Rights

Just as it was for the very first inhabitants of the Plateau over 10,000 years ago, access to water remains crucial for survival today. Over the course of the twentieth century, many irrigation projects were undertaken in an attempt to turn arid, dusty parts of the Plateau into suitable farmland. These were major projects that required considerable investment and planning and, as such, involved the federal government. In many cases, such as on the Yakama Reservation, the project was abandoned due to the costs involved. In others, such as the Flathead Irrigation Project, only 15,000 acres of 126,000 acres of irrigated land belonged to Native Americans.

Fish

The vast majority of the history of human habitation of the Plateau centres around the salmon runs. Whole cultures depended on this annual migration of spawning fish but, by the 1870s, a devastatingly efficient commercial fishing industry was established on the rivers of the Plateau. Mechanized fish wheels were constructed along the Columbia River which all but emptied the rivers and denied indigenous tribes access to their traditional fishing sites.

Access to fish was further damaged by the construction of many dams on the Plateau rivers. The Grand Coulee Dam, which was built in the 1930s on the upper Columbia River, included no fish ladder. This meant that the salmon and steelhead trout swimming up the Columbia no longer reached the Native fishing sites above it. It also created a lake that is more than 320 kilometres (200 miles) long and submerged both reservation lands and many traditional fishing sites. After desperate appeals to President Franklin Roosevelt, Congress approved plans to compensate the tribes that had lost lands to the lake. In addition, twenty-five per cent of the lake was designated as being available for use by Natives who had lost land beneath its water.

In 1968, two members of the Yakama tribe were arrested for fishing using a gill net. This is a method of fishing that has been used for centuries but was banned under Oregon State rules. The case became the focal point of campaigning by several tribes, including the Nez Percé and Yakama, and in 1969 a federal judge ordered that the state of Oregon had to ensure that Natives were given the opportunity to harvest their fair share of salmon.

This directly led to the formation of the Columbia River Inter-tribal Fish Commission in 1977. This works as an advocate for Native fishing rights as well as protecting the river as a natural resource to ensure it can remain central to the lives of their descendants for generations to come.

Indian Claims Commission

It is not just with regard to the rivers that the federal government has worked to rectify some of the wrongs committed in the nineteenth century. The Indian Claims Commission operated between 1946 and 1978 and heard more than 300 cases from various Native tribes involving the loss of land under treaties made with the government. It awarded over $800 million to tribes in recognition of violation of treaties and, where possible, returned land to them. Over 21,000 acres were returned to the Yakama by the federal government in 1972.

Gambling on Casinos

Many Plateau tribes have invested the funds they received from either treaties or judgments by the Indian Claims Commission in a variety of enterprises. These include holiday resorts, timber harvesting and wood processing. Like Native tribes in many parts of the United States, economic development has been built around casinos. This is largely due to the passing of the Federal Indian Gaming Regulation Act of 1988 (IGRA). This essentially ruled that reservations were sovereign entities whose residents were free to open casinos – even in states where gambling is illegal. The IGRA has been an undeniable financial boon for the indigenous peoples of North America and, after President Ronald Reagan signed it, Native revenue grew from $100 million in 1988 to $16.7 billion in 2006.

Following the Las Vegas model, many of the casinos are part of resorts which incorporate hotels, golf courses and other leisure activities. Such has been the success of these ventures that it has led to friction between various tribes and fears of supply for gambling resorts outstripping demand. In the Plateau states of Washington, Oregon and Idaho alone, there are over thirty casinos and there are concerns that they are all competing for the same gamblers.

Cultural Revival

There can be no doubt that the advent of the IGRA and the appearance of casinos on reservations has given many Native tribes the financial independence they were stripped of when they were divested of their lands. The money raised by the casinos has also been used to help preserve and protect their culture. Centres that preserve and celebrate Native heritage have been bankrolled by the gambling industry and built on reservation lands. Artefacts and cultural materials that had been collected by non-Natives have been returned and showcased with the money casinos have generated. This has helped to undo some of the damage caused by decades of US government policy that was designed to bring about assimilation.

Despite these advances and the reasons to be optimistic about the future, many Native Americans of the Plateau still live below the poverty line. Alcoholism and Type 2 diabetes are present at levels that are above the national average, in part due to a genetic predisposition to these conditions.

The impact of disease, the devastation of their fishing sites and the waging of war against them all failed to destroy the Native peoples of the Plateau. At the start of the twenty-first century, there were 42,738 members of Plateau tribes in the United States as well as those living across the border in Canada. Of these, over 8,000 are members of the Yakama, over 4,000 from the Nez Percé, and more than 3,000 are members of the Flathead tribe.

THE PLATEAU

AFTERWORD

The depressing repetition of events in this book is impossible to ignore. In every region, lives were being lived in balance with nature and in ways that had supported and sustained humans for thousands of years. Then, due to a combination of aggression, avarice and disease, these ways of life were suddenly and irrevocably shattered by the arrival of Europeans. The exact dates varied and so did the nationality of the Europeans who were responsible, but the same elements are present in the story of each geographical region.

Catastrophic as it undeniably was, it is important to emphasize that the arrival of the Europeans in the New World was in no way an endpoint for the Native peoples. They existed before and they existed after. They survived. The appalling devastation could be looked at in the context of other genocidal events that left the lives of those who survived for ever altered. It is estimated that Mao Zedong's Great Leap Forward cost the lives of somewhere between fifteen and fifty-five million Chinese people and, in four short years, shifted the country from being an agrarian economy into an industrialized society. Yet it would be utterly absurd to refer to the Chinese culture and people as if they only existed in the past tense. Millions of people in Central Europe perished during the Second World War. Many of those who survived emerged from the conflict living under communist regimes. The societies in which they lived were radically different from those that existed in the 1930s. In no way could the people and traditions of Central Europe be perceived as having disappeared.

Despite the parallels, many aspects of the Native American experience are unique. The subsistence cultures that had evolved over 13,000 years were suddenly and unceremoniously replaced by a ruthless and relentless capitalist way of life. Some have had as little as 150 years to make this drastic adjustment and many are still coming to terms with losing a life that moved with the seasons and usually left ample time for culture and leisure. The attempts to eradicate the very existence of the indigenous nations continued deep into the second half of the twentieth century. The new rules by which they had to live had to be learned, and so did the means by which they could fight back. And fight back they have.

INDIAN TERMINATION POLICY

As Cold War paranoia began to permeate all aspects of American society from the mid-1940s to the mid-1960s, anything perceived to favour the collective was looked on suspiciously. The Native American nations, with their common land and preference for making decisions that favoured the common good, looked too similar to communism for many Americans' liking. This belief heralded the adoption of the Indian Termination Policy, which sought to end the federal government's recognition of the sovereignty of tribes, something that had been legally established by the treaties of the nineteenth century.

Starting in 1953, Congress began passing Termination Acts on a tribe-by-tribe basis. These not only ended the federal recognition of the tribes as sovereign nations but also ended the government's trusteeship over the reservations. The exemptions that the members of tribes had previously enjoyed regarding laws and taxes also ended.

Between 1953 and 1964, over 100 tribes and bands had their recognition as sovereign dependent nations terminated. Around 10,000 square kilometres (3,800 square miles) of reservation land had its protected status removed and much of it was sold to non-Natives. More than 12,000 Native Americans had the rights they had previously enjoyed removed and the federal support for health care, education programmes and utility services was also brought to an end. Without this support, these services were no longer provided or available to the vast majority of tribes that had lost their sovereignty.

Allied with this, the Indian Relocation Act of 1956 provided support for indigenous people who wanted to leave reservations and move to cities. Many thousands, especially young people, decided to make the move. With their prospects so limited and a future on the reservation so seemingly bleak, it is easy to understand why. But for many, the move off the reservation heralded a permanent fissure with their history, culture and identity – exactly as those who designed the Indian Relocation Act intended it to.

THE CIVIL RIGHTS STRUGGLE

The American Indian Movement (AIM) was founded in the wake of these developments. This was a grassroots movement that was born in Minneapolis, Minnesota in July 1968 and was initially concerned with police brutality, poverty and discrimination suffered by Native people living in urban environments. In 1969, they participated with six other native movements in the occupation of the abandoned federal prison on Alcatraz Island.

After the prison was closed, some members of the Sioux attempted to legally claim the island under the terms of the 1868 Fort Laramie Treaty. According to the treaty, they argued, any land deemed surplus by the government could be claimed by the Sioux. Plans were drawn up for using the buildings on Alcatraz as a cultural centre but a perceived lack of progress and rumours of a commercial development of the island spurred some activists into action.

On the evening of 20 November, a party of eighty-nine Native Americans that included married couples and six children set out from Palo Alto with the intention of occupying Alcatraz. Most were intercepted by the US Coast Guard, but fourteen made it through to the island. More boats followed in the weeks and months after and, at its height, there were over 400 Native American activists occupying the island.

By June, a combination of a lack of electricity and water and the tragic death of a thirteen-year-old protester led to the occupation coming to an end. It may not have succeeded in gaining permanent ownership of the island for the Sioux people, but the protest generated a lot of publicity and created a blueprint for more Native American direct action.

In November 1970, on the 350th anniversary of the landing of the *Mayflower*, AIM members seized a British-made reproduction of the ship *Mayflower II* in protest against the poor treatment of Native Americans by the government. In 1972, the so-called Trail of Broken Treaties was a cross-country convoy of Native Americans that stretched for over four miles, contained over 700 activists from more than 200 tribes and travelled from Minnesota to Washington, DC to highlight their grievances.

In 1973, followers of AIM occupied the town of Wounded Knee for seventy-one days in protest against the failure of the US government to fulfil its treaty obligations and to demand the reopening of treaty negotiations. The protest became known as the Second Wounded Knee and garnered widespread public support and sympathy. In 1978, a 2,800-mile trek to Washington, DC set off from California with the aim of preventing the termination of the sovereignty of any more tribes. Hundreds of marchers were accompanied by thousands of supporters and, once in the capital, they paraded past the White House and camped on the grounds of the Washington Monument.

THE INDIAN SELF-DETERMINATION ACT OF 1975

The result of these struggles by AIM and other groups that fought for the civil rights of Native peoples was the Indian Self-Determination and Education Assistance Act of 1975. Their protests had made clear that the policy of termination was both unjust and a failure in terms of facilitating assimilation. Instead, the government decided to pursue a policy of self-determination. Under the terms of the act, tribes received federal funding depending on their specific needs, such as education, law enforcement, environmental protection, etc. In exchange, the tribes needed to meet federal requirements and guidelines.

NATIVE AMERICANS IN TWENTY-FIRST CENTURY AMERICA

The Indian Self-Determination Act was undoubtedly a step forward for indigenous nations and removed the threat of losing their sovereignty. But a great deal of damage was already done. Of all the Native people living in the United States in the twenty-first century, seventy-eight per cent live off-reservation. This means the Indian Self-Determination Act has had little or no impact on the lives of four out of five indigenous people. Reservations, which, during the nineteenth century, represented the loss of Native freedoms and the destruction of their culture, have in many ways become symbols of hope. With billions of dollars accrued due to the Indian Gaming Regulatory Act of 1988, culture centres, museums and education programmes have all been established on reservation land. There can be no doubt that environments have been protected, cultural items preserved and languages saved thanks to the continued existence of reservations and the revenue streams that the gambling operations run by 240 tribes have secured.

THE PROTEST AT STANDING ROCK

But it would be wrong to believe that the struggle between Native Americans and the US government is a thing of the past. The construction of the Dakota Access Pipeline in 2016 is proof that many of the forces that caused such trauma and destruction in the eighteenth and nineteenth centuries are still in play. The pipeline runs underground for 1,886 kilometres (1,172 miles) from North Dakota to Patoka, Illinois. Its original route was rejected due to fears of the impact a leak might have on municipal water sources, residential areas and roads. The alternative route, which gained approval, passed within half a mile of the Standing Rock Sioux Indian Reservation. An environmental report concluded that more than 800,000 acres of reservation land were at risk if there was a spill and that the waters the community relied upon would be severely impacted. Construction of the pipeline continued regardless.

In addition to the potential for environmental disaster, the construction of the pipeline also violated several archaeological sites that were held sacred by nations including the Sioux, Northern Cheyenne and Mandan. Pipeline resistance demonstrators flocked to the site. There were representatives of over 300 federally recognized tribes residing at the Sacred Stone Camps alongside thousands of other protesters who were there in defence of indigenous sovereignty.

Tribal representatives, including a descendant of Sitting Bull, addressed the United Nations and news of the dispute spread around the world. It did not stop the bulldozers and, when protesters moved on to private land that contained possible burial sites, a private security firm engaged by the oil company used pepper spray and dogs against them. Months later, amid reports of protesters setting up illegal roadblocks and trespassing on to private land, the police moved to clear out the protest camps with the help of the US National Guard. Water cannon, tear gas, rubber bullets and concussion grenades were all used and hundreds were reported injured.

In March 2020, a US district judge ruled there had not been adequate studies on the likely impact of the pipeline and ordered the United States Army Corps of Engineers to conduct a new environmental impact review. The pipeline was ordered to be emptied and shut down while the review took place. In August 2020, a US appeals court overturned the decision and the pipeline continues to operate and transports over 750,000 barrels of oil every single day.

NATIVE AMERICAN MASCOTS

During the twentieth century, one area of American culture where indigenous people were disproportionately represented was in the names of sports teams. Many teams, from those belonging to elementary schools to professional franchises, began to adopt Native-themed names and logos. Some were named after specific tribes such as the Sioux or Seminoles, whereas others had more generic names like 'Indians' or 'Chiefs'. Supporters of these teams often claimed that the names were chosen to pay homage and to honour the indigenous people of North America. Many Native peoples strongly disagreed.

AIM began to campaign against the use of Native stereotypes in sports teams in the 1960s but, in the face of strong resistance from both fans and team owners, there was little progress. In recent years, however, there have been significant developments in this area. In 2005, the National Collegiate Athletic Association (NCAA) banned teams from competing in its tournaments if they used Native-themed names or mascots. State governments have moved to ban the use of Native-themed mascots at school level with New York State ruling that schools would lose their funding if Native-themed mascots and names were not removed by 2025.

Professional sports have also begun to change. The Major League Baseball team that had been named the Cleveland Indians since 1915 changed its name to the Cleveland Guardians in 2022. The team retired its logo, which was widely considered to be a racist caricature, in 2018. Perhaps most famously of all, the NFL team known as the Washington Redskins since the 1960s became the Washington Commanders in 2022.

The names of sports teams may seem a particularly trivial note on which to end, but perhaps it provides insights into broader and more significant changes of attitudes within mainstream American society. These names had been considered crass, insulting and racist by indigenous peoples for many decades but it did not stop these teams from succeeding or being celebrated. For decades and in the face of frequent demonstrations, the owners of the Washington NFL team refused to consider changing the franchise's name. They were supported in this by most fans.

But in 2020, things suddenly changed. Sponsors such as Nike, FedEx and PepsiCo began responding to the wishes of their customers and expressed their reluctance to be associated with a brand that was widely believed to be racist. Major retailers then stopped selling Washington team merchandise from their stores and websites. Nike stopped selling Washington jerseys and hats and, on the same day, the stadium sponsor formally and publicly asked for the team's name to change. That change then became inevitable.

So the respective names of sports teams is not a trivial note, but an optimistic one. The adoption of a new name was not driven by a change of heart by the team's owner, or even in the boardrooms of the team's sponsors. It was brought about by a change in the attitude of the millions of people who could potentially purchase the products and services of these sponsors. The bottom line of these companies told them that racism towards indigenous people, casual, indirect or otherwise, was no longer acceptable to their customers. After several centuries when the opposite was manifestly true, this is indeed grounds for hope for a brighter future for the Native North Americans.

[illegible]

ANCIENT KINGS, LEADERS & PEOPLES

Ancient cultures often traded with and influenced each other, while others grew independently. This section provides key leaders, peoples or timelines from a number of regions, to offer comparative insights into developments across the ancient world.

NATIVE NORTH AMERICAN PEOPLES AT A GLANCE

General note: while the beliefs and research into the origins of Native North American peoples vary, what is largely undisputed is that there are ten main locations into which the different bands of peoples fall. These are listed below, including the major tribes for each area and information on their most significant locations. This list is not exhaustive and there may be differences in spellings or locations. It focuses on North American geographical areas. Some peoples are listed in more than one location due to groups splitting or settling in different places. ***Note:*** The term 'extinct' indicates that a group no longer exists as an intact tribal community – descendants may yet survive.

ARCTIC PEOPLES

Arctic peoples – sometimes known as Circumpolar peoples – originate or reside in the Arctic region which consists of parts of Norway, Sweden, Finland, Russia, Iceland, the United States and Canada.

Ancient Beringian (extinct; split into different peoples who largely settled in Siberia or Alaska)

Chukotko-Kamchatkan people, largely split into Chucki (Siberia, Russia) and Koryaks (Siberia, Russia)

Eskaleut, consisting of Eskimo (this term refers to both Inuit people based in Alaska, Canada and Greenland, and Aleut people from the Aleutian Islands), Yupik (Alaska and Russia), Alutiiq (Alaska), Yup'ik (Alaska), Siberian Yupik (Siberia, Russia), Inuit (Greenland, Northern Canada, Alaska), Aleut (Aleutian Islands)

Indo-European peoples, including Germanic, Icelanders, Norwegians, Swedes and Slavic peoples

Tungusic, largely consisting of Evenks (China, Mongolia, Russia) and Evens (Siberia, Russia)

Turkic, including Dolgans (Siberia, Russia) and Yakuts (Siberia, Russia)

Uralic, including Finno-Ugric (Eastern, Central and Northern Europe), Permians (Russia), Sámi (Norway, Sweden, Finland, Russia), Balto-Finnic (Finland, Norway, Russia). The Uralic group also includes Samoyedic, consisting of Nenets (Russia), Enets (Siberia, Russia), Nganasan (Siberia, Russia), Selkup (Siberia, Russia)

Yukaghirs (Siberia, Russia)

SUBARCTIC PEOPLES

Subarctic peoples originate from or reside in the Subarctic region which is south of the true Arctic. It consists of parts of Alaska, Canada, Iceland, Siberia, Russia, Fennoscandia and the Cairngorms in Scotland.

Ahtna (Copper River area, southern Alaska)

Aleut (Alaska, Russia)

Ancient Beringian (split into different peoples who largely settled in Siberia or Alaska)

Athabaskan (split into different peoples, including Carrier, Chipewyan Deg Hit'an, Dena'ina, Gwich'in, Han/Hwech'in, Holikachuk, Koyukon, Métis, Slave, Tanana, Upper Kuskokwim; Alaska, other parts of North America and Canada)

Atikamekw (Quebec)

Beothuk (Newfoundland; extinct)

Chugach Sugpiaq (Alaska)

Cree (of which there are several sub-groups; several parts of Canada, including Alberta, Saskatchewan, Manitoba, Ontario, British Columbia and Quebec)

Cup'ik (Alaska)

Dene (Northern Canada)

Eskimo (this term refers to both Inuit people based in Alaska, Canada and Greenland, and Aleut people from the Aleutian Islands)

Eyak (Copper River area and Cordova, Southern Alaska)

Haida (Haida Gwaii, off the coast of British Columbia)

Innu (Canada)

Iñupiat (Alaska)

Ojibwa (also known as Chippewa; Southern Canada, Midwestern US, Northern Plains)

Sugapiaq (also known as Alutiiq; Alaska)

Tlingit (Alaska, British Columbia, Yukon)

Tsimshian (Alaska, British Columbia)

Yup'ik (Alaska)

THE NORTHEAST

Peoples from the Northeast originate from or reside in the northeastern US, Midwestern US and parts of southeastern Canada.

Abenaki (significant locations include Quebec, Maine, New Brunswick, New Hampshire, Nova Scotia and Vermont)
Algonquin (Quebec, Ontario)
Anishinaabeg (Quebec, Ontario)
Assateague (Maryland; extinct)
Attawandaron (Ontario)
Beothuk (Newfoundland; extinct)
Chowanoke (North Carolina; extinct)
Choptank (Maryland; extinct)
Conoy (Virginia, Maryland)
Delaware (also known as Lenape; Pennsylvania, Delaware, New Jersey, Oklahoma, Ontario, formerly New York)
Doeg (also known as Tauxenent; Virginia)
Erie (Pennsylvania, New York)
Etchemin (Maine)
Fox (also known as Meskwaki; Michigan, Iowa)
Ho-Chunk (also known as Winnebago; Wisconsin, Illinois, Iowa, Nebraska)
Honniasont (Pennsylvania, Ohio, West Virginia; extinct)
Hopewell (Ohio, Illinois, Kentucky, Black River region; extinct)
Illinois (Illinois, Iowa, Missouri, Oklahoma)
Iroquis Confederacy, including Cayuga, Mohawk, Oneida, Onondaga and Seneca, later Tuscarora (Ontario, Quebec, New York, Oklahoma, Virginia, Wisconsin)

Kickapoo (Michigan, Illinois, Missouri, formerly New York, Ontario, Quebec)
Massachusett (Massachusetts; extinct)
Mi'kmaq (New Brunswick, Newfoundland, Nova Scotia, Prince Edward Island, Quebec, Maine)
Mohican (Connecticut, Massachusetts, New York, Vermont)
Mitchigamea (Illinois, Oklahoma; extinct)
Mohegan (Connecticut)
Monacan (Virginia)
Montaukett (New York)
Monyton (Virginia, West Virginia)
Nansemond (Virginia)
Nanticoke (Delaware, Maryland)
Narragansett (Rhode Island)
Niantic (Connecticut)
Nipmuc (Connecticut, Massachusetts, Rhode Island)
Nottaway (Virginia)
Occaneechi (Virginia)
Ojibwa (also known as Chippewa; Southern Canada, Midwestern US, Northern Plains)
Pamplico (North Carolina)
Patuxent (Maryland)
Paugussett (Connecticut)
Pawtucket (Massachusetts, New Hampshire)
Pequot (Connecticut)
Penobscot (Maine)
Petun (Ontario)
Piscataway (Maryland)
Pocumtuc (Massachusetts)
Podunk (New York, Hartford County, Connecticut)

Poospatuck (also known as Unquachog; Long Island, New York)
Powhatan Confederacy (Virginia)
Quapas (Ohio)
Quinnipiac (Connecticut, New York, New Jersey)
Rappahannock (Virginia)
Sauk (Michigan, Iowa, Oklahoma)
Schaghticoke (Connecticut)
Secotan (North Carolina)
Shawnee (formerly Ohio, Kentucky, Pennsylvania, Virginia, West Virginia, currently Oklahoma)
Shinnecock (New York)
Stegarake (Virginia)
Stuckanox (Virginia)
Susquehannock (also known as Conestoga; Maryland, Pennsylvania, New York, West Virginia)
Tunxis (Connecticut)
Tutelo (also known as Nahyssan; Virgnia)
Wabanaki (Maine, New Brunswick, Nova Scotia, Quebec)
Wampanoag (Massachusetts, Rhode Island)
Wangunk (Mattabeset, Connecticut)
Wenro (New York)
Wicocomico (Maryland, Virginia)
Wyachtonok (Connecticut, New York)
Wyandot (also known as Huron; Ontario, Quebec, Oklahoma, Kansas, Michigan)

THE SOUTHEAST

Peoples from the Southeast originate from or reside in the southeastern US and on the northeastern border of Mexico.

Acolapissa (Louisiana, Mississippi)
Ais (Florida)
Alafay (Florida)
Amacano (Florida)
Apalachee (Florida)
Atakapa (Louisiana, Texas)
Avoyel (Louisiana)
Bayogoula (Louisiana)
Caddo Confederacy (Arkansas, Louisiana, Oklahoma, Texas)
Calusa (Florida)
Cape Fear Indians (North Carolina)
Catawba (North Carolina, South Carolina)
Chakchiuma (Alabama, Mississippi)
Chatot People (Florida)
Chawasha (Louisiana)
Cheraw (North Carolina)
Cherokee (North Carolina, Tennessee, South Carolina, Alabama, Arkansas, Texas, Mexico, Oklahoma)
Chickanee (North Carolina)
Chickasaw (Alabama, Mississippi, Oklahoma)
Chicora (South Carolina)
Chine (Florida)
Chisca (Virginia, Florida)
Chitimacha (Louisiana)
Choctaw (Alabama, Louisiana, Mississippi, Oklahoma)

Chowanoc (North Carolina)
Congaree (South Carolina)
Coree (North Carolina)
Creek (also known as Muscogee; Alabama, Florida, Georgia, Mississippi, Oklahoma, Tennessee)
Croatan (North Carolina)
Cusabo (South Carolina)
Eno (North Carolina)
Etiwan (South Carolina)
Griga (Mississippi)
Guacata (Florida)
Guacozo (Florida)
Guale (Georgia)
Haw (North Carolina)
Houma (Louisiana, Mississippi)
Jaega (Florida)
Jaupin (North Carolina)
Jororo (Florida)
Keyauwee (North Carolina)
Koasati (Tennessee, Louisiana, Oklahoma, Texas)
Koroa (Mississippi)
Luca (Florida)
Lumbee (North Carolina)
Machapunga (North Carolina)
Matecumbe (Florida)
Mayaca (Florida)
Mayaimi (Florida)
Mayajuaca (Florida)
Miccosuke (Florida)
Mobila (Florida, Alabama)

Mocoso (Florida)
Mosopelea (also known as Ofo; Arkansas, Mississippi, Tennessee)
Mougoulacha (Mississippi)
Naniaba (Alabama, Florida)
Natchez (Louisiana, Mississippi, Oklahoma)
Neusiok (North Carolina)
Norwood Culture (Florida)
Okchai (Alabama)
Okelousa (Louisiana)
Opelousas (Louisiana)
Pacara People (Florida)
Pamlico (North Carolina)
Pascagoula (Mississippi)
Pee Dee (North Carolina, South Carolina)
Penascola (Alabama, Florida)
Poteskeet (North Carolina)
Quinipissa (Louisiana, Mississippi)
Roanoke (North Carolina)
Saluda (South Carolina)
Santee (South Carolina)
Santa Luces (Florida)
Saponi (North Carolina, Virginia)
Saura (North Carolina)
Saxapahaw (North Carolina)
Secotan (North Carolina)
Seminole (Florida, Oklahoma)
Sewee (South Carolina)
Shakori (North Carolina)
Shoccoree (North Carolina)

Sugeree (North Carolina, South Carolina)
Taensa (Mississippi)
Tawasa (Alabama)
Tequesta (Florida)
Timucua (Louisiana, Georgia)
Tioux (Mississippi)
Tocaste (Florida)
Tocobaga (Florida)
Tohomé (Alabama, Florida)
Tomahitan (Tennessee)
Topachula (Florida)
Tukabahchee Creek (Alabama)
Tunica (Arkansas, Mississippi)
Uzita (Florida)
Vicela (Florida)
Viscaynos (Florida)
Waccamaw (South Carolina)
Waccamaw Siouan (North Carolina)
Wateree (North Carolina)
Waxhaw (North Carolina, South Carolina)
Westo (South Carolina, Virginia)
Winyaw (South Carolina)
Woccon (North Carolina)
Yamasee (Florida, Georgia)
Yazoo (Arkansas, Louisiana, Mississippi)
Yuchi (Georgia, Oklahoma, Tennessee)

THE PLAINS

Peoples from the Plains originate from or reside in the Great Plains of the Central US and the Prairies of Western Canada.

Anishinaabe (Alberta, British Columbia, Manitoba, Minnesota, Montana, Ontario, Saskatchewan)
Apache (Oklahoma, New Mexico, Texas)
Arapaho (Colorado, Oklahoma, Wyoming)
Akikara (North Dakota)
Atsina (Montana)
Blackfoot (Alberta, Montana)
Cheyenne (Montana, Oklahoma)
Comanche (Oklahoma, Texas)
Plains Cree (Alberta, Manitoba, Montana, Saskatchewan)
Crow (also known as Absaroka; Montana)
Escanjaques (Oklahoma)
Hidasta (North Dakota)
Iowa (Kansas, Nebraska, Oklahoma)
Kaw (Kansas, Oklahoma)
Kiowa (Oklahoma)
Mandan (North Dakota)
Métis People (Alberta, Manitoba, North Dakota, Saskatchewan)
Missouri (Oklahoma)
Omaha (Nebraska)
Osage (Arkansas, Missouri, Oklahoma)
Otoe (Missouri, Oklahoma)
Pawnee (Oklahoma)
Ponca (Nebraska, Oklahoma)
Quapaw (Arkansas, Oklahoma)

Sioux, including Lakota or Teton Sioux (Montana, North Dakota, South Dakota, Saskatchewan), Santee (Minnesota, Montana, Nebraska, North Dakota, South Dakota, Manitoba, Saskatchewan), Yankton Sioux (South Dakota)
Teyas (Texas)
Tonkawa (Oklahoma)
Tsuu T'ina (Alberta)
Wichita People (Kansas, Oklahoma, Texas)

THE SOUTHWEST

Peoples from the Southwest originate from or reside in Arizona, California, Colorado, Nevada, New Mexico, Utah, and Chihuahua and Sonora in Mexico.

Ak Chin (Arizona)
Apache, including Eastern Apache peoples (spilt into several groups such as the Chiricahua, Jicarilla, Kiowa, Lipan and Mescalero Apache; Arizona, New Mexico, Oklahoma, Texas), Western Apache peoples (split into several groups such as the Cibecue, Coyotero, Mimbreño, San Carlos, Tonto, White Mountain; Arizona, Chihuahua, Sonora)
Aranama (Texas)
Coahuiltecan (northern Mexico, Texas)
Comecrudo (northern Mexico, Texas)
Halchidhoma (also known as Alchedoma; Arizona, California)
Hohokam (Arizona; extinct culture)
Hopi (northeastern Arizona, California, Colorado)
Karankawa (Texas)

La Junta (Chihuahua, Texas)
Navajo (Arizona, New Mexico, Utah)
Manso (Chihuahua, Texas)
Pima (Arizona, Chihuahua, Sonora)
Pima Bajo (Chihuahua, Sonora)
Pueblo, including Anasazi, Hopi-Tewa, Keres peoples (spilt into several groups such as the Acoma, Cochiti, Kewa, Laguna, San Felipe, Santa Ana and Zia Pueblos; New Mexico), Tewa peoples (split into several groups such as the Nambé, Ohkay Owingeh (also known as San Juan Pueblo, Pojoaque, San Ildefonso, Santa Clara, Tesuque Pueblos; New Mexico), Tiwa peoples (split into several groups such as the Isleta, Picuris, Piro, Sandia, Taos and Ysleta del Sur Pueblos; New Mexico, Texas), Towa peoples (spilt into several groups such as the Jemez and Pecos Pueblos; New Mexico), Zuni peoples (New Mexico)
Quems (Coahuila, Texas)
Solano (Coahuila, Texas)
Toboso (northern Mexico)
Tohono O'odham (Arizona, Mexico)
Yaqui (also known as Hiaki or Yoeme; Arizona, Sonora)
Yumans, including River Yumans (split into several groups such as the Cocopah, Maricopa, Mojave and Quechan; Arizona, California, Mojave Desert, northern Mexico), Upland Yumans (split into several groups such as the Hualapai, Havasupai, Kiiwa, Kumeyaay, Papa and Yavapai; Arizona, California, Baja California)

THE GREAT BASIN

Peoples from the Great Basin originate from or reside in parts of the Rocky Mountains and the Sierra Nevada Mountain range. Most groups speak Uto-Aztecan languages with the notable exception of the Washoe, who speak Hokan.

Bannock (affiliated with both Northern Paiute and Northern Shoshone people; southeastern California)
Mono (split into Eastern Mono and Western Mono, both in southeastern California)
Paiute people, including Northern Paiute (split into several groups; California, Idaho, Nevada, Oregon), Southern Paiute (split into several groups; Arizona, California, Nevada, Utah)
Shoshone people, including Eastern Shoshone (also known as Wind River Shoshone; split into several groups; Wind River Valley, Wyoming, Idaho), Western Shoshone (split into several groups, including some Goshute groups; California, Great Salt Desert, Great Salt Lake, Utah, Idaho, Nevada), Northern Shoshone (split into several groups; Great Salt Lake, Lemhi River, Idaho, Wyoming)
Ute people, including Northern Ute (split into several groups; central Utah, eastern Utah, and central and northern Colorado), White River Ute (also known as Parianuche, Yampa and Yamparika; Colorado and Utah), Southern Ute (split into several groups; Colorado and New Mexico), Ute Mountain Tribe (Colorado, Utah, New Mexico), Gouache (Rocky Mountains), Caputa (San Luis Valley), Weenuchiu (San Juan River Valley)
Washoe (Lake Tahoe, California and Nevada)

CALIFORNIA

Californian peoples originate from or reside within the current Californian boundaries and the Baja Peninsula of Mexico.

Astugewi (northeastern California)

Cahto (northwestern California)

Chemehuevi (eastern California)

Chumash (split into several groups; central and southern California)

Chilula (northwestern California)

Chimariko (northwestern California)

Cocopa (Baja California)

Eel River Athapaskan peoples (split into several groups; northwestern California)

Esselen (western-central California)

Hupa (northwestern California)

Karuk (northwestern California)

Kawaiisu (southeast-central California)

Maidu (split into several groups; northeastern and northern California)

Miwok (split into several groups; central and western California)

Mono (split into Eastern Mono and Western Mono, both in southeastern California)

Mojave (southeastern California)

Nisenan (eastern-central California)

Ohlone (formerly Costanoan; split into several groups; west-central California)

Pit River Tribe (northeastern California)

Pomo (northwestern and western California)

Quechan Yuman (southeastern California)

Salinan (central California)
Shastan (northwestern California)
Takic peoples (split into several groups; southern and southwestern California)
Timbisha (eastern California)
Tolowa (northwestern California)
Tubatulabal (south-central California)
Wappo (north-central California)
Whilkut (northwestern California)
Winton (split into several groups; northern and northwestern California)
Wiyot (northwestern California)
Yana (northeastern California)
Yokuts (split into several groups; central and southern California)
Yuki (split into several groups; northwestern California)
Yurok (northwestern California)

THE NORTHWEST

Peoples from the Northwest originate from or reside in Alaska, British Columbia, California, Oregon and Washington State.

Bella Coola (also known as Nuxalk; central coast of British Columbia)
Chimakum (Jefferson County, Washington)
Chinook (split into several groups; Northwest Coast, along the Columbia River, Oregon, southwest Washington)

Coast Salish (split into several groups; British Columbia, Oregon, Washington)
Da'naxda'xw Nation (Vancouver Island, British Columbia)
Ditidaht (Vancouver Island, British Columbia)
Eyak (Alaska, mainly near Cordova)
Gitxsan (British Columbia)
Haida (Alaska, British Columbia, Prince of Wales Island)
Haisla (British Columbia)
Heiltsuk (British Columbia)
Kwakiutl (also known as Kwakwaka'wakw (Vancouver Island, British Columbia)
Makah (Olympic Peninsula, Washington)
Nuu-chah-nulth (Vancouver Island)
Quileute (Olympic Peninsula, Washington)
Tillamook (Oregon Coast)
Tlingit (British Columbia, southeast Alaska)
Tsimshian (Alaska, British Columbia)
Willapa (southwestern Washington)
Wuikinuxv (British Columbia)

THE PLATEAU

Peoples from the Plateau originate from or reside in British Columbia, California, Idaho, Montana, Oregon and Washington State.

Cayuse (Oregon)
Chinook (split into several groups; Northwest Coast, along the Columbia River, Oregon, southwest Washington)

Cowlitz (split into several groups; Washington)
Flathead (split into several groups; Idaho, Montana)
Interior Salish (split into several groups; British Columbia, Idaho, Montana, Washington)
Kalapuya (split into several groups; Oregon)
Kalispel (Montana, Washington)
Klamath (Oregon)
Kutenai (British Columbia, Idaho, Montana)
Lake (also known as Sinixt; British Columbia, Idaho, Washington)
Modoc (California, Oregon)
Molala (Oregon)
Nespelem (Washington)
Okanagon (British Columbia, Washington)
Sahaptin (split into several groups; Idaho, Oregon, Washington)
Sanpoil (Washington)
Spokan (Washington)
Shuswap (also known as Secwepemc; British Columbia)
Thompson (often known as Nlaka'pamux; British Columbia)
Wenatchee (Washington)

MESOAMERICAN LEADERS

There is dispute about the dates and position of some Mesoamerican rulers due to a lack of cohesion within different cultures, especially in the earlier periods, partly because of migration. This list aims to provide an overview of the major Mesoamerican peoples of the Olmecs, Maya, Toltecs and Aztecs. It is not exhaustive and dates are approximate. There may also be differences in name spellings between different sources.

OLMEC LEADERS

Although it is clear from archaeological findings of the Olmecs that their society was organized and was likely hierarchical, little is known of its rulers, either legendary or historical, although some believe the many sculptures or colossal heads found were created to glorify their rulers. There is, however, no record such as the Maya *Popol Vuh* which lists specific rulers or the dates of their rule.

The Olmecs seemed to have worshipped a god similar to Quetzalcoatl, a figure seen in many other Mesoamerican cultures. Archaeological studies indicate they also worshipped deities which symbolized rain, maize and the earth; however, there is no confirmation whether these deities were thought to be legendary Olmec leaders.

MAYA LEADERS

There are numerous gods related to the Maya culture, as well as various interpretations of creation myths. Many of the Maya rulers took names associated with gods, such as K'awiil (God K, associated with fertility, maize and lightning), K'inich Ajaw (God G, associated with the sun), Chaak (associated with thunder and rain) and Kukulkan (serpent deity, sometimes considered a Maya ruler).

The following lists focus on several significant Maya cities. Cities are listed alphabetically. Where names are unknown, rulers are identified by numbers.

Caracol

Te' K'ab Chaak	*c.* 331–349 CE
K'ahk' Ujol K'inich I	*c.* 470 CE
Yajaw Te' K'inich I	484–514/531 CE
K'an I	531–*c.* 534 CE
Yajaw Te' K'inich II	553–*c.* 595/99 CE
Knot Ajaw	599–613/8 CE
K'an II	618–658 CE
K'ahk' Ujol K'inich II	658–*c.* 680/5 CE
Ruler VII	*c.* 700/2 CE
Tom Yohl K'inich	*c.* 744–793 CE
K'inich Joy K'awiil	*c.* 798/9
K'inich Tobil Yopaat	*c.* 810–830/5 CE

K'an III	c. 835–849 CE
Ruler XIII	c. 859 CE

Calakmul

Yuknoom Ch'een I	c. 484–520 CE
K'altuun Hix	c. 520/537–546 CE
Ut Chanal	c. 561–572 CE
Yax Yopaat	c. 572/3–579 CE
Uneh Chan	579–611 CE
Yuknoom Ti' Chan	c. 619 CE
Tajoom Uk'ab K'ahk'	622–630 BE
Yuknoom Head	630/1–636 CE
Yuknoom Ch'een II the Great	636–686 CE
Yuknoom Yich'aak K'ank'	686–c. 695/8 CE
Split Earth (co-ruler?)	c. 695 CE
Yuknoom Tok'	702–731/6 CE
Wamaw K'awiil	c. 736–741 CE
Bolon K'awiil	c. 751–771 CE
Great Serpent	c. 751 CE
Bolon K'awiil II	c. 771–789 CE
Kan Pet	c. 849 CE
Aj Tok'	c. 909 CE

Copan

K'inich Yax K'uk' Mo'	c. 426–435/7 CE
Ruler 2	c. 437–470 CE
Ruler 3	c. 455–465 CE
Ruler 4	c. 465/470–476 CE
Ruler 5	c. 475/480 CE
Ruler 6	c. 490 CE

Bahlam Nehn	*c*. 504–544 CE
Ruler 8	*c*. 532–551 CE
Ruler 9	551–553 CE
Tzi-Bahlam	553–578 CE
K'ak Chan Yopaat	578–628 CE
Chan Imix K'awiil	628–695 CE
Waxaklahun Ubah K'awiil	695–738 CE
K'ahk' Joplaj Chan K'awiil	738–749 CE
K'ahk' Yipyaj Chan K'awiil	749–761/3 CE
Yax Pasaj Chan Yopaat	763–*c*. 810/20 CE
Ukit Tok'	*c*. 822–830 CE

Naranjo

Tzik'in Bahlam	? CE
Naatz Chan Ahk	? CE
Tahjal Chaak	? CE
Aj Wosaaj Chan K'inich	546–615 CE
K'uxaj	615–631 CE
K'ahk' Xiiw Chan Chaahk	*c*. 644–680 CE
Wak Chanil of Dos Pilas	682–741 CE
K'ak' Tiliw Chan Chaak	*c*. 693–728 CE
Yax Mayuy Chan Chaak	*c*. 741–744 CE
K'ak' Yipiy Chann Chaak	746–? CE
K'ahk' Ukalaw Chan Chaak	755–780/4 CE
Itzamnaaj K'awiil	784–810 CE
Waxaklajuun Ub'aah K'awiil	*c*. 814–? CE

Palenque

K'uk' Bahlam I	431–435 CE
Casper	435–487 CE

B'utz Aj Sak Chilik	487–501 CE
Ahkal Mo'Nahb I	501–524 CE
K'an Joy Chitam I	529–565 CE
Ahkal Mo' Nahb II	565–570 CE
Kan Bahlam I	572–583 CE
Yohl Ik'nal	583–604 CE
Ajen Yohl Mat	605–612 CE
Sak K'uk'	612–615 CE
K'inich Janaab' Pakal I the Great	615–683 CE
K'inich Kan Bahlam II	684–702 CE
K'inich K'an Joy Chitam II	c. 702–721 CE
K'inich Ahkal Mo' Nahb III	c. 721–736/40 CE
K'inich Janaab Pakal II	c. 742–? CE
K'inich Kan Bahlam III	c. 751/761 CE
K'inich K'uk' Bahlam II	c. 764–783 CE
Janaab Pakal III	799–? CE

Tikal

Yax Ehb' Xook (founded Tikal lineage)	c. 90 CE
? Bahlam	c. 292
Sihyaj Chan K'awiil I	c. 300/7
Unen Bahlam	c. 317 CE
K'inich Muwaan Jol	?–369 CE
Chak Tok Ich'aak I	359/60–378 CE
Yax Nuun Ayiin I	379–404 CE
Sihyaj Chan K'awiil II	411–456/7 CE
K'an Chitam	458–486/8 CE
Chak Tok Ich'aak II	486–508 CE
Yo K'in (co-ruler)	511–527 CE
Kaloomte Bahlam (co ruler)	c. 511–527 CE

Bird Claw	*c.* 593 CE
Wak Chan K'awiil	537–562 CE
K'inich Waaw	562/593–628 CE
K'inich Wayaan	*c.* 635 CE
K'inich Muwaan Jol II	*c.* 645 CE
Nun Ujol Chaak	657–679 CE
Jasaw Chan K'awiil I	682–734 CE
Yik'in Chan K'awiil	734–760/6 CE
28th Ruler	*c.* 766 CE
Yax Nuun Ayiin II	768–790/4 CE
Nuun Ujol K'inich	*c.* 800 CE
Dark Sun	*c.* 810 or 849 CE
Jewel K'awiil	*c.* 849 CE
Jasaw Chan K'awiil II	*c.* 869 CE

Yaxchilan

Yopaat Bahlam I	*c.* 359 CE
Itzamnaaj Bahlam I	? CE
Yaxun Bahlam I	378–389 CE
Yax Deer-Antler Skull	389–402 CE
Ruler 5	402 BC
K'inich Tatb'u Jol I	? CE
Moon Skull	*c.* 454–467 CE
Yaxun Bahlam II	467–? CE
Joy Bahlam I	*c.* 508–518 CE
K'inich Tatb'u Jol II	526/37–550 CE
Joy Bahlam II	*c.* 560/4–570 CE
Itzamnaaj Bahlam II	*c.* 599–611 CE
K'inich Tatb'u Jol III	? CE
Yaxun Bahlam III	631–681 CE

Itzamnaaj Bahlam III	681–742 CE
Yopaat Bahlam II	c. 749 CE
Yaxun Bahlam IV	752–768 CE
Itzamnaaj Bahlam IV	769–800 CE
K'inich Tatb'u Jol IV	c. 808 CE

TOLTEC LEADERS

There is much dispute over the rulers of the Toltecs, both over who ruled and when. A sample of the records follow, which show the scale of discrepancies. As in other Mesoamerican cultures, the god Quetzalcoatl was worshipped and is sometimes considered as either the founder and first Toltec ruler, or its last ruler.

This list is from Fernando de Alva Ixtlilxochitl (1568/80–1648 CE), a nobleman of Aztec descent who chronicled indigenous Mesoamerican history.

Chalchiuhtlanetzin	510–562 CE
Ixtlilcuechahauac	562–614 CE
Huetzin	614–666 CE
Totepeuh	666–718 CE
Nacaxoc	718–770 CE
Tlacomihua	770–826 CE
Xihuiqueniitzin	826–830 CE
Tecpancaltzin Iztaccaltzin	830–875 CE
Meconetzin	875–927 CE
Mitl	927–979 CE
Xiuhtlaltzin	979–983 CE

Tecpancaltzin	983–1031 CE
Topiltzin	1031–1063 CE

This list is from the Anales de Cuauhtilan, part of the Codex Chimalpopoca, a record of pre-Hispanic Mesoamerican history and mythology which was written after the Spanish conquest. It is now thought to be lost.

Mixcoamazatzin	701–767 CE
Huetzin	767–782 CE
Ilhuitimal	783–821 CE
Ce Acatl Topiltzin Quetzalcoatl (mythological figure)	822–844 CE
Matlacxochitl	844–880 CE
Nauhyotzin	880–895 CE
Matlaccoatzin	896–924 CE
Tlilcoatzin	925–947 CE
Huemac (Atecpanecatl)	948–1023 CE

Most sources agree that Toltec society largely fell apart in the late eleventh and early twelfth centuries after a large-scale migration from Tollan, the capital city of the Toltec Empire. This was thought to be because of war and famine.

AZTEC LEADERS

Aztec creation myths say that people had lived through four great ages or iterations and that theirs was the fifth. Each previous age had ended in destruction when the gods decided the people were not worthy. In this age, known as the Fifth Sun, the gods Quetzalcoatl and Texcatlipoca came to earth to destroy the earth monster, Tlatecuhtli, whom they ripped in two to create the sky and the earth. Quetzalcoatl then restored humanity to the earth.

The following lists give the rulers of three major Aztec cities, Tenochtitlan, Texcoco and Tlacopan.

Tenochtitlan

Leaders of the Pre-Aztec Empire

Tenoch (legendary founder of the city of Tenochtitlan; preceded by the sun god Huitzilopochtli)	1325–1375 CE
Acamapichtli, first ruler of Tenochtitlan	c. 1367/76–1387 CE
Huitzilihuitl	1391–1415 CE
Chīmalpopōca	1415–1426/7 CE
Xihuitl Temoc	1427 (ruled for only 60 days)

Leaders of the Aztec Empire up to the Spanish Invasion

Itzcōātl (founding member of Aztec Empire)	1427–1440 CE
Motēuczōma I Ilhuicamīna	1440–1466/8 CE
Atotoztli	1466–1472 CE
Axayacatl	1469/72–1481 CE
Tizocic	1481–1486 CE
Āhuizotl	1486–1502 CE
Motēuczōma II Xocoyotzin	1502–1520 CE
Cuitlāhuac	1520 (80 days)
Cuāuhtemōc (partly under Spanish rule)	1520–1524

Texcoco

Leaders of the Pre-Aztec Empire

Quinatzin Tlaltecatzin (first known ruler)	1298–1357 CE
Techotlalatzin	1357 or 1377–1409 CE
Ixtlilxochitl Ome Tochtli	1409–1418 CE
Yancuiltzin (co-ruled)	1418–1431 CE
Tochpili (co-ruled)	1418–1431 CE

Leaders of the Aztec Empire up to the Spanish Invasion

Nezahualcoyōtl (founding member of Aztec Empire)	1431–1472 CE
Nezahualpilli	1472/3–1515 CE
Cacamatzin	1516–1519/20 CE
Cuicuizcatl (not officially recognized)	1519–1520 CE
Coanacoch	1520–1521 CE

Tlacopan

Leaders of the pre-Aztec Empire

Aculnahuacatl Tzaqualcatl (first known ruler)	*c*. 1400–1430 CE

Leaders of the Aztec Empire up to the Spanish Invasion

Totoquihuaztli I (founding member of Aztec Empire)	*c*. 1430–1469 CE
Chimalopopoca	*c*. 1469–1489 CE
Totoquihuaztli II	1489–1519 CE
Tetlepanquetzaltzin	1519–1524 CE

ANCIENT NEAR EAST LEADERS

This list concentrates on leaders with at least some proven legitimate claim. Dates are based on archaeological evidence as far as possible but are approximate. Where dates of rule overlap, rulers either ruled jointly or ruled in opposition to one another. There may also be differences in name spellings between different sources.

SUMER

The Sumerian list that follows is based on the *Sumerian King List* or *Chronicle of the One Monarchy*. The lists were often originally carved into clay tablets and several versions have been found, mainly in southern Mesopotamia. Some of these are incomplete and others contradict one another. Nevertheless, the lists remain an invaluable source of information.

After the kingship descended from heaven, the kingship was in Eridug.

Alulim	28,800 years (8 *sars**)
Alalngar	36,000 years (10 *sars*)

Then Eridug fell and the kingship was taken to Bad-tibira.

En-men-lu-ana 43,200 years (12 *sars*)
En-mel-gal-ana 28,800 years (8 *sars*)
Dumuzid the Shepherd (or Tammuz) 36,000 years (10 *sars*)
Then Bad-tibira fell and the kingship was taken to Larag.
En-sipad-zid-ana 28,800 years (8 *sars*)

Then Larag fell and the kingship was taken to Zimbir.

En-men-dur-ana 21,000 years (5 *sars* and 5 *ners*)

Then Zimbir fell and the kingship was taken to Shuruppag.

Ubara-Tutu 18,600 years (5 *sars* and 1 *ner**)

Then the flood swept over.

*A *sar* is a numerical unit of 3,600; a *ner* is a numerical unit of 600.

FIRST DYNASTY OF KISH

After the flood had swept over, and the kingship had descended from heaven, the kingship was in Kish.

Jushur 1,200 years Kullassina-bel 960 years

Nangishlisma 1,200 years
En-tarah-ana 420 years
Babum 300 years
Puannum 840 years
Kalibum 960 years
Kalumum 840 years
Zuqaqip 900 years
Atab (or A-ba) 600 years
Mashda (son of Atab) 840 years
Arwium (son of Mashda) 720 years
Etana the Shepherd 1,500 years
Balih (son of Etana) 400 years
En-me-nuna 660 years
Melem-Kish (son of Enme-nuna) 900 years
Barsal-nuna (son of Enme-nuna) 1,200 years
Zamug (son of Barsal-nuna) 140 years
Tizqar (son of Zamug) 305 years
Ilku 900 years
Iltasadum 1,200 years
Enmebaragesi 900 years (earliest proven ruler based on archaeological sources; Early Dynastic Period, 2900–2350 BCE)
Aga of Kish (son of Enmebaragesi) 625 years (Early Dynastic Period, 2900–2350 BCE)

Then Kish was defeated and the kingship was taken to E-anna.

FIRST RULERS OF URUK

Mesh-ki-ang-gasher (son of Utu) 324 years (Late Uruk Period, 4000–3100 BCE)

Enmerkar (son of Mesh-ki-ang-gasher) 420 years (Late Uruk Period, 4000–3100 BCE)

Lugal-banda the shepherd 1200 years (Late Uruk Period, 4000–3100 BCE)

Dumuzid the fisherman	100 years (Jemdet Nasr Period, 3100–2900 BCE)
Gilgamesh	126 years (Early Dynastic Period, 2900–2350 BCE)
Ur-Nungal (son of Gilgamesh)	30 years
Udul-kalama (son of Ur-Nungal)	15 years
La-ba'shum	9 years
En-nun-tarah-ana	8 years
Mesh-he	36 years
Melem-ana	6 years
Lugal-kitun	36 years

Then Unug was defeated and the kingship was taken to Urim (Ur).

FIRST DYNASTY OF UR

Mesh-Ane-pada	80 years
Mesh-ki-ang-Nuna (son of Mesh-Ane-pada)	36 years
Elulu	25 years
Balulu	36 years

Then Urim was defeated and the kingship was taken to Awan.

DYNASTY OF AWAN

Three kings of Awan	356 years

Then Awan was defeated and the kingship was taken to Kish.

SECOND DYNASTY OF KISH

Susuda the fuller	201 years
Dadasig	81 years
Mamagal the boatman	360 years
Kalbum (son of Mamagal)	195 years
Tuge	360 years
Men-nuna (son of Tuge)	180 years
Enbi-Ishtar	290 years
Lugalngu	360 years

Then Kish was defeated and the kingship was taken to Hamazi.

DYNASTY OF HAMAZI

Hadanish	360 years

Then Hamazi was defeated and the kingship was taken to Unug (Uruk).

SECOND DYNASTY OF URUK

En-shag-kush-ana	60 years (*c.* 25th century BCE)
Lugal-kinishe-dudu	120 years
Argandea	7 years

Then Unug was defeated and the kingship was taken to Urim (Ur).

SECOND DYNASTY OF UR

Nanni	120 years
Mesh-ki-ang-Nanna II (son of Nanni)	48 years

Then Urim was defeated and the kingship was taken to Adab.

DYNASTY OF ADAB

Lugal-Ane-mundu	90 years (*c.* 25th century BCE)

Then Adab was defeated and the kingship was taken to Mari.

DYNASTY OF MARI

Anbu	30 years
Anba (son of Anbu)	17 years
Bazi the leatherworker	30 years
Zizi of Mari, the fuller	20 years
Limer the 'gudug' priest	30 years
Sharrum-iter	9 years

Then Mari was defeated and the kingship was taken to Kish.

THIRD DYNASTY OF KISH

Kug-Bau (Kubaba)	100 years (*c.* 25th century BCE)

Then Kish was defeated and the kingship was taken to Akshak.

DYNASTY OF AKSHAK

Unzi	30 years	Ishu-Il	24 years
Undalulu	6 years	Shu-Suen (son of	
Urur	6 years	Ishu-Il)	7 years
Puzur-Nirah	20 years		

Then Akshak was defeated and the kingship was taken to Kish.

FOURTH DYNASTY OF KISH

Puzur-Suen (son of Kug-bau)	25 years (*c.* 2350 BCE)
Ur-Zababa (son of Puzur-Suen)	400 years (*c.* 2300 BCE)
Zimudar	30 years
Usi-watar (son of Zimudar)	7 years
Eshtar-muti	11 years
Ishme-Shamash	11 years
Shu-ilishu	15 years
Nanniya the jeweller	7 years

Then Kish was defeated and the kingship was taken to Unug (Uruk).

THIRD DYNASTY OF URUK

Lugal-zage-si	25 years (*c.* 2296–2271 BCE)

Then Unug was defeated and the kingship was taken to Agade (Akkad).

DYNASTY OF AKKAD

Sargon of Akkad	56 years (*c.* 2270–2215 BCE)
Rimush of Akkad (son of Sargon)	9 years (*c.* 2214–2206 BCE)
Manishtushu (son of Sargon)	15 years (*c.* 2205–2191 BCE)
Naram-Sin of Akkad (son of Manishtushu)	56 years (*c.* 2190–2154 BCE)
Shar-kali-sharri (son of Naram-Sin)	24 years (*c.* 2153–2129 BCE)

Then who was king? Who was not the king?

Irgigi, Nanum, Imi and Ilulu	3 years (four rivals who fought to be king during a three-year period; *c.* 2128–2125 BCE)
Dudu of Akkad	21 years (*c.* 2125–2104 BCE)
Shu-Durul (son of Duu)	15 years (*c.* 2104–2083 BCE)

Then Agade was defeated and the kingship was taken to Unug (Uruk).

FOURTH DYNASTY OF URUK

Ur-ningin	7 years (*c.* 2091?–2061? BCE)
Ur-gigir (son of Ur-ningin)	6 years
Kuda	6 years
Puzur-ili	5 years
Ur-Utu (or Lugal-melem; son of Ur-gigir)	6 years

Unug was defeated and the kingship was taken to the army of Gutium.

GUTIAN RULE

Inkišuš	6 years (*c*. 2147–2050 BCE)
Sarlagab (or Zarlagab)	6 years
Shulme (or Yarlagash)	6 years
Elulmeš (or Silulumeš or Silulu)	6 years
Inimabakeš (or Duga)	5 years
Igešauš (or Ilu-An)	6 years
Yarlagab	3 years
Ibate of Gutium	3 years
Yarla (or Yarlangab)	3 years
Kurum	1 year
Apilkin	3 years
La-erabum	2 years
Irarum	2 years
Ibranum	1 year
Hablum	2 years
Puzur-Suen (son of Hablum)	7 years
Yarlaganda	7 years
Si'um (or Si-u)	7 years
Tirigan	40 days

Then the army of Gutium was defeated and the kingship taken to Unug (Uruk).

FIFTH DYNASTY OF URUK

Utu-hengal	427 years / 26 years / 7 years (conflicting dates; *c*. 2055–2048 BCE)

THIRD DYNASTY OF UR

Ur-Namma (or Ur-Nammu)	18 years (*c*. 2047–2030 BCE)
Shulgi (son of Ur-Namma)	48 years (*c*. 2029–1982 BCE)
Amar-Suena (son of Shulgi)	9 years (*c*. 1981–1973 BCE)
Shu-Suen (son of Amar-Suena)	9 years (*c*. 1972–1964 BCE)
Ibbi-Suen (son of Shu-Suen)	24 years (*c*. 1963–1940 BCE)

Then Urim was defeated. The very foundation of Sumer was torn out. The kingship was taken to Isin.

DYNASTY OF ISIN

Ishbi-Erra	33 years (*c*. 1953–1920 BCE)
Shu-Ilishu (son of Ishbi-Erra)	20 years
Iddin-Dagan (son of Shu-Ilishu)	20 years
Ishme-Dagan (son of Iddin-Dagan)	20 years
Lipit-Eshtar (son of Ishme-Dagan or Iddin Dagan)	11 years
Ur-Ninurta (son of Ishkur)	28 years
Bur-Suen (son of Ur-Ninurta)	21 years
Lipit-Enlil (son of Bur-Suen)	5 years
Erra-imitti	8 years
Enlil-bani	24 years
Zambiya	3 years
Iter-pisha	4 years
Ur-du-kuga	4 years
Suen-magir	11 years
Damiq-ilishu (son of Suen-magir)	23 years

BABYLON

FIRST DYNASTY OF BABYLON (AMORITE, *c.* 1894–1595 BCE)

Sumu-abum	1894–1881 BCE
Sumulael	1880–1845 BCE
Sabium	1844–1831 BCE
Apil-Sin	1830–1813 BCE
Sin-muballit	1812–1793 BCE
Hammurapi	1792–1750 BCE
Samsu-iluna	1749–1712 BCE
Abi-eshuh	1711–1684 BCE
Ammi-ditana	1683–1647 BCE
Ammi-saduqa	1646–1626 BCE
Samsu-ditana	1625–1595 BCE

KASSITE DYNASTY (*c.* 1729–1155 BCE)

Gandash	1729–1704 BCE
Agum I	1703–1682 BCE
Kashtiliashu I	1681–1660 BCE
Abi-Rattash?	
Kashtiliash II?	
Urzigurumash	
Harba-Shipak?	
Shipta'ulzi?	
Burna-Buriash I	
Ulamburiash?	

Kashtiliash III?	
Agum III?	
Kara-indash	
Kadashman-Harbe I	
Kurigalzu I	
Kadashman-Enlil I	1374–1360 BCE
Burna-Buriash II	1359–1333 BCE
Kara-hardash	1333 BCE
Nazi-Bugash	1333 BCE
Kurigalzu II	1332–1308 BCE
Nazi-Maruttash	1307–1282 BCE
Kadashman-Turgu	1281–1264 BCE
Kadashman-Enlil II	1263–1255 BCE
Kudur-Enlil	1254–1246 BCE
Shagarakti-Shuriash	1245–1233 BCE
Kashtiliashu IV	1232–1225 BCE
Tukulti-Ninurta I of Assyria	1225 BCE
Enlin-nadin-shumi	1224 BCE
Kadashman-Harbe II	1223 BCE
Adad-shuma-iddina	1222–1217 BCE
Adad-shuma-usur	1216–1187 BCE
Meli-Shipak	1186–1172 BCE
Merodach-Baladan I	1171–1159 BCE
Zababa-shuma-iddina	1158 BCE
Enlil-nadin-ahi	1157–1155 BCE

DYNASTY OF ISIN (*c.* 1157–1026 BCE)

Marduk-kabit-ahheshu	1157–1140 BCE

Itti-Marduk-balatu	1139–1132 BCE
Ninurta-nadin-shumi	1131–1126 BCE
Nebuchadrezzar I	1125–1104 BCE
Enlil-nadin-apli	1103–1100 BCE
Marduk-nadin-ahhe	1099–1082 BCE
Marduk-shapik-zeri	1081–1069 BCE
Adad-apla-iddina	1068–1047 BCE
Marduk-ahhe-eriba	1046 BCE
Marduk-zer-X?	1045–1034 BCE
Nabu-shumu-libur	1033–1026 BCE

SECOND DYNASTY OF THE SEALAND (*c.* 1025–1005 BCE)

Simbar-Shipak	1025–1008 BCE
Ea-mukin-zeri	1008 BCE
Kashshu-nadin-ahhe	1007–1005 BCE

DYNASTY OF BAZI (*c.* 1004–985 BCE)

Eulmash-shakin-shumi	1004–988 BCE
Ninurta-kudurri-usur I	987–985 BCE
Shirikti-Shuqamuna	985 BCE

DYNASTY OF ELAM (*c.* 984–979 BCE)

Mar-biti-apla-usur	984–979 BCE

PERIOD OF MIXED DYNASTIES (*c.* 978–732 BCE)

Nabu-mukin-apli	978–943 BCE
Ninurta-kudurri-usur II	943 BCE
Mar-biti-ahhe-iddina	942–? BCE
Shamash-mudammiq	
Nabu-shuma-ukin I	
Nabu-apla-iddina	(33+ years)
Marduk-zakir-shumi I	(27+ years)
Marduk-balassu-iqbi	?–813 BCE
Baha-aha-iddina	812–? BCE
(interregnum)	
Ninruta-apl-X?	
Marduk-apla-usur	
Eriba-Marduk	(9+ years)
Nabu-shuma-ishkun	?–748 BCE (13+ years)
Nabonassar	747–734 BCE
Nabu-nadin-zeri	733–732 BCE
Nabu-shuma-ukin	732 BCE

NINTH DYNASTY OF BABYLON (*c.* 731–626 BCE)

Nabu-mukin-zeri	731–729 BCE
Tiglath-Pileser III of Assyria	728–727 BCE
Shalmaneser V of Assyria	726–722 BCE
Merodach-Baladan II	721–710 BCE
Sargon II of Assyria	709–705 BCE
Sennacherib of Assyria (first reign)	704–703 BCE
Marduk-zakir-shumi II	703 BCE

Merodach-Baladan II	703 BCE
Bel-ibni	702–700 BCE
Ashur-nadin-shumi	699–694 BCE
Nergal-ushezib	693 BCE
Mushezib-Marduk	692–689 BCE
Sennecherib of Assyria (second reign)	688–681 BCE
Esarhaddon of Assyria	680–669 BCE
Ashurbanipal of Assyria	668 BCE
Shamash-shuma-ukin	667–648 BCE
Kandalanu	647–627 BCE
(interregnum)	626 BCE

NEO-BABYLONIAN DYNASTY (*c.* 625–539 BCE)

Nabopolassar	625–605 BCE
Nebuchadrezzar II	604–562 BCE
Amel-Marduk	561–560 BCE
Neriglissar	559–556 BCE
Labashi-Marduk	556 BCE
Nabonius (co-ruler)	555–539 BCE
Belshazzar (co-ruler/regent)	555–539 BCE

ASSYRIA

PUZUR-ASHUR DYNASTY (2025–1809 BCE)

Puzur-Ashur I

Shalim-ahum	
Ilu-shuma	
Erishum I	1974–1935 BCE
Ikunum	1934–1921 BCE
Sargon I	1920–1881 BCE
Puzur-Ashur II	1880–1873 BCE
Naram-Sim	1872–1829 or 1819 BCE
Erishum II	1828 or 1818–1809 BCE

SHAMSHI-ADAD DYNASTY (1808–1736 BCE)

Shamshi-Adad I	1808–1776 BCE
Ishme-Dagan I	1775–1765 BCE
Mut-Ashkur	
Rimush	
Asinum	

NON-DYNASTIC USURPERS (1735–1701 BCE)

Puzur-Sin
Ashur-dugul
Ashur-apla-idi
Nasir-Sin
Sin-namir
Ipqi-Ishtar
Adad-salulu
Adasi

ADASIDE DYNASTY (1700–722 BCE)

Belu-bani	1700–1689 BCE
Libaya	1688–1672 BCE
Sharma-Adad I	1671–1660 BCE
Iptar-Sin	1659–1648 BCE
Bazaya	1647–1620 BCE
Lullaya	1619–1614 BCE
Shu-Ninua	1613–1600 BCE
Sharma-Adad II	1599–1597 BCE
Erishum III	1596–1584 BCE
Shamshi-Adad II	1583–1578 BCE
Ishme-Dagan II	1577–1562 BCE
Sharmshi-Adad III	1561–1546 BCE
Ashur-nirari I	1545–1520 BCE
Puzur-Ashur III	1519–1496 BCE
Enlil-nasir I	1495–1483 BCE
Nur-ili	1482–1471 BCE
Ashur-shaduni	1471 BCE
Ashur-rabi I	1470–1451 BCE
Ashur-nadin-ahhe I	1450–1431 BCE
Enlil-nasir II	1430–1425 BCE
Ashur-nirari II	1424–1418 BCE
Ashur-bel-nisheshu	1417–1409 BCE
Ashur-ra'im-nisheshu	1408–1401 BCE
Ashur-nadin-ahhe II	1400–1391 BCE
Eriba-Adid I	1390–1364 BCE

MIDDLE ASSYRIAN EMPIRE (1363–912 BCE)

Ashur-uballit I	1363–1328 BCE
Enlil-nirari	1327–1318 BCE
Arik-den-ili	1317–1306 BCE
Adad-nirari I	1305–1274 BCE
Shalmaneser I	1273–1244 BCE
Tukulti-Ninurta I	1243–1207 BCE
Ashur-nadin-apli	1206–1203 BCE
Ashur-nirari III	1202–1197 BCE
Enlil-kudurri-usur	1196–1192 BCE
Ninurta-apil-Ekur	1191–1179 BCE
Ashur-dan I	1178–1133 BCE
Ninurta-tukulti-Ashur	1132 BCE
Mutakkil-Nusku	1132 BCE
Ashur-resh-ishi I	1132–1115 BCE
Tiglath-Pileser I	1114–1076 BCE
Ashared-apil-Ekur	1075–1074 BCE
Ashur-bel-kala	1073–1056 BCE
Eriba-Adad II	1055–1054 BCE
Shamshi-Adad IV	1053–1050 BCE
Ashurnasirpal I	1049–1031 BCE
Shalmaneser II	1030–1019 BCE
Ashur-nirari IV	1018–1013 BCE
Ashur-rabi II	1012–972 BCE
Ashur-resh-ishi	971–967 BCE
Tiglath-Pileser II	966–935 BCE
Ashur-dan II	934–912 BCE

NEO-ASSYRIAN EMPIRE (911–609 BCE)

Adad-nirari II	911–891 BCE
Tukulti-Ninurta II	890–884 BCE
Ashurnasirpal II	883–859 BCE
Shalmaneser III	858–824 BCE
Shamshi-Adad V	823–811 BCE
Adad-nirari III	810–783 BCE
Shalmaneser IV	782–773 BCE
Ashur-dan III	772–755 BCE
Ashur-nirari V	754–745 BCE
Tiglath-Pileser III	744–727 BCE
Shalmaneser V	726–722 BCE

SARGONID DYNASTY (722–609 BCE)

Sargon II	721–705 BCE
Sennacherib	704–681 BCE
Esarhaddon	680–669 BCE
Ashurbanipal	668–627 BCE
Ashur-etil-ilani	626–623 BCE
Sin-shumu-lishir	623 BCE
Sin-shar-ishkun	622–612 BCE
Ashur-uballit II	611–609 BCE

(fall of Assyrian Empire 609 BCE)

PERSIA

ACHAEMENID DYNASTY (559–330 BCE)

Cyrus the Great	559–530 BCE
Cambyses	529–522 BCE
Smerdis	522 BCE
Darius I the Great	521–486 BCE
Xerxes I	485–465 BCE
Ataxerxes I (Longimanus)	464–424 BCE
Xerxes II	424 BCE
Sogdianus	424 BCE
Darius II (Nothus)	423–405 BCE
Ataxerxes II (Mnemon)	404–359 BCE
Ataxerxes III (Ochus)	358–338 BCE
Arses	337–336 BCE
Darius III (Codomannus)	335–330 BCE

(The Persian Empire ended when Alexander the Great invaded in 330 BCE*)*

PHOENICIA

ANCIENT TYRIAN LEADERS (MYTHOLOGICAL), (2050–1450 BCE)

Agenor (son of Posiedon or Belus)	*c.*2050–1450 BCE
Phoenix (son of Agenor, gave his name to Phoenicia)	?

LATE BRONZE AGE (1350–1335 BCE)

Abi-Milku	*c.*1350–1335 BCE

KINGS OF TYRE AND SIDON (990–785 BCE)

Abibaal	*c.*993–981 BCE
Hiram I	980–947 BCE
Baal-Eser I	946–930 BCE
Abdastartus	929–921 BCE
Astartus	920–901 BCE
Deleastartus	900–889 BCE
Astarymus	888–880 BCE
Phelles	879 BCE
Ithobaal I	878–847 BCE
Baal-Eser II	846–841 BCE
Mattan I	840–832 BCE
Pygmalion (Dido's brother, who formed Carthage in 814 BCE)	831–785 BCE

UNDER ASSYRIAN CONTROL (*c.* 750–660 BCE)

Ithobaal II	750–739 BCE
Hiram II	739–730 BCE
Mattan II	730–729 BCE
Elulaios	729–694 BCE
Abd Melqart	694–680 BCE
Baal I	680–660 BCE

AFTER ASSYRIAN CONTROL (*c.* 592–573 BCE)

Ithobaal III	591–573 BCE

(Overthrow of monarchy in favour of oligarchic government)

RESTORATION OF MONARCHY (551–532 BCE)

Hiram III	551–532 BCE

UNDER PERSIAN CONTROL (539–411 BCE)

Mattan IV	*c.*490–480 BCE
Boulomenus	*c.*450 BCE
Abdemon	*c.*420–411 BCE

UNDER CYPRIOT CONTROL (SALAMIS, 411–374 BCE)

Evagoras of Salamis	411–374 BCE

UNDER PERSIAN CONTROL (374–332 BCE)

Eugoras	*c.*340s
Azemilcus	*c.*340–332 BCE

(The Phoenician Empire ended when Alexander the Great invaded in 332 BCE)

ANCIENT EGYPTIAN PHARAOHS

There is dispute about the dates and position of pharaohs within dynasties due to several historical sources being incomplete or inconsistent. This list aims to provide an overview of the ancient Egyptian dynasties, but is not exhaustive and dates are approximate. There may also be differences in name spellings between different sources. Also please note that the throne name is given first, followed by the personal name – more commonly they are known by the latter.

ANCIENT EGYPTIAN DEITIES

Ancient Egyptian gods and goddesses were worshipped as deities. They were responsible for maat (divine order or stability), and different deities represented different natural forces, such as Ra the Sun God. After the Egyptian state was first founded in around 3100 BCE, pharaohs claimed to be divine representatives of these gods and were thought to be successors of the gods.

While there are many conflicting Egyptian myths, some of the significant gods and goddesses and their significant responsibilities are listed here.

Amun/Amen/Amen-Ra	Creation
Atem/Tem	Creation, the sun

Ra	The sun
Isis	The afterlife, fertility, magic
Osiris	Death and resurrection, agriculture
Hathor	The sky, the sun, motherhood
Horus	Kingship, the sky
Set	Storms, violence, deserts
Maat	Truth and justice, she personifies *maat*
Anubis	The dead, the underworld

PREDYNASTIC AND EARLY DYNASTIC PERIODS (*c.* 3000–2686 BCE)

First Dynasty (*c.* 3150–2890 BCE)

The first dynasty begins at the unification of Upper and Lower Egypt.

Narmer (Menes/M'na?)	c. 3150 BCE
Aha (Teti)	c. 3125 BCE
Djer (Itej)	54 years
Djet (Ita)	10 years
Merneith (possibly the first female Egyptian pharaoh)	c. 2950 BCE
Khasti (Den)	42 years
Merybiap (Adjib)	10 years
Semerkhet (Iry)	8.5 years
Qa'a (Qebeh)	34 years
Sneferka	c. 2900 BCE
Horus-Ba (Horus Bird)	c. 2900 BCE

Second Dynasty (*c.* 2890–2686 BCE)

Little is known about the second dynasty of Egypt.

Hetepsekhemwy (Nebtyhotep)	15 years
Nebra	14 years
Nynetjer (Banetjer)	43–45 years
Ba	unknown
Weneg-Nebty	*c.* 2740 BCE
Wadjenes (Wadj-sen)	*c.* 2740 BCE
Nubnefer	unknown
Senedj	*c.* 47 years
Peribsen (Seth-Peribsen)	unknown
Sekhemib (Sekhemib-Perenmaat)	*c.* 2720 BCE
Neferkara I	25 years
Neferkasokkar	8 years
Horus Sa	unknown
Hudejefa (real name missing)	11 years
Khasekhemwy (Bebty)	18 years

OLD KINGDOM (*c.* 2686–2181 BCE)

Third Dynasty (*c.* 2686–2613 BCE)

The third dynasty was the first dynasty of the Old Kingdom. Its capital was at Memphis.

Djoser (Netjerikhet)	*c.* 2650 BCE
Sekhemkhet (Djoser-Teti)	2649–2643 BCE
Nebka? (Sanakht)	*c.* 2650 BCE
Qahedjet (Huni?)	unknown
Khaba (Huni?)	2643–2637 BCE
Huni	2637–2613 BCE

Fourth Dynasty (*c.* 2613–2498 BCE)

The fourth dynasty is sometimes known as the 'golden age' of Egypt's Old Kingdom.

Snefru (Nebmaat)	2613–2589 BCE
Khufu, or Cheops (Medjedu)	2589–2566 BCE
Djedefre (Kheper)	2566–2558 BCE
Khafre (Userib)	2558–2532 BCE
Menkaure (Kakhet)	2532–2503 BCE
Shepseskaf (Shepeskhet)	2503–2498 BCE

Fifth Dynasty (*c.* 2498–2345 BCE)

There is some doubt over the succession of pharaohs in the fifth dynasty, especially Shepseskare.

Userkaf	2496/8–2491 BCE
Sahure	2490–2477 BCE
Neferirkare-Kakai	2477–2467 BCE
Neferefre (Izi)	2460–2458 BCE
Shepseskare (Netjeruser)	few months between 2458 and 2445 BCE
Niuserre (Ini)	2445–2422 BCE
Menkauhor (Kaiu)	2422–2414 BCE
Djedkare (Isesi)	2414–2375 BCE
Unis (Wenis)	2375–2345 BCE

Sixth Dynasty (*c.* 2345–2181 BCE)

Teti	2345–2333 BCE
Userkare	2333–2332 BCE
Meryre (Pepi I)	2332–2283 BCE

Merenre I (Nemtyemsaf I)	2283–2278 BCE
Neferkare (Pepi II)	2278–2183 BCE
Merenre II (Nemtyemsaf II)	2183 or 2184 BCE
Netjerkare (Siptah I) or Nitocris	2182–2179 BCE

FIRST INTERMEDIATE PERIOD (*c.* 2181–2040 BCE)

Seventh and Eighth Dynasties (*c.* 2181–2160 BCE)

There is little evidence on this period in ancient Egyptian history, which is why many of the periods of rule are unknown.

Menkare	c. 2181 BCE
Neferkare II	unknown
Neferkare III (Neby)	unknown
Djedkare (Shemai)	unknown
Neferkare IV (Khendu)	unknown
Merenhor	unknown
Sneferka (Neferkamin I)	unknown
Nikare	unknown
Neferkare V (Tereru)	unknown
Neferkahor	unknown
Neferkare VI (Peiseneb)	unknown to 2171 BCE
Neferkamin (Anu)	c. 2170 BCE
Qakare (Ibi)	2175–2171 BCE
Neferkaure	2167–2163 BCE
Neferkauhor (Khuwihapi)	2163–2161 BCE
Neferiirkkare (Pepi)	2161–2160 BCE

Ninth Dynasty (*c.* 2160–2130 BCE)

There is little evidence on this period in ancient Egyptian history which is why many of the periods of rule are unknown.

Maryibre (Khety I)	2160 BCE to unknown
Name unknown	unknown
Naferkare VII	unknown
Seneh (Setut)	unknown

The following pharaohs and their dates of rule are unknown or widely unconfirmed.

Tenth Dynasty (*c.* 2130–2040 BCE)

Rulers in the Tenth dynasty were based in Lower Egypt.

Meryhathor	2130 BCE to unknown
Neferkare VIII	2130–2040 BCE
Wahkare (Khety III)	unknown
Merykare	unknown to 2040 BCE
Name unknown	unknown

Eleventh Dynasty (*c.* 2134–1991 BCE)

Rulers in the eleventh dynasty were based in Upper Egypt.

Intef the Elder	unknown
Tepia (Mentuhotep I)	unknown to 2133 BCE
Sehertawy (Intef I)	2133–2117 BCE
Wahankh (Intef II)	2117–2068 BCE
Nakhtnebtepefer (Intef III)	2068–2060/40 BCE

MIDDLE KINGDOM (*c.* 2040–1802 BCE)

Eleventh Dynasty Continued (*c.* 2134–1991 BCE)

This period is usually known as the beginning of the Middle Kingdom.

Nebhepetre (Mentuhotep II) 2060–2040 BCE as king of Upper Egypt, 2040–2009 BCE as King of Upper and Lower Egypt

Sankhkare (Mentuhotep III)	2009–1997 BCE
Nebtawyre (Mentuhotep IV)	1997–1991 BCE

Twelfth Dynasty (*c.* 1991–1802 BCE)

The twelfth dynasty was one of the most stable prior to the New Kingdom, and is often thought to be the peak of the Middle Kingdom.

Sehetepibre (Amenemhat I)	1991–1962 BCE
Kheperkare (Senusret I / Sesostris I)	1971–1926 BCE
Nubkaure (Amenemhat II)	1929–1895 BCE
Khakheperre (Senusret II / Sesostris II)	1898–1878 BCE
Khakaure (Senusret III / Sesostris III)	1878–1839 BCE
Nimaatre (Amenemhat III)	1860–1815 BCE
Maakherure (Amenemhat IV)	1815–1807 BCE
Sobekkare (Sobekneferu/Nefrusobek)	1807–1802 BCE

SECOND INTERMEDIATE PERIOD (*c.* 1802–1550 BCE)

Thirteenth Dynasty (*c.* 1802–*c.* 1649 BCE)

There is some ambiguity on the periods of rule of the thirteenth dynasty, but it is marked by a period of several short rules. This dynasty is often combined with the eleventh, twelfth and fourteenth dynasties under the Middle Kingdom.

Sekhemre Khutawy (Sobekhotep I)	1802–1800 BCE
Mehibtawy Sekhemkare (Amenemhat Sonbef)	1800–1796 BCE
Nerikare (Sobek)	1796 BCE
Sekhemkare (Amenemhat V)	1796–1793 BCE
Ameny Qemau	1795–1792 BCE
Hotepibre (Qemau Siharnedjheritef)	1792–1790 BCE
Lufni	1790–1788 BCE
Seankhibre (Amenemhat VI)	1788–1785 BCE
Semenkare (Nebnuni)	1785–1783 BCE
Sehetepibre (Sewesekhtawy)	1783–1781 BCE
Sewadijkare I	1781 BCE
Nedjemibre (Amenemhat V)	1780 BCE
Khaankhre (Sobekhotep)	1780–1777 BCE
Renseneb	1777 BCE
Awybre (Hor)	1777–1775 BCE
Sekhemrekhutawy Khabaw	1775–1772 BCE
Djedkheperew	1772–1770 BCE
Sebkay	unknown
Sedjefakare (Kay Amenemhat)	1769–1766 BCE
Khutawyre (Wegaf)	*c.* 1767 BCE
Userkare (Khendjer)	*c.* 1765 BCE
Smenkhkare (Imyremeshaw)	started in 1759 BCE
Sehetepkare (Intef IV)	*c.* 10 years
Meribre (Seth)	ended in 1749 BCE
Sekhemresewadjtawy (Sobekhotep III)	1755–1751 BCE
Khasekhemre (Neferhotep I)	1751–1740 BCE

Menwadjre (Sihathor)	1739 BCE
Khaneferre (Sobekhotep IV)	1740–1730 BCE
Merhotepre (Sobekhotep V)	1730 BCE
Knahotepre (Sobekhotep VI)	c. 1725 BCE
Wahibre (Ibiau)	1725–1714 BCE
Merneferre (Ay I)	1714–1691 BCE
Merhotepre (Ini)	1691–1689 BCE
Sankhenre (Sewadjtu)	1675–1672 BCE
Mersekhemre (Ined)	1672–1669 BCE
Sewadjkare II (Hori)	c. 5 years
Merkawre (Sobekhotep VII)	1664–1663 BCE
Seven kings (names unknown)	1663–? BCE

Note: the remaining pharaohs of the thirteenth dynasty are not listed here as they are either unknown or there is a lot of ambiguity about when they ruled.

Fourteenth Dynasty (*c.* 1805/1710–1650 BCE)

Rulers in the fourteenth dynasty were based at Avaris, the capital of this dynasty.

Sekhaenre (Yakbim)	1805–1780 BCE
Nubwoserre (Ya'ammu)	1780–1770 BCE
Khawoserre (Qareh)	1770–1745 BCE
Aahotepre ('Ammu)	1760–1745 BCE
Maaibre (Sheshi)	1745–1705 BCE
Aasehre (Nehesy)	c. 1705 BCE
Khakherewre	unknown
Nebefawre	c. 1704 BCE
Sehebre	1704–1699 BCE

Merdjefare	*c.* 1699 BCE

Note: the remaining pharaohs of the fourteenth dynasty are not listed here as they are either unknown or there is a lot of ambiguity about when they ruled.

Fifteenth Dynasty (*c.* 1650–1544 BCE)

The fifteenth dynasty was founded by Salitas and covered a large part of the Nile region.

Salitas	*c.* 1650 BCE
Semqen	1649 BCE to unknown
'Aper-'Anat	unknown
Sakir-Har	unknown
Seuserenre (Khyan)	*c.* 30 to 35 years
Nebkhepeshre (Apepi)	1590 BCE?
Nakhtyre (Khamudi)	1555–1544 BCE

Sixteenth Dynasty (*c.* 1650–1580 BCE)

Rulers in the sixteenth dynasty were based at Thebes, the capital of this dynasty. The name and date of rule of the first pharaoh is unknown.

Sekhemresementawy (Djehuti)	3 years
Sekhemresemeusertawy (Sobekhotep VIII)	16 years
Sekhemresankhtawy (Neferhotep III)	1 year
Seankhenre (Mentuhotepi)	less than a year
Sewadjenre (Nebiryraw)	26 years
Neferkare (?) (Nebiryraw II)	*c.* 1600 BCE
Semenre	*c.* 1600 BCE

Seuserenre (Bebiankh)	12 years
Djedhotepre (Dedumose I)	c. 1588–1582 BCE
Djedneferre (Dedumose II)	c. 1588–1582 BCE
Djedankhre (Montensaf)	c. 1590 BCE
Merankhre (Mentuhotep VI)	c. 1585 BCE
Seneferibre (Senusret IV)	unknown
Sekhemre (Shedwast)	unknown

Seventeenth Dynasty (*c.* 1650–1550 BCE)

Rulers in the seventeenth dynasty ruled Upper Egypt.

Sekhemrewahkhaw (Rahotep)	c. 1620 BCE
Sekhemre Wadjkhaw (Sobekemsaf I)	c. 7 years
Sekhemre Shedtawy (Sobekemsaf II)	unknown to c. 1573 BCE
Sekhemre-Wepmaat (Intef V)	c. 1573–1571 BCE
Nubkheperre (Intef VI)	c. 1571–1565 BCE
Sekhemre-Heruhirmaat (Intef VII)	late 1560s BCE
Senakhtenre (Ahmose)	c. 1558 BCE
Seqenenre (Tao I)	1558–1554 BCE
Wadkheperre (Kamose)	1554–1549 BCE

NEW KINGDOM (*c.* 1550–1077 BCE)

Eighteenth Dynasty (*c.* 1550–1292 BCE)

The first dynasty of Egypt's New Kingdom marked the beginning of Ancient Egypt's highest power and expansion.

Nebpehtire (Ahmose I)	c. 1550–1525 BCE
Djeserkare (Amenhotep I)	1541–1520 BCE

Aakheperkare (Thutmose I)	1520–1492 BCE
Aakheperenre (Thutmose II)	1492–1479 BCE
Maatkare (Hatshepsut)	1479–1458 BCE
Menkheperre (Thutmose III)	1458–1425 BCE
Aakheperrure (Amenhotep II)	1425–1400 BCE
Menkheperure (Thutmose IV)	1400–1390 BCE
Nebmaatre 'the Magnificent' (Amehotep III)	1390–1352 BCE
Neferkheperure Waenre (Amenhotep IV)	1352–1336 BCE
Ankhkheperure (Smenkhkare)	1335–1334 BCE
Ankhkheperure mery Neferkheperure (Neferneferuaten III)	1334–1332 BCE
Nebkheperure (Tutankhamun)	1332–1324 BCE
Kheperkheperure (Aya II)	1324–1320 BCE
Djeserkheperure Setpenre (Haremheb)	1320–1292 BCE

Nineteenth Dynasty (*c.* 1550–1292 BCE)

The nineteenth dynasty is also known as the Ramessid dynasty as it includes Ramesses II, one of the most famous and influential Egyptian pharaohs.

Menpehtire (Ramesses I)	1292–1290 BCE
Menmaatre (Seti I)	1290–1279 BCE
Usermaatre Setpenre 'the Great', 'Ozymandias' (Ramesses II)	1279–1213 BCE
Banenre (Merneptah)	1213–1203 BCE
Menmire Setpenre (Amenmesse)	1203–1200 BCE
Userkheperure (Seti II)	1203–1197 BCE
Sekhaenre (Merenptah Siptah)	1197–1191 BCE
Satre Merenamun (Tawosret)	1191–1190 BCE

Twentieth Dynasty (*c.* 1190–1077 BCE)

This, the third dynasty of the New Kingdom, is generally thought to mark the start of the decline of Ancient Egypt.

Userkhaure (Setnakht)	1190–1186 BCE
Usermaatre Meryamun (Ramesses III)	1186–1155 BCE
Heqamaatre Setpenamun (Ramesses IV)	1155–1149 BCE
Heqamaatre Setpenamun (Ramesses IV)	1155–1149 BCE
Usermaatre Sekheperenre (Ramesses V)	1149–1145 BCE
Nebmaatre Meryamun (Ramesses VI)	1145–1137 BCE
Usermaatre Setpenre Meryamun (Ramesses VII)	1137–1130 BCE
Usermaatre Akhenamun (Ramesses VIII)	1130–1129 BCE
Neferkare Setpenre (Ramesses IX)	1128–1111 BCE
Khepermaatre Setpenptah (Ramesses X)	1111–1107 BCE
Menmaatre Setpenptah (Ramesses XI)	1107–1077 BCE

Twenty-first Dynasty (*c.* 1077–943 BCE)

Rulers in the twenty-first dynasty were based at Tanis and mainly governed Lower Egypt.

Hedjkheperre-Setpenre (Nesbanadjed I)	1077–1051 BCE
Neferkare (Amenemnisu)	1051–1047 BCE
Aakkheperre (Pasebakhenniut I)	1047–1001 BCE
Usermaatre (Amenemope)	1001–992 BCE
Aakheperre Setepenre (Osorkon the Elder)	992–986 BCE
Netjerikheperre-Setpenamun (Siamun)	986–967 BCE
Titkheperure (Pasebakhenniut II)	967–943 BCE

Twenty-second Dynasty (*c.* 943–728 BCE)

Sometimes called the Bubastite dynasty. Its pharaohs came from Libya.

Hedjkheneperre Setpenre (Sheshonq I)	943–922 BCE
Sekhemkheperre Setepenre (Osorkon I)	922–887 BCE
Heqakheperre Setepenre (Sheshonq II)	887–885 BCE
Tutkheperre (Sheshonq Llb)	c. the 880s BCE
Hedjkheperre Setepenre (Takelot I Meriamun)	885–872 BCE
Usermaatre Setpenre (Sheshonq III)	837–798 BCE
Hedjkheperre Setepenre (Sheshonq IV)	798–785 BCE
Usermaatre Setpenre (Pami Meriamun)	785–778 BCE
Aakheperre (Sheshonq V)	778–740 BCE
Usermaatre (Osorkon IV)	740–720 BCE

Twenty-third and Twenty-fourth Dynasties (*c.* 837–720 BCE)

These dynasties were led mainly by Libyans and mainly ruled Upper Egypt.

Hedjkheperre Setpenre (Takelot II)	837–813 BCE
Usermaatre Setpenamun (Meriamun Pedubaste I)	826–801 BCE
Usermaatre Meryamun (Sheshonq VI)	801–795 BCE
Usermaatre Setpenamun (Osorkon III)	795–767 BCE
Usermaatre-Setpenamun (Takelot III)	773–765 BCE
Usermaatre-Setpenamun (Meriamun Rudamun)	765–762 BCE
Shepsesre (Tefnakhte)	732–725 BCE
Wahkare (Bakenrenef)	725–720 BCE

Twenty-fifth Dynasty (*c.* 744–656 BCE)

Also known as the Kushite period, the twenty-fifth dynasty follows the Nubian invasions.

Piankhy (Piye)	744–714 BCE
Djedkaure (Shebitkku)	714–705 BCE
Neferkare (Shabaka)	705–690 BCE
Khuinefertemre (Taharqa)	690–664 BCE

LATE PERIOD (*c.* 664–332 BCE)

Twenty-sixth Dynasty (*c.* 664 – 525 BCE)

Also known as the Saite period, the twenty-sixth dynasty was the last native period before the Persian invasion in 525 BCE.

Wahibre (Psamtik I)	664–610 BCE
Wehemibre (Necho II)	610–595 BCE
Neferibre (Psamtik II)	595–589 BCE
Haaibre (Apreis)	589–570 BCE
Khemibre (Amasis II)	570–526 BCE
Ankhkaenre (Psamtik III)	526–525 BCE

Twenty-seventh Dynasty (*c.* 525–404 BCE)

The twenty-seventh dynasty is also known as the First Egyptian Satrapy and was ruled by the Persian Achaemenids.

Mesutre (Cambyses II)	525–1 July 522 BCE
Seteture (Darius I)	522–November 486 BCE
Kheshayarusha (Xerxes I)	November 486–December 465 BCE
Artabanus of Persia	465–464 BCE
Arutakhshashas (Artaxerxes I)	464–424 BCE
Ochus (Darius II)	July 423–March 404 BCE

Twenty-eighth Dynasty (*c.* 404–398 BCE)

The twenty-eighth dynasty consisted of a single pharaoh.

Amunirdisu (Amyrtaeus)	404–398 BCE

Twenty-ninth Dynasty (*c.* 398–380 BCE)

The twenty-ninth dynasty was founded following the overthrow of Amyrtaeus.

Baenre Merynatjeru (Nepherites I)	398–393 BCE
Khnemmaatre Setepenkhnemu (Hakor)	*c.* 392–391 BCE
Userre Setepenptah (Psammuthis)	*c.* 391 BCE
Khnemmaatre Setepenkhnemu (Hakor)	*c.* 390–379 BCE
Nepherites II	*c.* 379 BCE

Thirtieth Dynasty (*c.* 379–340 BCE)

The thirtieth dynasty is thought to be the final native dynasty of Ancient Egypt.

Kheperkare (Nectanebo I)	*c.* 379–361 BCE
Irimaatenre (Teos)	*c.* 361–359 BCE
Snedjemibre Setepenanhur (Nectanebo II)	*c.* 359–340 BCE

Thirty-first Dynasty (*c.* 340–332 BCE)

The thirty-first dynasty is also known as the Second Egyptian Satrapy and was ruled by the Persian Achaemenids.

Ochus (Artaxerxes III)	*c.* 340–338 BCE
Arses (Artaxerxes IV)	338–336 BCE
Darius III	336–332 BCE

MACEDONIAN/ARGEAD DYNASTY (*c*. 332–309 BCE)

Alexander the Great conquered Persia and Egypt in 332 BCE.

Setpenre Meryamun (Alexander III of Macedon 'the Great')	332–323 BCE
Setpenre Meryamun (Philip Arrhidaeus)	323–317 BCE
Khaibre Setepenamun (Alexander IV)	317–309 BCE

PTOLEMAIC DYNASTY (*c*. 305–30 BCE)

The Ptolemaic dynasty in Egypt was the last dynasty of Ancient Egypt before it became a province of Rome.

Ptolemy I Soter	305–282 BCE
Ptolemy II Philadelphos	284–246 BCE
Arsinoe II	c. 277–270 BCE
Ptolemy III Euergetes	246–222 BCE
Berenice II	244/243–222 BCE
Ptolemy IV Philopater	222–204 BCE
Arsinoe III	220–204 BCE
Ptolemy V Epiphanes	204–180 BCE
Cleopatra I	193–176 BCE
Ptolemy VI Philometor	180–164, 163–145 BCE
Cleopatra II	175–164 BCE, 163–127 BCE and 124–116 BCE
Ptolemy VIII Physcon	171–163 BCE, 144–131 BCE and 127–116 BCE
Ptolemy VII Neos Philopator	145–144 BCE

Cleopatra III	142–131 BCE, 127–107 BCE
Ptolemy Memphites	113 BCE
Ptolemy IX Soter	116–110 BCE
Cleopatra IV	116–115 BCE
Ptolemy X Alexander	110–109 BCE
Berenice III	81–80 BCE
Ptolemy XI Alexander	80 BCE
Ptolemy XII Auletes	80–58 BCE, 55–51 BCE
Cleopatra V Tryphaena	79–68 BCE
Cleopatra VI	58–57 BCE
Berenice IV	58–55 BCE
Cleopatra VII	52–30 BCE
Ptolemy XIII Theos Philopator	51–47 BCE
Arsinoe IV	48–47 BCE
Ptolemy XIV Philopator	47–44 BCE
Ptolemy XV Caesar	44–30 BCE

In 30 BCE, Egypt became a province of the Roman Empire.

ANCIENT GREEK MONARCHS

This list is not exhaustive and dates are approximate. Where dates of rule overlap, emperors either ruled jointly or ruled in opposition to one another. There may also be differences in name spellings between different sources.

Because of the fragmented nature of Greece prior to its unification by Philip II of Macedon, this list includes mythological and existing rulers of Thebes, Athens and Sparta as some of the leading ancient Greek city-states. These different city-states had some common belief in the mythological gods and goddesses of ancient Greece, although their accounts may differ.

KINGS OF THEBES (*c.* 753–509 BCE)

These rulers are mythological. There is much diversity over who the kings actually were, and the dates they ruled.

Calydnus (son of Uranus)
Ogyges (son of Poseidon, thought to be king of Boeotia or Attica)
Cadmus (Greek mythological hero known as the founder of Thebes, known as Cadmeia until the reign of Amphion and Zethus)
Pentheus (son of Echion, one of the mythological Spartoi, and Agave, daughter of Cadmus)

Polydorus (son of Cadmus and Harmonia, goddess of harmony)
Nycteus (like his brother Lycus, thought to be the son of a Spartoi and a nymph, or a son of Poseidon)
Lycus (brother of Nyceteus)
Labdacus (grandson of Cadmus)
Lycus (second reign as regent for Laius)
Amphion and Zethus (joint rulers and twin sons of Zeus, constructed the city walls of Thebes)
Laius (son of Labdacus, married to Jocasta)
Oedipus (son of Laius, killed his father and married his mother, Jocasta)
Creon (regent after the death of Laius)
Eteocles and Polynices (brothers/sons of Oedipus; killed each other in battle)
Creon (regent for Laodamas)
Laodamas (son of Eteocles)
Thersander (son of Polynices)
Peneleos (regent for Tisamenus)
Tisamenus (son of Thersander)
Autesion (son of Tisamenes)
Damasichthon (son of Peneleos)
Ptolemy (son of Damasichton, 12 century BCE)
Xanthos (son of Ptolemy)

KINGS OF ATHENS

Early legendary kings who ruled before the mythological flood caused by Zeus, which only Deucalion (son of Prometheus) and a few others survived (date unknown).

Periphas (king of Attica, turned into an eagle by Zeus)
Ogyges (son of Poseidon, thought to be king of either Boeotia or Attica)
Actaeus (king of Attica, father-in-law to Cecrops I)

Erechtheid Dynasty (1556–1127 BCE)

Cecrops I (founder and first king of Athens; half-man, half-serpent who married Actaeus' daughter)	1556–1506 BCE
Cranaus	1506–1497 BCE
Amphictyon (son of Deucalion)	1497–1487 BCE
Erichthonius (adopted by Athena)	1487–1437 BCE
Pandion I (son of Erichthonius)	1437–1397 BCE
Erechtheus (son of Pandion I)	1397–1347 BCE
Cecrops II (son of Erechtheus)	1347–1307 BCE
Pandion II (son of Cecrops II)	1307–1282 BCE
Aegeus (adopted by Pandion II, gave his name to the Aegean Sea)	1282–1234 BCE
Theseus (son of Aegeus, killed the minotaur)	1234–1205 BCE
Menestheus (made king by Castor and Pollux when Theseus was in the underworld)	1205–1183 BCE
Demophon (son of Theseus)	1183–1150 BCE
Oxyntes (son of Demophon)	1150–1136 BCE
Apheidas (son of Oxyntes)	1136–1135 BCE
Thymoetes (son of Oxyntes)	1135–1127 BCE

Melanthid Dynasty (1126–1068 BCE)

Melanthus (king of Messenia, fled to Athens when expelled)	1126–1089 BCE
Codrus (last of the semi-mythological Athenian kings)	1089–1068 BCE

LIFE ARCHONS OF ATHENS (1068–753 BCE)

These rulers held public office up until their deaths.

Medon	1068–1048 BCE	Pherecles	864–845 BCE
Acastus	1048–1012 BCE	Ariphon	845–825 BCE
Archippus	1012–993 BCE	Thespieus	824–797 BCE
Thersippus	993–952 BCE	Agamestor	796–778 BCE
Phorbas	952–922 BCE	Aeschylus	778–755 BCE
Megacles	922–892 BCE	Alcmaeon	755–753 BCE
Diognetus	892–864 BCE		

From this point, archons led for a period of ten years up to 683 BCE, then a period of one year up to 485 CE. Selected important leaders – including archons and tyrants – in this later period are as follows:

SELECTED LATER LEADERS OF ATHENS

Peisistratos 'the Tyrant of Athens'	561, 559–556, 546–527 BCE
Cleisthenes (archon)	525–524 BCE
Themistocles (archon)	493–492 BCE
Pericles	c. 461–429 BCE

KINGS OF SPARTA

These rulers are mythological and are thought to be descendants of the ancient tribe of Leleges. There is much diversity over who the kings actually were, and the dates they ruled.

Lelex (son of Poseidon or Helios, ruled Laconia) c. 1600 BCE
Myles (son of Lelex, ruled Laconia) c. 1575 BCE
Eurotas (son of Myles, father of Sparta) c. 1550 BCE

From the Lelegids, rule passed to the Lacedaemonids when Lacedaemon married Sparta.
Lacedaemon (son of Zeus, husband of Sparta)
Amyklas (son of Lacedaemon)
Argalus (son of Amyklas)
Kynortas (son of Amyklas)
Perieres (son of Kynortas)
Oibalos (son of Kynortas)
Tyndareos (first reign; son of Oibalos, father of Helen of Troy)
Hippocoon (son of Oibalos)
Tyndareos (second reign; son of Oibaos, father of Helen of Troy)

From the Lacedaemons, rule passed to the Atreids when Menelaus married Helen of Troy.

Menelaus (son of Atreus, king of Mycenae, and husband of Helen) c. 1250 BCE
Orestes (son of Agamemnon, Menelaus' brother) c. 1150 BCE
Tisamenos (son of Orestes)
Dion c. 1100 BCE

From the Atreids, rule passed to the Heraclids following war.

Aristodemos (son of Aristomachus, great-great-grandson of Heracles)

Theras (served as regent for Aristodemes' sons, Eurysthenes and Procles)

Eurysthenes c. 930 BCE

From the Heraclids, rule passed to the Agiads, founded by Agis I. Only major kings during this period are listed here.

Agis I (conceivably the first historical Spartan king) c. 930–900 BCE

Alcamenes c. 740–700 BCE, during First Messenian War

Cleomenes I (important leader in the Greek resistance against the Persians) 524 – 490 BCE

Leonidas I (died while leading the Greeks – the 300 Spartans – against the Persians in the Battle of Thermopylae, 480 BCE) 490–480 BCE

Cleomenes III (exiled following the Battle of Sellasia) c. 235–222 BCE

KINGS OF MACEDON

Argead Dynasty (808–309 BCE)

Karanos	c. 808–778 BCE	Alcetas I	c. 576–547 BCE
Koinos	c. 778–750 BCE	Amyntas I	c. 547–498 BCE
Tyrimmas	c. 750–700 BCE	Alexander I	c. 498–454 BCE
Perdiccas I	c. 700–678 BCE	Alcetas II	c. 454–448 BCE
Argaeus I	c. 678–640 BCE	Perdiccas II	c. 448–413 BCE
Philip I	c. 640–602 BCE	Archelaus I	c. 413–339 BCE
Aeropus I	c. 602–576 BCE	Craterus	c. 399 BCE

Orestes	c. 399–396 BCE	Perdiccas III	c. 368–359 BCE
Aeropus II	c. 399–394/93 BCE	Amyntas IV	c. 359 BCE
Archelaus II	c. 394–393 BCE	Philip II	c. 359–336 BCE
Amyntas II	c. 393 BCE	Alexander III 'the Great' (also King of Persia and Pharaoh of Egypt by end of reign)	c. 336–323 BCE
Pausanias	c. 393 BCE		
Amyntas III	c. 393 BCE; first reign		
Argeus II	c. 393–392 BCE	Philip III	c. 323–317 BCE
Amyntas III	c. 392–370 BCE	Alexander IV	c. 323/317–309 BCE
Alexander II	c. 370–368 BCE		

Note: the Corinthian League or Hellenic League was created by Philip II and was the first time that the divided Greek city-states were unified under a single government.

Post-Argead Dynasty (309–168 BCE, 149–148 BCE)

Cassander	c. 305–297 BCE
Philip IV	c. 297 BCE
Antipater II	c. 297–294 BCE
Alexpander V	c. 297–294 BCE

Antigonid, Alkimachid and Aeacid Dynasties (294–281 BCE)

Demetrius	c. 294–288 BCE
Lysimachus	c. 288–281 BCE
Pyrrhus	c. 288–285 BCE; first reign

Ptolemaic Dynasty (281–279 BCE)

Ptolemy Ceraunus (son of Ptolemy I of Egypt)	c. 281–279 BCE
Meleager	279 BCE

Antipatrid, Antigonid, Aeacid Dynasties, Restored (279–167 BCE)

Antipater	*c.* 279 BCE
Sosthenes	*c.* 279–277 BCE
Antigonus II	*c.* 277–274 BCE; first reign
Pyrrhus	*c.* 274–272 BCE; second reign
Antigonus II	*c.* 272–239 BCE; second reign
Demetrius II	*c.* 239–229 BCE
Antigonus III	*c.* 229–221 BCE
Philip V	*c.* 221–179 BCE
Perseus (deposed by Romans)	*c.* 179–168 BCE
Revolt by Philip VI (Andriskos)	*c.* 149–148 BCE

SELEUCID DYNASTY (*c.* 320 BCE–63 CE)

Seleucus I Nicator	*c.* 320–315, 312–305, 305–281 BCE
Antiochus I Soter	*c.* 291, 281–261 BCE
Antiochus II Theos	*c.* 261–246 BCE
Seleucus II Callinicus	*c.* 246–225 BCE
Seleucus III Ceraunus	*c.* 225–223 BCE
Antiochus III 'the Great'	*c.* 223–187 BCE
Seleucus IV Philopator	*c.* 187–175 BCE
Antiochus (son of Seleucus IV)	*c.* 175–170 BCE
Antiochus IV Epiphanes	*c.* 175–163 BCE
Antiochus V Eupater	*c.* 163–161 BCE
Demetrius I Soter	*c.* 161–150 BCE
Alexander I Balas	*c.* 150–145 BCE
Demetrius II Nicator	*c.* 145–138 BCE; first reign
Antiochus VI Dionysus	*c.* 145–140 BCE

Diodotus Tryphon	*c.* 140–138 BCE
Antiochus VII Sidetes	*c.* 138–129 BCE
Demetrius II Nicator	*c.* 129–126 BCE; second reign
Alexander II Zabinas	*c.* 129–123 BCE
Cleopatra Thea	*c.* 126–121 BCE
Seleucus V Philometor	*c.* 126/125 BCE
Antiochus VIII Grypus	*c.* 125–96 BCE
Antiochus IX Cyzicenus	*c.* 114–96 BCE
Seleucus VI Epiphanes	*c.* 96–95 BCE
Antiochus X Eusebes	*c.* 95–92/83 BCE
Demetrius III Eucaerus	*c.* 95–87 BCE
Antiochus XI Epiphanes	*c.* 95–92 BCE
Philip I Philadelphus	*c.* 95–84/83 BCE
Antiochus XII Dionysus	*c.* 87–84 BCE
Seleucus VII	*c.* 83–69 BCE
Antiochus XIII Asiaticus	*c.* 69–64 BCE
Philip II Philoromaeus	*c.* 65–63 BCE

Ptolemaic Dynasty (305–30 BCE)

The Ptolemaic dynasty in Greece was the last dynasty of Ancient Egypt before it became a province of Rome.

Ptolemy I Soter	305–282 BCE
Ptolemy II Philadelphos	284–246 BCE
Arsinoe II	*c.* 277–270 BCE
Ptolemy III Euergetes	246–222 BCE
Berenice II	244/243–222 BCE
Ptolemy IV Philopater	222–204 BCE
Arsinoe III	220–204 BCE
Ptolemy V Epiphanes	204–180 BCE

Cleopatra I	193–176 BCE
Ptolemy VI Philometor	180–164, 163–145 BCE
Cleopatra II	175–164 BCE, 163–127 BCE and 124–116 BCE
Ptolemy VIII Physcon	171–163 BCE, 144–131 BCE and 127–116 BCE
Ptolemy VII Neos Philopator	145–144 BCE
Cleopatra III	142–131 BCE, 127–107 BCE
Ptolemy Memphites	113 BCE
Ptolemy IX Soter	116–110 BCE
Cleopatra IV	116–115 BCE
Ptolemy X Alexander	110–109 BCE
Berenice III	81–80 BCE
Ptolemy XI Alexander	80 BCE
Ptolemy XII Auletes	80–58 BCE, 55–51 BCE
Cleopatra V Tryphaena	79–68 BCE
Cleopatra VI	58–57 BCE
Berenice IV	58–55 BCE

In 27 BCE, Caesar Augustus annexed Greece and it became integrated into the Roman Empire.

ANCIENT ROMAN LEADERS

This list is not exhaustive and some dates are approximate. The legitimacy of some rulers is also open to interpretation. Where dates of rule overlap, emperors either ruled jointly or ruled in opposition to one another. There may also be differences in name spellings between different sources.

KINGS OF ROME (753–509 BCE)

Romulus (mythological founder and first ruler of Rome)	753–716 BCE
Numa Pompilius (mythological)	715–672 BCE
Tullus Hostilius (mythological)	672–640 BCE
Ancus Marcius (mythological)	640–616 BCE
Lucius Tarquinius Priscus (mythological)	616–578 BCE
Servius Tullius (mythological)	578–534 BCE
Lucius Tarquinius Superbus (Tarquin the Proud; mythological)	534–509 BCE

ROMAN REPUBLIC (509–27 BCE)

During this period, two consuls were elected to serve a joint one-year term. Therefore, only a selection of significant consuls are included here.

Lucius Junius Brutus (semi-mythological)	509 BCE
Marcus Porcius Cato (Cato the Elder)	195 BCE
Scipio Africanus	194 BCE
Cnaeus Pompeius Magnus (Pompey the Great)	70, 55 and 52 BCE
Marcus Linius Crassus	70 and 55 BCE
Marcus Tullius Cicero	63 BCE
Caius Julius Caesar	59 BCE
Marcus Aemilius Lepidus	46 and 42 BCE
Marcus Antonius (Mark Anthony)	44 and 34 BCE
Marcus Agrippa	37 and 28 BCE

PRINCIPATE (27 BCE–284 CE)

Julio-Claudian Dynasty (27 BCE–68 CE)

Augustus (Caius Octavius Thurinus, Caius Julius Caesar, Imperator Caesar Divi filius)	27 BCE–14 CE
Tiberius (Tiberius Julius Caesar Augustus)	14–37 CE
Caligula (Caius Caesar Augustus Germanicus)	37–41 CE
Claudius (Tiberius Claudius Caesar Augustus Germanicus)	41–54 CE
Nero (Nero Claudius Caesar Augustus Germanicus)	54–68 CE

Year of the Four Emperors (68–69 CE)

Galba (Servius Sulpicius Galba Caesar Augustus) 68–69 CE
Otho (Marcus Salvio Otho Caesar Augustus) Jan–Apr 69 CE
Vitellius (Aulus Vitellius Germanicus Augustus) Apr–Dec 69 CE

Note: the fourth emperor, Vespasian, is listed below.

Flavian Dynasty (66–96 CE)

Vespasian (Caesar Vespasianus Augustus) 69–79 CE
Titus (Titus Caesar Vespasianus Augustus) 79–81 CE
Domitian (Caesar Domitianus Augustus) 81–96 CE

Nerva-Antonine Dynasty (69–192 CE)

Nerva (Nerva Caesar Augustus) 96–98 CE
Trajan (Caesar Nerva Traianus Augustus) 98–117 CE
Hadrian (Caesar Traianus Hadrianus Augustus) 138–161 CE
Antonius Pius (Caesar Titus Aelius Hadrianus Antoninus Augustus Pius) 138–161 CE
Marcus Aurelius (Caesar Marcus Aurelius Antoninus Augustus) 161–180 CE
Lucius Verus (Lucius Aurelius Verus Augustus) 161–169 CE
Commodus (Caesar Marcus Aurelius Commodus Antoninus Augustus) 180–192 CE

Year of the Five Emperors (193 CE)

Pertinax (Publius Helvius Pertinax) Jan–Mar 193 CE
Didius Julianus (Marcus Didius Severus Julianus) Mar–Jun 193 CE

Note: Pescennius Niger and Clodius Albinus are generally regarded as usurpers, while the fifth, Septimius Severus, is listed below

Severan Dynasty (193–235 CE)

Septimius Severus (Lucius Septimus Severus Pertinax) 193–211 CE
Caracalla (Marcus Aurelius Antonius) 211–217 CE
Geta (Publius Septimius Geta) Feb–Dec 211 CE
Macrinus (Caesar Marcus Opellius Severus Macrinus Augustus) 217–218 CE
Diadumenian (Marcus Opellius Antonius Diadumenianus) May–Jun 218 CE
Elagabalus (Caesar Marcus Aurelius Antoninus Augustus) 218–222 CE
Severus Alexander (Marcus Aurelius Severus Alexander) 222–235 CE

Crisis of the Third Century (235–285 CE)

Maximinus 'Thrax' (Caius Julius Verus Maximus) 235–238 CE
Gordian I (Marcus Antonius Gordianus Sempronianus Romanus) Apr–May 238 CE
Gordian II (Marcus Antonius Gordianus Sempronianus Romanus) Apr–May 238 CE
Pupienus Maximus (Marcus Clodius Pupienus Maximus) May–Aug 238 CE
Balbinus (Decimus Caelius Calvinus Balbinus) May–Aug 238 CE
Gordian III (Marcus Antonius Gordianus) Aug 238–Feb 244 CE
Philip I 'the Arab' (Marcus Julius Philippus) 244–249 CE
Philip II 'the Younger' (Marcus Julius Severus Philippus) 247–249 CE
Decius (Caius Messius Quintus Traianus Decius) 249–251 CE
Herennius Etruscus (Quintus Herennius Etruscus Messius Decius) May/Jun 251 CE

Trebonianus Gallus (Caius Vibius Trebonianus Gallus) 251–253 CE
Hostilian (Caius Valens Hostilianus Messius Quintus) Jun–Jul 251 CE
Volusianus (Caius Vibius Afinius Gallus Veldumnianus Volusianus) 251–253 CE
Aemilian (Marcus Aemilius Aemilianus) Jul–Sep 253 CE
Silbannacus (Marcus Silbannacus) Sep/Oct 253 CE
Valerian (Publius Licinius Valerianus) 253–260 CE
Gallienus (Publius Licinius Egnatius Gallienus) 253–268 CE
Saloninus (Publius Licinius Cornelius Saloninus Valerianus) Autumn 260 CE
Claudius II Gothicus (Marcus Aurelius Claudius) 268–270 CE
Quintilus (Marcus Aurelius Claudias Quintillus) Apr–May/Jun 270 CE
Aurelian (Luciua Domitius Aurelianus) 270–275 CE
Tacitus (Marcus Claudius Tacitus) 275–276 CE
Florianus (Marcus Annius Florianus) 276–282 CE
Probus (Marcus Aurelius Probus Romanus; in opposition to Florianus) 276–282 CE
Carus (Marcus Aurelias Carus) 282–283 CE
Carinus (Marcus Aurelius Carinus) 283–285 CE
Numerian (Marcus Aurelius Numerianus) 283–284 CE

DOMINATE (284–610)

Tetrarchy (284–324)

Diocletian 'Lovius' (Caius Aurelius Valerius Diocletianus) 284–305
Maximian 'Herculius' (Marcus Aurelius Valerius Maximianus; ruled the western provinces) 286–305/late 306–308

Galerius (Caius Galerius Valerius Maximianus; ruled the eastern provinces) 305–311

Constantius I 'Chlorus' (Marcus Flavius Valerius Constantius; ruled the western provinces) 305–306

Severus II (Flavius Valerius Severus; ruled the western provinces) 306–307

Maxentius (Marcus Aurelius Valerius Maxentius) 306–312

Licinius (Valerius Licinanus Licinius; ruled the western, then the eastern provinces) 308–324

Maximinus II 'Daza' (Aurelius Valerius Valens; ruled the western provinces) 316–317

Martinian (Marcus Martinianus; ruled the western provinces) Jul–Sep 324

Constantinian Dynasty (306–363)

Constantine I 'the Great' (Flavius Valerius Constantinus; ruled the western provinces then whole) 306–337

Constantine II (Flavius Claudius Constantinus) 337–340

Constans I (Flavius Julius Constans) 337–350

Constantius II (Flavius Julius Constantius) 337–361

Magnentius (Magnus Magnentius) 360–353

Nepotianus (Julius Nepotianus) Jun 350

Vetranio Mar–Dec 350

Julian 'the Apostate' (Flavius Claudius Julianus) 361–363

Jovian (Jovianus) 363–364

Valentinianic Dynasty (364–392)

Valentinian I 'the Great' (Valentinianus) 364–375

Valens (ruled the eastern provinces) 364–378

Procopius (revolted against Valens)	365–366
Gratian (Flavius Gratianus Augustus; ruled the western provinces then whole)	375–383
Magnus Maximus	383–388
Valentinian II (Flavius Valentinianus)	388–392
Eugenius	392–394

Theodosian Dynasty (379–457)

Theodosius I 'the Great' (Flavius Theodosius)	Jan 395
Arcadius	383–408
Honorius (Flavius Honorius)	395–432
Constantine III	407–411
Theodosius II	408–450
Priscus Attalus; usurper	409–410
Constantius III	Feb–Sep 421
Johannes	423–425
Valentinian III	425–455
Marcian	450–457

Last Emperors in the West (455–476)

Petronius Maximus	Mar–May 455
Avitus	455–456
Majorian	457–461
Libius Severus (Severus III)	461–465
Anthemius	467–472
Olybrius	Apr–Nov 472
Glycerius	473–474
Julius Nepos	474–475
Romulus Augustulus (Flavius Momyllus Romulus Augustulus)	475–476

Leonid Dynasty (East, 457–518)

Leo I (Leo Thrax Magnus)	457–474
Leo II	Jan–Nov 474
Zeno	474–475
Basiliscus	475–476
Zeno (second reign)	476–491
Anastasius I 'Dicorus'	491–518

Justinian Dynasty (East, 518–602)

Justin I	518–527
Justinian I 'the Great' (Flavius Justinianus, Petrus Sabbatius)	527–565
Justin II	565–578
Tiberius II Constantine	578–582
Maurice (Mauricius Flavius Tiberius)	582–602
Phocas	602–610

LATER EASTERN EMPERORS (610–1059)

Heraclian Dynasty (610–695)

Heraclius	610–641
Heraclius Constantine (Constantine III)	Feb–May 641
Heraclonas	Feb–Nov 641
Constans II Pogonatus ('the Bearded')	641–668
Constantine IV	668–685
Justinian II	685–695

Twenty Years' Anarchy (695–717)

Leontius	695–698
Tiberius III	698–705

Justinian II 'Rhinometus' (second reign)	705–711
Philippicus	711–713
Anastasius II	713–715
Theodosius III	715–717

Isaurian Dynasty (717–803)

Leo III 'the Isaurian'	717–741
Constantine V	741–775
Artabasdos	741/2–743
Leo V 'the Khazar'	775–780
Constantine VI	780–797
Irene	797–802

Nikephorian Dynasty (802–813)

Nikephoros I 'the Logothete'	802–811
Staurakios	July–Oct 811
Michael I Rangabé	813–820

Amorian Dynasty (820–867)

Michael II 'the Amorian'	820–829
Theophilos	829–842
Theodora	842–856
Michael III 'the Drunkard'	842–867

Macedonian Dynasty (867–1056)

Basil I 'the Macedonian'	867–886
Leo VI 'the Wise'	886–912
Alexander	912–913
Constantine VII Porphyrogenitus	913–959
Romanos I Lecapenus	920–944

Romanos II	959–963
Nikephoros II Phocas	963–969
John I Tzimiskes	969–976
Basil II 'the Bulgar-Slayer'	976–1025
Constantine VIII	1025–1028
Romanus III Argyros	1028–1034
Michael IV 'the Paphlagonian'	1034–1041
Michael V Kalaphates	1041–1042
Zoë Porphyrogenita	Apr–Jun 1042
Theodora Porphyrogenita	Apr–Jun 1042
Constantine IX Monomachos	1042–1055
Theodora Porphyrogenita (second reign)	1055–1056
Michael VI Bringas 'Stratioticus'	1056–1057
Isaab I Komnenos	1057–1059

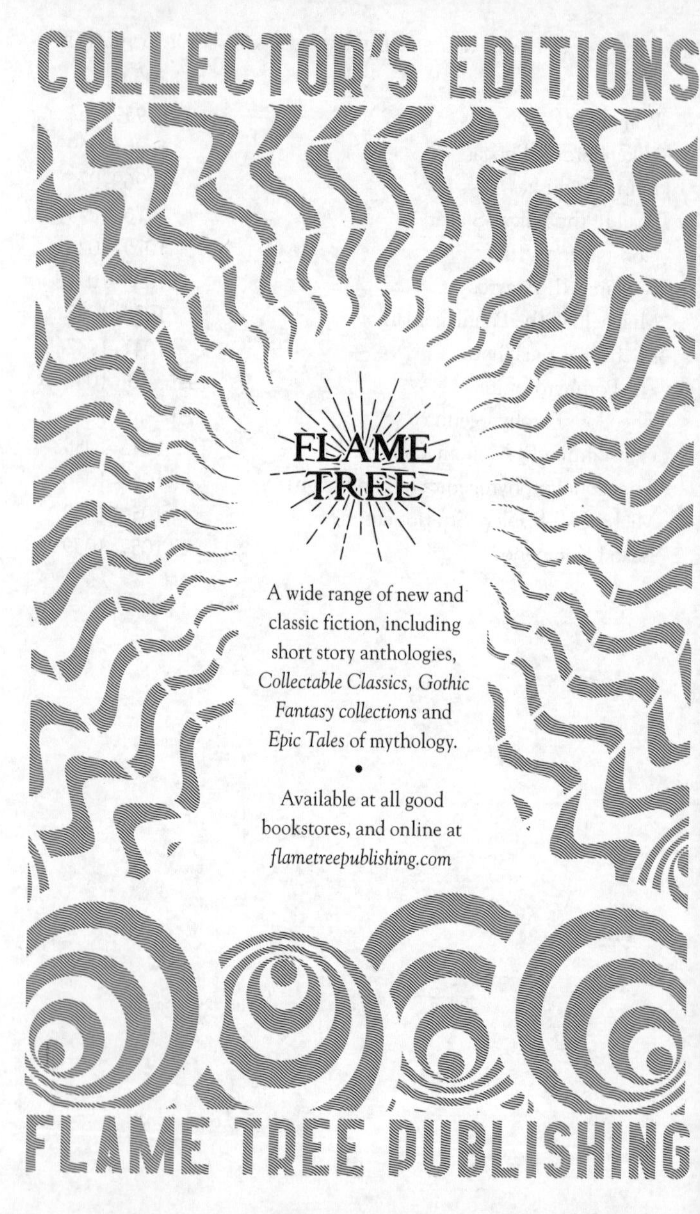
COLLECTOR'S EDITIONS
FLAME TREE
A wide range of new and classic fiction, including short story anthologies, *Collectable Classics*, *Gothic Fantasy collections* and *Epic Tales* of mythology.
•
Available at all good bookstores, and online at *flametreepublishing.com*
FLAME TREE PUBLISHING